Trinity in Hum

C000182025

Cover image:
With the Father under-girding, bearing up the Trinity, the Son resting in the Father's hand and the Holy Spirit anointing all.

Trinity in Human Community

Exploring Congregational Life in the Image of the Social Trinity

Peter R. Holmes

Paternoster:
thinking faith

Copyright © 2006 Peter R. Holmes

12   11   10   09   08   07   06   7   6   5   4   3   2   1

First published in 2006 by Paternoster Press
Paternoster Press is an imprint of Authentic Media
9 Holdom Avenue, Bletchley, Milton Keynes, Bucks, MK1 1QR
285 Lynnwood Avenue, Tyrone, GA 30290, USA
OM Authentic Media
Medchal Road, Jeedimetla Village, Secunderabad 500 055 A. P.
www.authenticmedia.co.uk
Authentic Media is a division of Send the Light Ltd. (registered charity no. 270162).

The right of Peter R. Holmes to be identified as the author of this work has been
asserted by him in accordance with the Copyright, Designs and Patents Act 1988.

All rights reserved. No part of this publication may be reproduced, stored in a
retrieval system, or transmitted in any form or by any means, electronic, mechanical,
photocopying, recording or otherwise, without the prior permission of the publisher or
a licence permitting restricted copying. In the UK such licences are issued by the
Copyright Licensing Agency, 90 Tottenham Court Road,
London, W1P 9HE.

British Library Cataloguing in Publication Data

A catalogue record for this book is available from
the British Library.

ISBN-13 978-1-84227-470-5
ISBN-10 1-84227-470-8

Designed by James Kessell for Scratch the Sky Ltd. (www.scratchthesky.com)
Cover photo by Ian Giles – www.iangilesphotos.co.uk
Print Management by Adare Carwin
Printed in Great Britain by J.H. Haynes and Co., Sparkford

Julie, Graham, James, Christabel, Jessica, Megan, Tim, David, Alasdair, Jane, Richard, Jenny, Dawn, Catriona, Robert, Ruth, Joel, Amy, Raymond, Fiona, James, Clare, Eliciah, Martin, Nicola, Michael, Deborah, Semra, Shaun, Sandra, Amber, Jacob, Simon, Wendy, Emily, Richard, Ann, George, Yvonne, Sally, Sarah, Joy, Patrick, Anna, Peter, Daimen, Margaret, Jane, Simon, Leanne, Chloe, John, Jenny, Anne, Matthew, Ruth, Helen, Carl, Jean, John, Brian, Carl, Annie, Helen, Roman, Rachael, Sophie, Tony, Kathy, Jim, Lauren, Victoria, Maggie, Melody, Phil, Rosemary, Ray, Kate, Hannah, Charlotte, Grace, Carissa,

Dedication
To all the members of Christ Church Deal, past and present

Robert, Yvonne, Maria, Kasim, Hazel, Shemuel, Yusha, Yosef, Matt, Camilla, Phoebe, Arthur, Jack, William, Ethan, Eleri, Gillian, Daniel, Loquessa, Dominique, Nicola-Jane, Samuel, Irena, Ann, Gerard, Nicola, Joseph, Harry, Michael, Martin, Elaine, Sam, Sarah, Sue, Susan, Nathalie, Robert, Jason, Stacey, Jon, Carlton, Paivi, Karlie, Mark, Noëlla, Janis, Mike, Mary, Mary-Beth, John, Margaret, Adele, Annika, Kristina, Rebekka, Dorothy, Monty, Derry, Marlyce, Naomi, John, Mike, Rebecca, Kaya, Rachel, Richard, Lorraine, Jana, Liz, Francis, Marigold, Wendy, Maria Luisa, Laurence, Jillian, Bob, Dorothy, Meg, John, Brenda, Mike, Julie, Kathleen, Laura, Jana, Ruth, John, Ralf, Sabine, Anna-Lena, Laura, Emma, Joshua, Elle, Paul, Jenelle, Mike, Nick, Maria, Amy, Zoe, Yvonne, Andrew, Tanya, Eleanor, Alexandra, Ruby, Steven, Rachel, Katie, David, Gareth, Peter, Mary, Christopher, Jason, Louise, Andy, Elizabeth, Imogen, Charis, Isobelle, Andrew, Christine, Benjamin, Steven, Lee, Daniel, Elaine, Simon, Alison, Benjamin, Oliver, Jennifer, Max, Gus, Wendy, Rose-Marie, Chris, Fred, Christine, Andrew, Julie, Joe, Max, Don, Mary-Ann, Heather, Sandra, David, Steve, Rebecca, Rebekah, Alaister, Harry, Diana, Trevor, Caroline, Barbara, Emy, Colleen, Helen, Rebecca, Claire, Malindi, Colin, Kaye, Jemma, Barry, Lyn, Paddy, Paul, Maureen, Angela, Edward, Florence, Ruth, Annmarie, Michael, Chris, Zahria, Wendy, M. Louisa, Diane, Jay, Jessie, Bonnie, Natalija, Shoshana, Jon, Janice, Hamish, Karen, Liz, Philippa, Chris, Sue, Linda, Frank, Georgia, Neville, Trevor, Conway, David, Brian, Christine, Julie, Nesh, Eddy, Magda, Hope, Tony, Rita, Adrian, Sylvia, Lamees, Kama, Abi, Elaine, Tony, Kathy, Chris, Michael, Jillian, Jean, Helen, Pam, Roman, Sandra, Carlie, Bob, Dorothy, Naomi, Dave, Barry, Courtney, Andrea, Daniel, Nandini, Tim, Chris, Mandy, Christian, Felicity, Elisa, Joy, Kyle, Franklin, Robert, Boaz, Charlotte, Bridie, Maurice, Sully, Jade, Peter, Elisabeth, Michael, John, Christine, Dick, Julien, David, Chloe, Nyall, Jakob, Joseph, Samuelle

'Thank You'

Although I am the author, I am not the maker of this book. This has been the fruit of much labour by many people over a number of years. Firstly, I want to thank all the members of Christ Church Deal (CCD), past and present, who have been willing to be part of our explorations in congregational life. I have dedicated this book to all those I can remember since the congregation was formed in 1998. Many of the ideas presented here were not mine, but have become part of the folklore of life in Christ Church Deal.

There are also a number of individuals who have contributed in a very direct way. Mary my wife has shared the whole adventure with me as a fellow founding member of the congregation. Several people read the first draft and gave me invaluable comment, so you, the reader, can have a much easier voyage journeying through the text. First of all, I would like to thank Dr Knut Heim of the Queen's Foundation, University of Birmingham, UK, a Hebrew scholar and friend. How he found the time I do not know, but he read the text like the scholar and gentleman that he is, giving me numerous invaluable comments that helped me navigate through some very dangerous waters. All opinions and views, however, remain mine.

Some members of CCD read the entire first draft and gave me honest and very constructive comment. I thank especially Rachel Hayes for her intuitive honesty and ability to see the core issues. Also Margaret Dove, graduate of London Bible College and one of the few theology graduates in our community. Thank you, Margaret, for casting your keen eye over the text. Both were able to agree with me that it did reflect what we have been trying to do in CCD, but with qualifications that I then included in the rewrite. I also need to thank Archie Ferguson, who ploughed through the earlier version. Thank you! And thanks to Derry Long, from Portland, Oregon, USA, friend, former pastor and lifelong learner, for his astute observations, possible only from a friend of over twenty-five years who one is still journeying with.

Having then rewritten the book, I called on volunteers in our congregation to read it with comments. I gave each of them a specific challenge. Christabel Allen looked at the draft from the young mum's perspective, Nicola Jane Soen from a student's perspective, Don Meston from the perspective of a Christian of many years, and Ruth Evans from the young person's perspective. Elaine Todd took up the challenge of reading it as if she were a Christian leader, and Jenelle Hall as an American Christian. Finally, Jane Dryden, with her impeccable style, noted numerous flaws others had missed!

Finally, I need to thank Susan Williams, friend of many years, who tirelessly read through the whole text in both its initial draft, and after my extensive revisions. I have already authored books with her and assume her contribution to this one will not be her last.

Peter R Holmes
Walmer, Kent, UK

Contents

Introducing the Themes of the Book

This book brings together the themes of Trinity, community and explorations in congregational life. It is a book about my growing beliefs, the learning journey of exploring them, and how we have experimented with applying some of these ideas in our faith community.

The book begins with a brief outline of the 'Trinitarian problem', seeking to set the tone in the language of theology. But then it shifts to a confession of my own prejudices regarding the idea of 'community'. My somewhat arrogant attitude toward 'community' really shocked me and became a block to positive change in both my life and that of our congregation. From this point the book moves into two separate streams: Old and New Testament teaching, and our experience in Christ Church Deal (CCD) in implementing some of these ideas. Both are woven into each other throughout the remaining text. But, first, a comment on the term 'community'.

A great deal is being said today about 'community', but in this book I am using the term very specifically. In contemporary life we talk about Islamic, Christian, Buddhist and Hindu 'communities'. Likewise, we talk about community as something we have lost today, and about virtual communities such as those on the internet. The term is badly over-used and much abused in many ways. In this book I will be using 'community' to refer to two specific things. One is a way of describing the social Trinity as 'Trinity community', and I will be developing this idea throughout the book. The other is in talking about local congregational life, and my desire to describe this as 'faith community'.

So let me outline the way this book holds together. The opening theme is the theological journey I have been on as I have worked through a range of ideas focused around social Trinity and the implications of this thinking for faith community today. Social Trinity is the idea that God as Trinity is a relationship of three unique persons, all living within one another. I focus on both Cappadocian ideas regarding social Trinity, and the loss of authentic community over the last several hundred years. By Cappadocian ideas, I refer to Basil the Great, Gregory of Nyssa[1] and Gregory Nazianzus, who, while having some abstractions themselves, borrowed from Athanasius[2] and achieved several steps in the development of a view of Trinity that until recently the Western Church[3] had largely ignored. In Cappadocian thinking there is no 'being' of God except the dynamic of *persons in relation*. The two aspects, person and relation, are one and the same. If you have read my book *Becoming More Human*, you will recognize some of the theological sections that I have borrowed from this text, where I have explored these ideas in more academic depth.[4]

The second stream in this book is the ongoing experience of trying to live some of these ideas as a faith community in Christ Church Deal, Kent, UK. This makes it a difficult book to write, since it talks about Church life in our own local congregation. By using CCD, I am not claiming we have it right. We are not a perfect church. That is not what this book is saying. On the contrary, as both a leadership and as church members we have made lots of mistakes whilst journeying together to see what social Trinity might look like in human community. These mistakes have themselves helped us to gain greater understanding. So I will be looking at some of the theology, then commenting on some of the implications of trying to live this in a local congregation.

The book therefore has two complementary streams: blocks of academic journeying woven into sections of my personal experience as part of CCD, seeking to live out some of the principles I am noting. Both need each other. By mentioning the theology first, I am not suggesting that these theological ideas led to the practice. In fact, it was often the other way round. Through the process of social research in the community, mainly by means of focus groups and questionnaires, which were then coded and analysed, Susan

Williams and I discovered that the community was adopting new values and ways of living that surprised us. But once we had identified precisely what these ideas were, as a community we then tried to find a theological or Biblical framework for them.

My own background in both professional Christian work and business helps to explain these 'experiments' in contemporary Church. When five of us as leaders planted CCD in 1998, we brought to it a basic business pragmatism that undergirded all we did. For instance, we went for a 'minimalist' Sunday morning meeting of only three parts – a block of worship in music, community notices and birthdays, and a short preach. The meeting was no longer than an hour. But as members we placed an emphasis on relationship before and after the meeting, supporting this by refreshments. In so doing, we did not try to follow any other tradition, preferring to make our own.

Adopting business thinking for the running of the community meant, for instance, that because we had few wage earners in membership, we used local (inexpensive) community buildings. We invested instead in people, focusing around a network of volunteers with no full-time paid staff. This has allowed us to avoid reproducing the sort of substantial building maintenance overheads that a number of us had previously been familiar with. It gave us a focus on being earthed in human need, which was the reality of who we wanted to become.

So alongside the theological dialogue, and my own journey, part of the second stream of the book includes blocks of quotations taken from focus groups and questionnaires of sociological research conducted here in CCD in 2002.[5] This collected data forms the basis of a range of research and its findings in CCD. The quotes illustrate some of the points I make in the book. I have taken them from either the verbatim notes of the focus groups, or from written answers in a reflective questionnaire undertaken in the community. I believe they illustrate well people's reactions to some of the distinctives in CCD, as well as some of the historic pain and frustration that members brought into the community when they arrived. My apologies for the colloquial language in some of the quotes. It is lifted directly, unchanged, from the sources. I have made no attempt to 'correct' it or make it more acceptable. It is the way people talk and often write.

The quotations are of two types: either in blocks made up of short bullet points lifted from the text, or brief paragraphs of one person's thoughts. Let me illustrate how this works. What follows is a block of mixed quotes from both men and women who were talking about their impressions of what it is like to live in CCD as a community. It begins with a single quote that is slightly longer, then continues with a series of brief thoughts, random ideas collected from a range of people who contributed to our research. Where the ♦ symbol appears, another person is talking. Let me illustrate.

What community is for members of Christ Church Deal

> ♦ Community for me is people just being around me, people prepared to listen to me, people wanting friendship, people wanting relationship, acceptance, non-judgmental. That is community ♦ Hard ♦ Servant-hood ♦ Get yourself healed ♦ Relationship, mirrors ♦ Choosing ♦ Isolation or community ♦ We all belong to each other ♦ You find yourself in community ♦ Other people see you, as you don't see yourself ♦ They show you the real you ♦ Learning to love and be loved ♦ Going the extra mile for people when you don't feel like you can ♦ Always somewhere to go ♦ Never being on your own ♦ An extended family that you hoped for but you never actually had ♦ Safety in knowing there is other people doing the same thing ♦ They will understand what you are doing ♦ We are all in it together ♦ People accept you for whatever state you are in ♦ Being aware of other people's needs ♦ Hurt people tend to withdraw and build walls around themselves and those walls need to be demolished ♦ Exposure and vulnerability ♦ Normally everyone would go towards the slowest, but here everyone goes towards the fastest ♦ Loving yourself while looking at the bad in you ♦ Stop blaming others ♦ Everyone seems to share the same vision, culture ♦ You need all the parts of the body to be complete ♦ (Most valuable) It would probably be the community aspect ♦ That was the most important thing to each one of us. That is the thing that most people want and don't ever find

At first I hesitated to use quotes because they can give the impression that we have a community who are living out the ideas of the book. But this is *not* the case. Please note that this book is about what we *believe* and *seek to live* as a community. So often we fail to live in the way that we believe. I will be expanding on this at several places in the book.

If you jump in the car, train or bus and come to see us, please do not expect to see all that we are talking about in this book. We do believe it, truly, but we are still on the journey – learning how to live it, and our ideas are continuing to mature. If some of the quotes sound too sweet, sloppy, idealistic or too good to be true, then some of them probably are!

But I must also take a moment to thank everyone who is and has been part of CCD. They did not always know that *they* were the experiment. I also found myself ambushed by discovering the direction we as a community were exploring. Maybe some will be surprised, and even exclaim, 'Oh, now I know what he was doing!' I am sorry I did not always make my thoughts known in an adequate way. Many times I only figured them out later. Thank you for being so brave and for the enormous support you have shown me in this adventure.

I must also thank the *Rapha* community, all those who have attended workshops, over two thousand people to date. Many are spread across three continents, and have endured my own journey and its most difficult learning curve. I thank them also for their willingness to be part of this living laboratory of biblical ideas and human experiences (I will be introducing *Rapha* in Chapter 5).

Notes

1 In some ways Gregory was the key Cappadocian. For a critical introduction to his thinking, see S. Coakley, 'Rethinking Gregory of Nyssa: Introduction – gender, Trinitarian analogies and the pedagogy of "The Song"', *Modern Theology* 18 (2002), 4.431–444.
2 P.M. Collins, *Trinitarian Theology: West and East, Karl Barth, the Cappadocian Fathers and John Zizioulas* (Oxford: Oxford University Press, 2001), 136.

[3] I will be using the word 'church' in a range of ways throughout the book. When speaking of the universal Church, I will capitalize it 'Church'. When speaking of the local congregation, I will use the lower case 'church'. When speaking of our own congregation, I will call it Christ Church or CCD.

[4] P.R. Holmes, *Becoming More Human: Exploring the interface of spirituality, discipleship and therapeutic faith community* (Milton Keynes: Paternoster, 2005).

[5] For the academic background to this data see S.B. Williams, 'Journeys of Personal Change in a Therapeutic Faith Community: A congregational study of Christ Church Deal,' M.Phil. thesis (Department of Theology: University of Birmingham, UK, 2002).

How It All Began . . .

It was in the autumn of 1998 that Christ Church Deal (CCD) was planted and we also held our first *Rapha* workshop here at Waterfront, my wife Mary's and my home in Walmer, Kent, UK. The congregation had just 24 adults and their children, and none of us realized at the time the journey we were all beginning. Our modest goal was to create a congregation that was a safe space for others and ourselves, and to do our wholeness journey, learning from the Lord and one another. What we did not know was that we were joining a global wave of emerging churches.[1]

But from these small beginnings the congregation grew, though the growth was not the most intriguing factor, since watching congregations grow was something I was familiar with. What was new was the type of faith community we were becoming. Most of us had come from sick and damaged pasts. Many of us had suffered lots of abuse. So we got on with the job of working through our baggage. By baggage I mean 'the old determinants called tapes, programmes, or scripts, from which we derive all our values and heritage from childhood'.[2] It is the lasting bitter fruit of the toxic experiences of our childhood, parents, people, life and often, also, church.

But the success of what we were experiencing began to attract other people wanting similar help. A few were local, others from farther afield. Many had traumatic pasts or personal damage in their lives. So a significant number of those joining CCD were already admitting that they needed to change, and began or continued their journey when they arrived. At the core of our community life was a kind of therapeutic culture of ongoing positive personal change, therapeutic in the sense that as members we had an emphasis on relationality, openness, honesty and a need to change the way we had been living. So what was this journey we were doing?

Since the late 1960s I have had a personal interest in helping people who have either felt stuck in their relationship with the Lord, or who have a background of mental and emotional illness. I have always done this in a lay pastoral capacity, learning from those the Lord has brought to me. As I continued into the late 1970s patterns began to emerge for me of how some of this illness was constructed, and the manner in which the Lord wanted to free people who sought His help. By the mid 1980s this model was fairly developed. So when Susan Williams came to see me in 1989, going through her second 'nervous breakdown', with Mary's support I began to help her in the way I had helped folk in the past. But I already had an inkling that she would be unlike others who had come before her.

When Susan first approached me I had a conversation with Mary telling her that if we both decided to help her, Susan would be likely to initiate a whole new wave of people seeking help. I added that we would need to open our home to her so that she could learn fast, as her need was urgent. I asked Mary whether she was willing to let this happen. She thought about it for a few days, and, bless her, said yes. The rest is history.

Working with Susan was different. She was one of the first to insist that I teach her how I was able to help her, and, specifically, how I was able to anticipate her need, and then in each session touch precisely into an area that she needed to work on next. She wanted to know how I was able to clarify the issue for her and tell her how to apply this knowledge in a clinical way so that she could be free from the pain, trauma, or other damage involved. So after I had thought about it for a while, I began to teach her how I had seen the situation, and how I had heard from the Lord about her need to unravel this particular issue or that layer next.

After several months, I began to require that Susan herself seek this knowledge from the Lord, practising the principles I had taught her, and coming to me only if she was stuck. The consistency and success of the sequential unravelling of issue after issue over two to three years really fascinated her. The help I gave was a combination of many years' experience of drawing on the patterns I had observed in people needing help, guided by the Lord's perspective on the issues concerned. During this time I also began to write up Bible notes as background to the issues as Susan dealt with them. These were on a range of subjects, including our need for revenge because of the pain we might be in, feeling is healing, the importance of the human spirit, and how our body suffers from the sins of our heart. Susan's journey, together with the principles she learnt along the way are documented in our book, *Letting God Heal.*[3]

At this time a number of other people from Christian, post-Christian and unchurched backgrounds came to me seeking pastoral help. To help these folk, I invited Susan to sit in the session with me and type verbatim notes of what was said. These notes could then be taken away and used to help with the 'homework' before the next session. By 'homework', I mean the personal effort and time we give to allowing the Lord to talk to us about what He sees is wrong with us and how He wants us to grow. The process of learning from others about how they have worked through similar problems.

Over the next few years Susan and I did several thousand sessions this way. Not only were others helped, but Susan herself was taught a variety of approaches and ways of helping people in need. Inevitably, it was not long before she was offering people – mainly women – extensive support as she shared what she was learning. This grew into doing sessions herself. As I had done with her, she found someone else to sit in and 'scribe', or alternatively she would record the session on tape. This method has continued for both of us to the present day. Women generally prefer tapes, and men written notes.

In 1996, because of corporate theft (another story!), I lost my business and found myself with a highly mortgaged but lovely home in Walmer, Kent. I took some time out to research this 'hobby' of mine from the perspectives of theology and psychology. By 1998 I had a long list of people wanting to see me, friends of people I had already been able to help. So Susan, Mary and I decided to hold a workshop, here in our home, to which we invited 25 women for a weekend of training and sharing. Susan did most of the teaching, taking the 12 key areas that she had found most helpful in her own personal journey into wholeness. I did a session saying sorry to all the ladies for the abuse from men in their lives. We expected this workshop to shorten our waiting list, but a number went off and told their friends how much it had helped them, so the list grew and we needed to repeat the workshop. We have continued holding workshops ever since, here in the UK, Europe and the USA. The original introductory workshop is now one of a range that *Rapha* offers, including how to do a personal journey, living in wholeness, mentoring, and meeting Jesus.

In what can only have been God's timing, the first workshop coincided with the planting of Christ Church Deal. Our view was that if the congregation met a need in the lives of people, then together we would keep going. If not, then we would let it die. In the first year it almost doubled, and amazing stories began to emerge of deep positive change in people's lives. In the second year it grew again, on into its third year. These members were taking the teaching of the workshops and the sessions we were doing with them, and applying it to their own lives. The distinctive, that I was to learn later, was that in doing this together they were creating the beginnings of a 'therapeutic community' focused around congregational life. It was only as I continued my academic research that this process became clear. The members together were creating a social process of deep healing relationships. People were choosing to make themselves vulnerable to each other.

By 'social process' I am describing what happens as people relate to each other. This process creates, in turn, a range of social rules that help guide relationships. These 'social rules', which are formed at a subliminal level when any group begins to meet together, are the unwritten values that a group adopts and chooses to live by. Guided by Scripture, members of CCD were creating and adopting values as they worked together on their journey. At the same time, the social process offered them so much more than they had found on a private journey of healing. These values and processes have helped form the foundation in Christ of our faith community. Let me illustrate this.

Describing some of the social rules

‣ They have given me a framework to work to, and within which to be able to undertake my healing journey ‣ The rules are constantly changing as we change, and so is the language. We are the ones who are writing the social rules ‣ The one that I find most challenging is the idea that my behaviour impacts everyone else ‣ It has given me a freedom to be honest about where I'm at ‣ I have been able to relax ‣ More willing to forgive and forget, not bearing a grudge ‣ At first they made me feel excluded. Now I understand and value them ‣ Don't dump. Leave your baggage outside ‣ Feeling is healing. Getting real. Not letting the past steal the future ‣ Don't say, 'I'm fine' when you're not – let out how you really feel ‣ Don't get embarrassed when I tell you the truth about myself. Listen ‣ Total honesty – even if it hurts! ‣ What is best for the other person? ‣ People giving without expecting anything back

Some of the benefits of the social rules

‣ These 'insights' or 'social rules' I find a great relief ‣ Transparency has helped me to stop having my own agenda ‣ Helped me find boundaries and taught me how to practise honouring myself and others ‣ Being able to make mistakes and it not being the 'end of the world' has given a lot of freedom to move on ‣ Taught me how to honour people and myself ‣ It is a case of are you buying into it or not? I've realized that you can't do it half and half ‣ Seeing spiritually what's going on, where most people don't have a clue ‣ Ordinary language cuts through the religious language that clouds reality ‣ They have allowed me to deal with emotions as and when they happen – in the past they were bottled up inside 'being brave' etc., but now I know that it is OK to feel scared, it's OK to ask for help, it's OK for others to see how you are feeling – it doesn't make you less of a person

Looking back today on this evolving process, I now see that in seeking to help others on a one-to-one basis, Susan and I brought into our congregation the experience of our own learning journey. But when this knowledge of how to find healing from our pasts began to be adopted relationally, it had the ability to expand organically in both its effectiveness, pace and results. The way this worked is evident from our diaries. In the first year or so Susan and I did sessions most days, even though the group was small, but as people learned, and after the leadership adopted a mentoring scheme whereby people were more and more committed to helping each other, Susan and I were needed less and less. This mentoring programme gave people permission to try and help others who were needing support and teaching. Over the years a number of people in CCD and *Rapha* have become 'experts by experience', and this is now a substantial resource in our work. Some protest that I call them experts, but they do not realize how much they have learned. The few people we did meet regularly were, and are, mainly newcomers or those with more intractable problems. Not those already on the journey or being helped by mentors.

Members were birthing a faith community where many were doing a journey, because we all admitted to ourselves and each other that we needed to change. We could no longer remain the way we were. As the community journeyed, we learned more, and increasingly began to share the 'short cuts' being learned. By late 2005 we had a community moving toward two hundred members, plus kids, with a very high IQ of how to overcome, with the Lord's help, a significant range of problems. Both in our relationship with the Lord, as well as a range of mental and emotional disorders. Two 60-minute BBC documentaries were broadcast showing the community and the journey in action in the lives of a couple who joined with serious addictive disorders, and a young man who visited temporarily.[4]

This knowledge or 'healing IQ' has become available to any new member joining the community. As an example of the resulting increased effectiveness, when Susan first came to Mary and me for help, she took about five years to work through the basic historic baggage, mainly because she was doing it alone and we were learning together. But once we had planted the church, we saw similar people taking less time to work through these basic issues. With each generation of pilgrims on this journey the experience of finding ways to unravel the damage has increased as we continue to find numerous short cuts to assist newcomers.

What has emerged is a whole range of simple practical ideas of how to live faith community. But as you can already see, this was not a preconceived clever plan, nor any one person's genius. It is entirely down to the wisdom of God and the desire of a group of people who together have been doing a journey, learning new things as they go. This book is a record of some of the interesting things that we continue to learn. Let me illustrate this from comments of members of the community.

Characteristics of the CCD community

• I struggle with the community and everything else that goes on, but the one consistent thing for me is that someone at any time of the night has always been on the end of the phone, that if you are in deep do-da, really upset, there is always that pleasant voice on the end of the phone that can help

• (When asked to comment on the word community) That really makes me squirm. I have got to get over my emotions of that before I can discuss it. I tell you what it does to me when I hear the word, I feel like running. I guess because it implies for me a level of honesty and intimacy that I fear

• For me it is the relationships, they are all different I thought when I came here I'd move into equal relationships, feel safe with everybody, but that wasn't the case. But what has happened is that relationships like that have been built on forgiveness and it is just open and deep and real. It has enabled me to start to become a human being with other human beings, no facades, or less facades. And that is everything

• And I would say to someone else that it is sometimes a very hard place to be a part of, but it is also the most fulfilling community that I have ever lived in because it helps me to see who I really am and also who I can be. I don't think there is a better reason to live your life than to find out who you can be

♦ I was witness to at least 5 churches getting smaller . . . Christ Church has the opposite polarity, trying to keep people away whilst at the same time the church gets bigger and bigger

♦ But in Christ Church we had both, community as we had never known it before and teaching which is out of this world, incredible

♦ In a sense I had never moved into community, although I had been part of the Church for about a year. I had actually never really moved into community, I had never actually become, it might sound strange, I have never become a member of the church, I was always holding back

♦ We assume when we use community that everybody understands what we mean by that word, but I think our experiences of community are all very different . . . but I just didn't know what community was. And I have been a member of the church for nearly two years and I am only just starting to have appreciation for that

♦ You can't stay in isolation

Notes

[1] D. Carson, *Becoming Conversant with the Emerging Church* (Grand Rapids: Zondervan, 2005).
[2] G.G. May, *Care of Mind, Care of Spirit: Psychiatric dimensions of spiritual direction* (San Francisco: Harper & Row, 1982), 51.
[3] S.B. Williams and P.R. Holmes, *Letting God Heal: From emotional illness to wholeness* (Milton Keynes, UK: Authentic Media, 2004).
[4] Copies of the documentaries are available from our church office, 3 Stanhope Road, Deal, Kent, CT14 6AB, UK.

1.

A Problem in the Contemporary Church

Ongoing change seems to be one of the few certain things in our postmodern age. Some of it is good, some bad. In technological terms society is moving like an inter-city express pounding down the tracks, seemingly without interest in the countryside, coast-lands and beauty around. So for me one of my greatest needs, intimidated as I am by all that is changing, is to stop, take time out and think. But even the desire to take space can itself be a source of conflict, torn as we all are by the demands of the urgent, intransigent and hopeless.

I have had to learn the hard way that it is essential to take time out in order to manage the tyranny of change, even change in lit-tle things like learning a new computer skill or how to type. If not, change can suddenly cease to be a friend, becoming instead a taskmaster. Adjusting to ongoing change is essential if we are to remain citizens of the world, for change as a lifestyle is becoming one of the holy grails of contemporary life. Without some level of cooperation from us, some willingness to change, we all lose out.

Deciding how to change and which areas to focus on is becom-ing the warp and weft of modern life, for our struggles to change in a positive way go beyond our personal lives. For instance, the Church, like all other institutions, has been greatly impacted by the demands of change, being the victim of huge sociological changes in our culture.[1] Yet as well as being the victim, the Church has in some ways been its own enemy. I agree that some parts of the Church seem to be holding steady under the rolling waves of turbulent change and some are even managing to ride the billows and take new ground.[2] Others are giving us the impression that they think they can turn back the tide by merely increasing efforts through old ways, or that by tickling the management structures they can accommodate this threatening leviathan called change.

Overall, the picture of the Church in Western Europe is a sad one, with either an inability or an unwillingness to change, thereby inviting *rigor mortis*. I still love the Church, and although I quote people who are now part of the 'emerging' Church, I do not share their condemnation of traditional confessional Christianity. A Church that has survived and prospered for two thousand years is a remarkable achievement, with or without God. As Christians we should not allow this long and rich history to be lost in a postmodern frenzy to be contemporary. Finding an appropriate response that can build on such a valuable legacy is essential.

Here in the UK a church building is closing every day, and several hundred thousand people are leaving the traditional denominations every year.[3] Some have even suggested that the next decade threatens to see the end of the Church as we know it.[4] These falling numbers in traditional churches suggest that few of us in the Church know how to respond to this worsening situation. Some are just bored so they leave.[5] Other members get abused,[6] while others seem merely to ignore the situation, standing by and watching the Church age rather than seeking to learn and change because of what is happening. Although an emerging Church is responding to this problem,[7] spirituality is also alive and well outside the Church[8] while within traditional church communities many seem disillusioned and apathetic.

Traditional Church dogma sees God as immutable, so in reflecting this image some Christians seek to be faithful and immovable in the face of 'threatening' change. For many years I was part of the culture in the Church that, in believing God is faithful, trusts He will save our congregations if we pray hard and long enough. Surely He will turn this situation around, and eventually send people in through the doors when we open them (at the times we choose)? In some parts of the traditional Church sadly this is not proving to be the case, and for the last four decades I have pondered on this increasing problem.

Despite my efforts I have discovered few solutions, and I soon learned that even those I thought I had found were either not new, or unworkable. I personally have found no new theologies or fairy-tale answers that give postmodern people the motivation to attend church and follow Christ. Among other things I have felt ashamed of the way we as Christians can inadvertently give the impression to contemporary people that they must either join our congregations on our terms, or stay away.

Behind such an attitude lurks the idea that maintaining traditional ways of doing things is mirroring God and His unchangeableness. We seem to believe that not changing is the most spiritual way forward. For over thirty years I was within mainstream churches and part of such a belief system, a system that will frequently put the institution first. But during this same period I saw my values and my responses changing. I increasingly found myself asking people what they wanted from the Lord, me and the Church. Sitting in my old oak chair in our lounge at Waterfront, looking across the room I would ask them, 'What do you want from the Lord?', or, 'How can I help you?' I have found few answers to the huge problems facing the Western Church, but what does resonate with people is that simple question, 'How can I serve you?'

In noting hundreds of people's responses over the years I have become convinced that asking questions about how we can serve people is what we need to do much more of. I have concluded that one of the main purposes of the Church is to love and serve those willing to receive our love and support, and to do this regardless of their history, creed or background. Part of the role of the Church is to serve people in meaningful, wholeness-giving relationships, and particularly to care for hurting people who are already sharing in congregational life, helping them become more human[9] so they can become more like Christ. The power of such love is enormous, delectable. As Christians we have already talked for decades about a revolution of love, deeper relationships and the need for all of us to let God love us. But what I am suggesting is that this idea be placed at the centre of congregational life, where the relationships are more important than the rules. For this to happen our attitude to God and to human relationships has got to fundamentally change. Let some of the members of CCD speak for themselves about the ways they are seeking to live this.

Changing attitudes to relationships

◆ People genuinely care about me, and I can begin to let down my defences and welcome others into my life ◆ My mentor is kind, caring, and friendly. I'm not used to this in my life, so when I see her and talk about absolutely anything, it's like a breath of fresh air ◆ It has the potential to be my family – if I allow it! ◆ I can see now that I was actually moving further and further away from what I wanted, and I was actually not connecting with people in church, at work or in my family ◆ Learning that we are all part of each other ◆ In relationship I see my sin much clearer ◆ Others show me my true self ◆ Relationship helps me to see the damage in my life ◆ To learn to trust in relationships, not to feel condemned ◆ Friendships and hospitality – it's where the rubber hits the road ◆ They loved me and thought more of me than I did. Some people refused to believe I couldn't change, even when I thought I couldn't ◆ As I find relationships so hard, it reflects my relationship with God ◆ Seeing people change, isn't it quite exciting.

I believe that as Christians we are called to serve, not dictate to others how they should live or serve God (and us). I am suggesting that meeting human need at the place people are is one of the ways that would help to slow down the loss of people from the Church. If we could offer people solutions on their terms to both their daily concerns and identified needs, then God's love would become more relevant to them. But to be a congregation that exists to serve those who come to it is not an easy task, for we cannot give what we do not have.

For me one of the obstacles was the way I perceived God, for the way we see God directly impacts the way we as people see ourselves and others. When I first became a Christian I used to believe that He was remote, far off and not particularly helpful to me. Although I declared a love for Him, I expected Him to treat me as badly as my father had. So I kept my distance from Him and regarded Him as irrelevant to my daily life. It took me some ten years, into the 1970s, before I began to unpack this flawed view of God. I now realize that only as we can see God in a more intimate, personable light are we able to see others and ourselves in this way.

Over the last few years I have been intrigued to realize the difference that a theology that understands God as social Trinity makes both to individuals and to faith communities. Instead of having an image of God as remote and individual (promoting a private one-to-one faith), it enables us to embrace a healthier image of a Trinity committed to promoting harmonic relationship. As Christians we begin to love a God who is never alone. This perception also creates a view of God that generates trust in relationships because He is already fully committed to permanent relationships. He already lives Trinity relationally. Consequently, since, however tarnished we may be, we are human beings made 'in His image'. We are intentionally created to thrive in the mutual giving and receiving of relationships. Like our Maker, we are all created for relationships. Such a view of God has the potential to transform us and all our 'relationships'.

For the rest of this chapter, and over the next several chapters, I would like to consider the implications of various Trinitarian theologies that the Church has adopted. I will be suggesting that, far from being a set of beliefs that are interesting only for those deeply immersed in theology, our view of the nature of God fundamentally determines how we as people live and love in a changing world. Every one of us has a view of who God is and how He relates, or does not relate to us. Many of us also think we know enough from Scripture about the Trinity to have a relationship with Him. This book is intended to challenge this assumption. What we do not experience we cannot pass on.

Introducing the Problem of Trinity

In speaking of the Trinity I am aware that we are not dealing with a concept that is explicit in Scripture, but a second-level reflection.[10] By 'second level' I mean a doctrine that is built up on the evidence of Scripture, but is not directly stated in Scripture. Once the idea of Trinity is accepted, I believe the real task facing

modern theology is to identify a unique description of the personhood of the Christian God. In a manner understandable from
the human perspective. In a contemporary world of competing
religious pluralism. For instance, Jenson has argued that the
Western Church must either renew its Trinitarian consciousness,
or experience increasing impotence and confusion.[11] Pinnock *et
al.*[12] made a similar call.

The late Colin Gunton reinforced this idea, suggesting that we
need to reconsider the problem of Western 'Theism',[13] that is, the
idea that God is one. He suggested that only through our understanding of the kind of being that God is can we learn what kind
of beings we are.[14] Our image of the Deity has been formed in a
dualistic way in the crucible of Greek philosophical structures of
either/or.[15] Today we are therefore hindered in understanding and
experiencing both a relational God of three persons able to connect
with us, and our own relational potential of personhood. Despite
these observations and others, for most of my life I have not questioned the traditional view of Trinity described in the creeds of the
Early Church – one God in three persons. More recently, however,
I have conceded that traditional Church dogma, and its inadequa-
cies in describing a social Trinity, are today obstructing helpful new
thinking. My personal conclusion has been that the prevalent
Constantinian paradigm of Trinity has cramped alternative theological thought. (The Constantinian paradigm is the teaching of the
Western Church that had evolved by the time of Constantine. I will
introduce this viewpoint in more detail later in the chapter.)

In his seminal book *The Trinity*, Rahner noted the seriousness
of the legacy of this Constantinian paradigm to contemporary
Christianity. He comments: 'Should the doctrine of the Trinity
have to be dropped as false, the major part of religious literature
could well remain virtually unchanged.'[16] At a clinical pastoral
level, where one is seeking to help a person who is hurt or damaged, the consequence of holding to the traditional Church view
of a 'remote' unchanging Trinity is that one has few ways of
describing the intimacy of a helpful, personable God. Likewise, it
is hard to imagine how this God might help us in all our other
damaged relationships. With our traditional view of God we
have little to convince people that God might want to talk to
them or even help them. Traditional views of Trinity, which

embrace ideas such as the unchangeableness of God, suggest His incapacity to relate to us in our pain and need.

Nevertheless, despite such difficulties the Trinity has always been a key topic in the Church. Schadel,[17] for instance, listed some 4,656 titles on the theme of Trinity, but even he missed what for me have been some of the key texts, such as Hartshorne[18] and Ogden.[19] Some of these titles have suggested that when we speak about God in Trinity as immanent reality we should be cautious. I agree that it is indeed a perilous task, though not for the traditional reasons, suggested by Greek categories, that one cannot penetrate the veil of His being. Instead, I tend to agree with Gunton that there is always a danger of what he described as 'objectifying' God, 'of turning him into a static and impersonal object, to be subjected to our unfettered intellectual control'.[20] Gunton further suggested that this is something the Church seems to have done throughout history.[21] In the following chapters I will be unpacking something of what this 'objectifying' has come to mean for us today.

I do accept that it is possible within the traditional Church to speak of one's spiritual experiences, and of engaging with God. An emphasis on the experience of God has always been with the Church, but for a range of reasons has been pushed to the fringes in the quest for an intellectual knowing of God. Probably because of concerns similar to my own, other authors have also noted the Trinitarian problem at both a theological and practical level.[22]

A typical example of the experience of God within the Church is the practical mysticism of the Shakers, who 'experience and recognize the mystery of Christ-in-us our hope of Glory (Col. 1:27) travelling from gift to Gift, and glory to Glory'.[23] We see a similar emphasis in the mystic movements within the Church, which have always sought the experience of a relationship with the living God.[24] Calvin and Luther likewise emphasized a living union with Christ.[25] But the very fact that numerous authors have made such emphases in their writings and practice merely suggests to me that they are seeking to compensate for the underlying view of a static, isolated or transcendent God.

What also seems to be missing today is a practical, hands-on application of how thinking about Trinity can be applied to both the individual and to everyday congregational life. In some way this is the theme of this book. But the idea of engaging with a social

God has been further complicated by questions about how we get to 'know' God at a practical level. How do we as Christians understand relationship with God? How do we explain it? I would like to suggest that until recently we have had a flawed Trinitarian theology that has failed to give us a framework to comprehend a personable God who is intimately knowable. What we cannot imagine as people we will be unlikely to possess (experience).

The Church cannot offer the contemporary world what it is not itself first enjoying. In losing a relational Trinity we lose a relational God. For instance, the Church's current teaching on accepting Christ does not make this dependent on *engaging* God, but on *making an intellectual decision* to follow Him. Much of the time experience of God is not thought to be part of this process: accepting Christ is *about* Him, rather than relationship *with* Him. For this reason, T.F. Torrance[26] argued that it is not divine personhood but worship that should be the starting point for any new thinking regarding God. These same themes were further developed by A.J. Torrance.[27]

To illustrate this problem I will now outline some aspects of the classical (Augustinian/Constantinian) view of the Trinity, showing how it has structured our view of God's nature, especially the doctrine of the Holy Spirit. Also, I will consider how this lack of emphasis on the person and work of the Holy Spirit has contributed to the loss of lived spirituality and community in the contemporary Church. I will then very briefly look at three twentieth-century responses to the problem of this Greek legacy before outlining an alternative model of Trinity. One more able, I believe, to support a theology of change and relationship as it is sought in the twenty-first century. But first we must understand the Greek culture within which these theological ideas regarding Trinity were birthed.

The Womb of Christianity

The womb of Christianity was initially *both* Hebrew and Greek.[28] But by the time of Christ Greek-Roman thinking was dominating the Near East, and Christ was born into a multilingual culture; as well as Aramaic, He was probably able to speak Greek, and maybe even some Latin. He lived on the edge of one of the largest cosmopolitan new cities in the Middle East, Sepphoris, which was being built while He was in Nazareth.

I am using the words 'Hebrew' and 'Greek' to talk about systems of thought and this might suggest one set of comprehensive ideas in each tradition. This is hardly the case, though we do seem to think that way. In actual fact there were many types of Greek thought, just as there are many types of 'British attitudes'. Hebrew thought introduces us to the Old Testament and is the language of the text. I use the term 'Greek thought', therefore, simply by contrast, and am not suggesting that just one set of ideas alone existed.

At Pentecost (Acts 2 – 3) the Church was born into a Greek-Roman world, but with local languages of Aramaic and Hebrew. Over time, as the Church expanded, it began to let go of its Hebrew roots, and became more Greek-Roman. This process occurred gradually as the number of Jewish believers decreased. The watershed was probably the time of the Christian apologist Justin Martyr in the second century, a period when fewer and fewer Jewish believers were being added to the Gentile Church.[29]

During the early centuries Christianity, understandably, increasingly relied on Greek philosophical categories, accepting the bifurcation of Western intellectualism into subject/object, essence/existence, substance/accident, noumenal/phenomenal and theoretical/practical.[30] These classical Greek either/or ideas were mainly static – essences, snapshots and single pictures. This is how Greek thought was expressed. It can be compared with twenty-first century philosophy and its 'postmodernity', which has evolved from a single snapshot way of thinking to a changing landscape or movie pictures.

The Western Church, however, has changed very little over the centuries in its way of thinking. The influence of great theologians such as Augustine (354–430) and Aquinas (1224/5–1274), men with giant intellects, has been such that much of this Greek framework has remained in place. In the past this was not a problem. Augustine, as a man of his time, left us a huge theological legacy with the largest single corpus of extant writings of any theologian from the Patristic period. Although he is normally known for his *Confessions*, one of his most significant works was *On the Trinity* (399–early 420s), written in response to the Arian controversy.[31] This book set the standard on how to view the

Godhead. Through this and other writings Augustine achieved huge progress in developing a way of talking about Christ to his contemporaries. But as we shall note later, his system of doctrine has its flaws.

Aquinas likewise, in what is now called Scholastic thought, successfully reconstructed, in the language of his day, many of the Church's ideas. But what was once good has now in various ways become ballast in the Church. Modern society has abandoned some aspects of traditional Greek ways of thinking in favour of a range of more contemporary ways of expressing the self. This means that either/or dualistic categories are no longer helpful in the way they once were. Today people are more likely to talk in quantum or holistic terms about their views and experiences.

So the contemporary Church struggles to engage in dialogue with contemporary people. Greek cultural thinking continues to form part of the fibre of the Church's tradition and theology, whereas new spiritualities frequently do not accept the dualistic notions of Greek thought. Neither do contemporary people accept dogmatic teaching about objective absolutes such as good and evil, preferring instead an approach based on 'situation ethics' or 'relativism'. This creates conflicts of value systems and a widening of the gap between the ideas of the Western Church and contemporary society. In our community at Christ Church Deal and its teaching ministry we have a number of unchurched people who are either referred to us or find their way to us. In order to talk with them in a way that they understand the community, when introducing them to biblical thinking, will instinctively use the language of psychology and sociology that un-churched people have learned. We talk, for example, of 'human spirit' (the Biblical *pneuma*), 'good and bad emotion' (the Hebrew idea that every feeling has both a good and a bad side to it), and 'baggage' (so avoiding the term 'sin' at too early a stage in our relationship with them).

It is very important to stress that the use of Greek categories has been enormously helpful to the Church in the past. For instance, in the Early Church Greek language and the way it was structured allowed the gospel to move freely from England to India.[32] In the West the peace between Greek and Roman cultures gave the early believers a way of talking to the whole known world, through either Greek or Latin categories. But times have changed, and contemporary unchurched people's ideas are now challenging traditional ones, especially within Western society. Dualism is giving way to holism,[33] relationality questioning individualism,[34] and change replacing conformity and compliance. By examining certain features of the Church's Greek heritage I will suggest that although this was helpful in the past the Church not now needs to move on, acknowledging that such Greek categories could be a hindrance.

The Classical Western View of Trinity

As we have already noted in the case of Greek language and culture, any speculative theologizing about the knowledge of God is necessarily carried out in the context of the philosophical teaching and cultural assumptions of the time.[35] The philosophical outlook of the wider culture at any one time or place therefore becomes the landscape for Christian theologizing. For instance, Giles argued that the Trinitarian thinking of the first three centuries has been lost until recently.[36] So it is necessary always to see the ideas of Trinity in the light of the culture of the time.

The classical view of Trinity grew out of orthodox or conventional thinking, by which I mean theology as it was formed in the first three centuries of the Early Church. The early creeds, or confessional doctrinal statements of the Church led to doxology, ways of expressing in poetry and song what these creeds were intended to teach. For instance, the Nicene Creed focuses on *homoousios*, 'of the same substance', the oneness and indivisibility of the Godhead. The Athanasian Creed affirms that God is triune, not only in His activities, but in His essential, eternal nature. Whilst being distinct in their own individual perspectives, both creeds interpret the Trinity as a means of understanding God's nature, emphasizing a technical rather than a relational viewpoint. We can summarize this consensus, the orthodox view, in one simple phrase, 'one God in three persons'.

In time this orthodox thinking divided into several 'schools'. Cobb saw four Trinitarian theologies. The first Eastern (e.g. Greek Orthodox), the second Augustinian (classical Western), the third a non-metaphysical view that used the horizons of human language and experience, and the fourth an 'economic' Trinity, where the discrimination of three functions did not necessarily imply much about differentiations within the divine life itself.[37] Within all these schools one theme emerges – God's being is defined through the various ways of viewing His relationality, that is, God is defined by His interest or will for relationship, not just by His essence.

Our Western Church has largely inherited the classical Western Trinitarian approach which states that God's essential 'sociality' is defined within God's self, but His relationship with the world is contingent, a matter of divine choice. Sometimes He may, other times He may not. This suggests that His Trinitarian sociality does not intrinsically extend to human beings. This is a problem because although as Christians we believe His nature to be personable, we have no theological or conceptual structure to build or illustrate this.

In current Western Trinitarian theology there are limited ways of describing the concept of the sociality of God within both material reality and personal relationality. Jesus is the traditional contact point, but He came then went. Then the Holy Spirit came, but He is very difficult either to describe or visualize. As a result, God becomes known by His offer of salvation in the next life, not the potential of relationship as we know it today. I believe that this is an area of deep pain and disappointment for many Christians.

Here in the West the Church inherited, primarily through Augustine of Hippo's use of Greek language and ideas, the idea of a static, transcendent Trinity. Because of the Greek idea of dualistic worlds – the material and spiritual worlds as separate realities – such a Trinity largely fails in its promise of being a personally experienced God. It also makes it more difficult for us to imagine the possibility of engaging with our spirituality, and knowing an intimate relationship with God.

So how did Augustine's teaching come about? Eastern or Byzantine Orthodoxy began with an affirmation of belief in the Father, Son and Holy Spirit, according to Scripture, with a focus on *hypostasis* (personhood). This gave priority to God's personhood. But, in contrast Augustine of Hippo thought it better to begin with the unity of the divine, as this was a truth that could be demonstrated by reason.[38] This loss of emphasis on the personhood of

God makes it harder to conceive of an experience of relationship with God.

Augustine, though African, is today seen as a 'Western' man, since his background training in the Greek classics, and all of his ideas, were constructed within the framework of Greek categories. Augustine is seen as one of the leading formative thinkers of the Western Church's theology, but he did this, as we all do, within the framework of his education and culture. So, as we have seen, his thinking, along with that of many other intellectuals of his time, brought into the Church of Europe an intellectual framework that was Greek in origin. As an example, Greek Stoic philosophers had a problem with the expression of emotion, suggesting that it obstructed pure intellectual thought. Likewise, although the human body was admired, it was considered inferior to spirit. Until recently these ideas and assumptions seem not to have been a significant problem for the Church.

Gunton, building on McKenna's observation, proposed that we needed to go behind Augustine's thinking to his (Greek) suspicion of material reality, illustrated in his Christology.[39] Gunton suggested that Augustine was reluctant to give due weight to the full physical authenticity of Christ's incarnation as a fully human person. Likewise, despite some literary exceptions, Western theology has for the most part failed to develop adequate conceptual tools to ensure that due prominence be accorded to Christ's full humanity. To illustrate this, Gunton referred to the numerous Old Testament theophanies of Christ, suggesting that Augustine appeared to be rather embarrassed, as some Greek philosophers were, by too close an involvement of God in physical human life.

Augustine's problem has become our problem, as it weakens the full impact of the finished work of Christ, and His incarnation, resurrection and ascension, all within material reality. The failure to acknowledge fully Christ's total humanity and complete involvement with our world had the tendency to distance God from the world, re-emphasizing Greek dualistic separatism. It suggests a static Deity remote from His creation. In response to this Schwobel and Gunton wrote, 'The revelation of God in Christ is the foundation for what it means to be human. This implies, secondly, that the true humanity of Christ is understood as the paradigm for true knowledge of human being.'[40]

Augustine's avoidance of Christ's humanity hinders our own theological exploration of the humanity of ourselves and others.

Gunton further noted that Augustine seems either not to have understood the Trinitarian theology of his predecessors in both East and West, or to have had his perspective distorted by Neoplatonic assumptions.[41] Augustine's brilliance in helping construct the foundations of Western Christian dogmatics seems to have hidden, until now, these deep flaws in his thinking.[42] For instance, his firm stress on the mind, following Greek thought, has had unhelpful consequences for the Western Church. It encouraged the idea that knowledge of God was to be found primarily, and adequately, in the mind instead of being known and experienced emotionally. Such a view is not appealing to spiritually engaged and experientially aware contemporary people with much more interest than Augustine in emotion and relationships.

Augustine lost sight of God-in-man-in-Christ-on-earth, and focused more on Christ's transcendence and deity. He looked at God from his Greek perspective, not from the perspective of the nature of deity itself. Greek thought saw the necessity to describe and understand everything, giving it shape and form, thereby drawing Augustine toward the idea that God's character was fixed and unchanging. It was this view of God that inadvertently drew the Church, through Augustine and others, toward the view that He was static, lacking the faculties for being part of our world now.

If as Christians we follow Augustine's teaching on the intellectual knowing of God, we are tempted to believe that when we know ourselves correctly (intellectually/cognitively) we will also know God in the same act, 'the man who knows how to love himself, loves God'.[43] Gunton, following Nicholas Bradbury, called the idea that we can know God simply through a better understanding of ourselves a 'decadent mysticism',[44] a degrading anthropomorphism that fails to perceive God's nature on His terms as God within human experiential reality. Such thinking is in danger of merely flattering our intellectual capacity for a self-knowing of our nature, and of God's. McCoy called the idea that we can know God by this route a metaphysics of divine stasis.[45] Put in contemporary language, it is our belief that we are able to cognitively know about God but that He remains static and distant, rather than giving us a personal knowing of God that is relationally authentic, present and dynamic. What the Church has failed to see is that God is *three*, meaning that He has the experience of relationship and wants to impart this idea and experience to everyone willing to learn from Him, the social Trinity.

I am suggesting that the visible Church should resonate with the *dynamic* of the relations between the three persons, who together constitute deity. This means that the sociality of the Trinity should in some way permit the eternal God – the eternally inter-animating energies of the three – to provide the basis of the personal dynamics of human/divine relationship.[46] The idea here is that we are able to make social Trinity more than merely an intellectual theology. Social Trinity can and should be a vibrant example of what human relationships can become, especially within the Body of Christ. Such thinking allows a 'social' Trinity to be more 'involved' in both Church and contemporary society. The Constantinian Trinity's failure has meant that the Church is left with a type of Christianity that does not fully support the experience of 'intimacy with God'. Christians get started but discover that God is far away, so quit. We worship Him but do not experience Him. But another problem also haunts us.

Does God Change?

Central to the idea of relationship with God is the question of whether or not God changes. A great deal of debate is currently under way on the idea of whether God either can, does or does not change. I leave this whole debate to process theologians and those who disagree with them. In one of my earlier books I make it very clear that I am not a process theologian.[47] From the Christian perspective, however, we do need to admit that we have a problem, inherited from Constantinian theology. The problem is that it is difficult to see how an unchangeable (e.g. unresponsive) God can have a relationship with changeable human beings. This conflict is now a very real issue in our contemporary world. Let us note some of the reasons.

All human relationships are about making choices. Most of us make mundane choices of little consequence and sometimes

even important decisions in a spontaneous way, without thinking them through. We are unpredictable, emotional. We are
changing all the time, for example, we are growing up or old,
and we keep changing our minds. So from our perspective, for
God to be in relationship with us, we need Him to have the
capacity to respond to this continual change in us. But if He can
respond, how can He do so while remaining unchanging? Surely
He must be changing in some ways Himself in acknowledging
that we are changing our minds or our choices? To view Him as
impassive in the face of our impetuosity suggests an absence of
personal relationship. For instance, when we pray, does He
know every word we say before we say it? Has He already
answered or ignored our prayers? Or is He able to change or
adjust His plans on the basis of our prayers? The answer seems
to be that in one sense He does seem to have the capacity to
change, for example, in responding to us, while in another sense
He remains unchanging.

In the past many sought to resolve this problem. One such person is Lee, who suggested that change itself is the most meaningful expression of God's *is-ness* in the world of constant change
and becoming. But he also noted that it is not only that God's
nature is change in itself, but also that in changing He remains
changeless. According to his view of God, God might be described
as being like the stationary axle of the moving wheel of a cart: all
the spokes are moving, but the spindle remains fixed. The axle,
God, does not move. For Lee, the element of changelessness in
God is His faithfulness to Himself. It is found in change itself, in
the 'living God'.[48] To this I would add that God's immutability is
also in His consistency regarding covenant relationship with His
people.

Put this way, God has the capacity to respond to a changing
world, for change is His familial relational nature. Creation
expresses and mirrors this change. Continual change itself constitutes covenant in continual process with human beings. The
covenant in process facilitates creation in process. In mentioning creation I am suggesting a God-created order and evolving
harmonic inter-relationship within nature. Thus the material
world is in the process of becoming.[49] This perspective, though
not entirely comfortable for everyone, does offer a helpful

foundation from which to respond to the modern spiritual search for transcendent relationship with God.[50] By emphasizing, through our use of the concepts of traditional theology, God's unchangeableness, omniscience, and omnipresence, we as Christians can be in danger of suggesting that God is some 'brass Buddha' who remains unflinching in the face of our appalling human pain, trauma and suffering. Instead, we need as a Church to find ways of describing God that enable us to perceive Him as capable of warm relationships. What I am suggesting is not that we abandon traditional teaching about the nature of God, but that alongside that we develop ideas that emphasize His imminence and capacity for love and intimacy. For example the use of Abba – calling God 'Daddy' (Mk. 14:36), Jesus as friend (Mt. 20:13; Lk. 5:20), Jesus' calling of the little children (Mt. 19:14), etc. Describing this ability in God to respond to us, Lee said, '"Oneness in three and threeness in one" is the perfect symbol of divine nature, suggesting not only relationship, but an inner process of change.'[51] What people do with the gift of life they are given makes a difference to God, for His actions are shaped to some extent by the actions of His creatures (e.g. Je. 22:1–5).[52]

Therefore, in speaking of 'change' in God and the Church, and based on some of the ideas later introduced in this book, one could say the following: 'Within Trinitarian relations in local faith community, change is His endless capacity,[53] guided by His unchanging covenant commitment, to support our continual becoming through both the *Rapha* principle, and His facilitating this in our life in Christ.'

Let some of the members of CCD speak for themselves on this idea of following Christ and being in relationship with Him and one another.

Being a Christian in CCD

♦ Really [in my other churches] I didn't feel different to most of the non-Christians I knew, except that I believed in God, and I knew the Bible, but had hardly experienced any of it. The only way that I could cope with this bitter disappointment was by deceiving myself and (some) others that I was fine and full of the fruit of the Spirit!

♦ Prior to CCD I thought being a Christian was like having a label, being part of a club you attended once a week, and used the membership to judge others by. It was empty and false. But since being at CCD, I understand that being a Christian is about how you live your life every day – it's in you, about living in truth and loving each other, belonging

♦ It's a journey and not an event ♦ A whole way of life ♦ Not a doctrine, a creed or a rulebook ♦ More about an emotionally-led relationship with God based on Him talking with me about myself ♦ I used to think being a Christian was about things you did (or didn't do!) rather than a quality of being ♦ Things that I have known in my head have started to become more real in my spirit ♦ Relationships, relationships, relationships. And I now understand what it's about from God's perspective ♦ The knowledge of our sin yet to be discovered, and to be free ♦ Loving God, loving people, loving myself. It's a discipleship journey, not a one-off for Christ ♦ Seeing Christ's perspective

♦ Christianity is not about achieving and doing to get to heaven, or for God to love you or for you to love God more. But about being in yourself and in Christ. Being who God desires for you to be, and to get rid of whatever is hindering you

♦ I understand what is needed for me to find God now. I understand more than ever my personal role in that. The journey to discovering myself has meant that I can welcome God, even as I am welcoming myself. I am also developing a much greater understanding of sin and its effects on me and others

(Speaking of experienced Christians) ♦ They want to come and change us [CCD]. But actually they wouldn't, because they would go through the workshops, and then they would find their own homework, and God would start changing them

Ways Augustinian Thinking Has Impacted Us Today

As we have seen, Augustine contributed to our contemporary view of a static and distant God. As a result, relationship with God has become a theological system that is believed and yet frequently not experienced. Congregational meetings can look like the classroom, faith being a thing we learn to do intellectually. We often stand in rows to worship God. We are told how to live and what to do in order to please this God. Likewise, in our life with others we have surrounded ourselves with rules that govern the way we live, how we spend our time and money, and even who we can and cannot be friends with. Life becomes so structured for some of us that we even carry a genuine fear of meeting people who are not Christians, who live in the 'sinful' world outside the Church, who smell of alcohol and tobacco, use 'bad' language and have no 'class'. It is almost as if we believe that we must keep away from such people in case their 'sin' rubs off on us or our children. We are even taught to fear other religions and New Age thinking, or to see Islam as the 'enemy' with 'darkness' behind it.

God is holy, so as Christians we have been taught that to be holy we need to be separate from the world, no longer directly involved in it. To achieve this, some have even gone to great lengths to create a whole 'Christian' sub-culture that includes 'Christian' cinema, television, dance, clubs and retreat centres. We send our kids to 'Christian' schools, give them a 'Christian' education, and teach them to be like us. We rarely stop, however, to think that we have failed to live up to our own expectation of Christianity, and that having 'faith in Christ' has not delivered the type of intimacy with Christ that the Church has promised. The Church becomes known for what it does not do, rather than for what it can offer. Yet this has not stopped us wanting our children to live just as we do. It may not have worked for us, but we still believe in it, so we pressure our Christian friends, as well as our children, to make it work for them. Sadly (or perhaps not so sadly), many of our children are 'postmodern', so are much more frank and honest about their own and others' expectations. They therefore escape at the earliest possible time and sometimes continue their quest for God in more experiential contemporary ways, having rejected our type of Christianity.[54]

In an Evangelical tradition, when people say to us that they would like to meet Jesus, we enthusiastically tell them they can, wishing to teach them all we know. But this activity, much of the time, is more based on what we have been taught than what we have personally experienced. To reinforce our statement that they really can know Jesus, we quote a range of people from books and sermons, citing remarkable experiences about how *they* met Jesus. What we often fail to see is that we are quoting others because we have little personal experience of our own that we can talk about. When enquirers press us more on the 'how to', we will often pass them on to others who we hope can show them some answers.

Of course I am deliberately exaggerating the problem, but I have done so to make a point. I am suggesting that the foundations of our way of believing in God are seriously flawed. Not only can this be a cause of instability and dissatisfaction in us as Christians, it appears to have resulted in a failure to attract those outside the Church. An intellectual faith, being one that is constructed on ideas, not upon relationship, does not respond well to the stresses and strains of daily life. Let me give you two contrasting examples from my pastoral work.

A man lost his daughter in a car accident. He was a career Christian, having served the Lord for many years, but he had no faith framework, even intellectually, for such a 'betrayal' by God. So he quit his Christian job and cursed God for allowing such a thing to happen. He was very angry and in deep pain. He was lost long-term to both the Church and the Lord. Part of his problem was that he was unschooled emotionally in expressing this pain to God, and in letting Him and others love and comfort him through this crisis. In holding on to the trauma of God's 'betrayal', he became bitter and isolated.

This reaction is in marked contrast to another man who lost his wife to cancer and sought help from me. When he arrived at my home, he cried, and cried, and cried. He cried for several weeks, pouring his heart out to God and to anyone who would sit with him. His grief came in waves. He did not understand why his wife had died, but he was sure that God was taking his pain and receiving his tears. He was emotionally aware that the Lord was available and empathic toward his grief. He told me some time later that he loved the Lord, and so would not let even the death of his wife separate him from the Lord.

The first man had an intellectual faith that gave him no emotional structures to process his loss. The other man had a faith rooted in personal experience or relationship with Christ. He had already learned and believed that although he did not understand why the Lord had allowed this, he would not emotionally let go of God. The first man's faith failed him, the other man's deepened his love and dependence on the Lord.

Some would argue that such responses may be put down to individual temperaments, but Dr Knut Heim of the Queen's Foundation put it concisely to me when I was recently talking with him. Wrong theology leads to a wrong (or no) relationship; a wrong head leads to a wrong heart. A right head leads to a right heart; right theology leads to a right relationship. A social Trinity knows a lot about right relationality.

Another characteristic of the impact on us of our belief in a far-away God is the separating of our 'worship' from our daily lives. The two bifurcate: on Sundays we go to church and worship God, then we spend the rest of the week outside of this faith setting. Our life as a whole is not seen by us as worship. Instead, our idea of worship is focused around an hour on Sunday morning and perhaps a midweek meeting or two. This polarization means that outside church meetings, we do not feel the need to live in either God or His values. As a result, much of the time we live outside His orbit of relationality. Though intellectually we still believe in God, relationship with Him becomes less and less relevant to our daily lives. This can be especially true in times of stress and need, when our first thought will not be to invite the Lord into the situation. He is at church, how can He help us?

A further example of the legacy of the Western view of Trinity is that, despite the clear evidence of Scripture, we believe that this transcendent and static, unchanging God is not given to expressing emotion or responding to what we are and do, unless it be to throw a lightening bolt of anger or judgement. This apparent unchangeableness on God's part, fed for many of us by our need to live by rules, has become one of our greatest obstacles to knowing God. When we find ourselves in a difficult situation, we *think* of what to do, rather than *feel* how we should respond. Many of us tenaciously hold on to beliefs and practices as though they are sacred. Trusting Christ can become little more than an unchanging intellectual belief system, with little room for our feelings. We have the opportunity to change by building a faith in Christ, which, while being intellectually understood, is also personally and relationally experienced. Heart and head work together. We need both intellect and emotion working harmoniously together in order to live well. We need a return to a place where we understand God to be a 'person' who responds to us, and has the capacity for empathic intimacy. Likewise, we need a more positive understanding of our human emotion and its capacity to guide us in positive ways. As Christians we will never *experience* God if we do not first have a framework for believing we can do so.

In using Greek categories, Augustine allowed into his theology ideas that suggest that at the core of one's being there is not communion/relationship with others, but something else underlying it.[55] Augustine, like all of us, was a child of his time, so he embraced the dualistic tension of which Barth and Rahner, among others, have made us aware. This is the tension between God's being and God's becoming, between the one God and the triune God.[56] Augustine failed to observe that God is wholly in relationship within Himself and, by implication, with the whole created world, including us. If He chooses to create, He is necessarily related to what He creates, while what He creates will also have some of this potential relationality. As human beings we all realize ourselves primarily in and through others.

This weakness in Augustine has led to misconceptions about God and His relation to material reality. Some members of CCD have been clear that the relationship they were seeking with God was something they had not previously found.

Disappointment in formal church

> ◆ My view of church was extremely negative, to the point where I would not even venture in one. A year later to be playing in the worship band is quite a turn-around ◆ People here are more honest – but I'm still angry / anti-church ◆ For me I now believe in church ◆ Church is in a very real way community ◆ It's how it should be ◆ It has put a whole new

perspective on my view of church. It is exciting ✦ Changed view of church? Yes, I think it has given me hope to believe that church life can be what I really always knew it was meant to be. A community of Christians living together in reality, rather than just going to a Sunday club ✦ I thought church was a farce, and a hiding place for people who thought they were better than everyone else ✦ Church is people, relationships, walking a journey together, in brokenness. CCD is a safe place to do it ✦ It allowed me to begin to make peace with myself ✦ Yes. I had come to the conclusion that church didn't work, and people didn't change. Now I know I was wrong

Notes

1 D. Maclaren, *Mission Implausible: Restoring credibility to the church* (Milton Keynes: Paternoster, 2004).
2 M. Yaconelli (ed.), *Stories of Emergence: Moving from absolute to authentic* (El Cajon, CA: Emergent YS, 2003).
3 See P. Brierley, *The Tide is Running Out: What the English church attendance survey reveals* (London: Christian Research, 2000) and P. Brierley, *UK Church Religious Trends*, Number 4 2003–2004 (London: Christian Research, 2003).
4 Brierley, *Tide*, 27.
5 Brierley, *Tide*, 87, 200.
6 D. Johnson and J. Van Vonderen, *The Subtle Power of Spiritual Abuse; Recognising and escaping spiritual manipulation and false spiritual authority within the church* (Minneapolis: Bethany House, 1991).
7 For example, S. Rabey, *In Search of Authentic Faith: How emerging generations are transforming the Church* (New York: Random House, 2001), P. Ward, *Liquid Church: A bold vision of how to be God's people in worship and mission – A flexible fluid way of being church* (Milton Keynes: Paternoster, 2002) and D. Kimball, *The Emerging Church* (Grand Rapids: Zondervan, 2003).
8 See J. Chu, 'O Father, Where Art Thou?' Time Magazine 161 (16 June 2003), 24.22–30 and P.R. Holmes, 'Spirituality: some disciplinary perspectives' in K. Flanagan and P.C. Jupp (eds.), *The Sociology of Spirituality* (to be published – 2006).

[9] I am aware that 'becoming more human' is often interpreted to mean growing in our ungodly character. In this book I will be suggesting that becoming more human is a process of discovering and re-enabling the *imago Dei* as the dignity of divinity in humanity.

[10] For example, D.B. Burrell, *Knowing the Unknowable God: Ibn-Sina, Maimonides, Aquinas* (Notre Dame: University of Notre Dame Press, 1986) and B.J. Lee, 'An "Other" Trinity' in J.A. Bracken and M.H. Suchocki (eds.), *Trinity in Process: A relational theology of God* (New York: Continuum, 1997), 191–214, 191.

[11] See R.W. Jenson, *The Trinity Identity* (Philadelphia: Fortress Press, 1982), ix, quoted in C.E. Gunton, *The Promise of Trinitarian Theology* (Edinburgh: T&T Clark, 1991), 18.

[12] C. Pinnock, *et al.*, *The Openness of God: A Biblical challenge to the traditional understanding of God* (Downers Grove, IL: InterVarsity Press, 1994).

[13] See Gunton, *Promise*, 1–2, Collins, *Trinitarian Theology* and C.E. Gunton, *The One, the Three and the Many: God, creation and the culture of modernity* (Cambridge: Cambridge University Press, 1993).

[14] Gunton, *Promise*, vii.

[15] By this I mean that where we have to choose between two mutually exclusive options, we are thinking in an either/or way. Such thinking reduces our scope for thinking of the Trinity, along with many other aspects of spiritual reality.

[16] K. Rahner, *The Trinity* (London: Burn & Oates, 1970), 11. See also N. Ormerod, 'Wrestling with Rahner on the Trinity', *Irish Theological Quarterly* 69 (2003), 213–227 *passim*.

[17] E. Schadel (ed.), *Biblitheca Trinitariorum: The international bibliography of Trinitarian theology* (London: K.G. Saur, 1984).

[18] C. Hartshorne, *The Divine Relativity: A social conception of God* (New Haven: Yale University Press, 1948).

[19] S.M. Ogden, *The Reality of God and Other Essays* (London: SCM Press, 1967).

[20] Gunton, *Promise*, 162.

[21] See C.E. Gunton, *Enlightenment and Alienation: An essay towards a Trinitarian theology* (Grand Rapids: Eerdmans, 1985) and Gunton, C.E., *The One, the Three and the Many: God, Creation and the Culture of Modernity* (Cambridge: Cambridge University Press, 1993).

22 For example, from the Catholic perspective, see D.L. Gelpi, *The Turn to Experience in Contemporary Theology* (New York: Paulist Press, 1994), Liberation Theology's 'praxis' in A.T. Hennelly, *Liberation Theologies: The global pursuit of justice* (Mystic, Connecticut: 23rd Publications, 1997) and the concept of 'experience' in *Process Theology and Transcendental Thomism*. Gelpi helpfully summarized a number of these. Likewise, with an Eastern tradition there is Zizioulas, who wrote a significant book, J.D. Zizioulas, *Being as Communion: Studies in personhood and the church* (New York: St Vladimir's Seminary Press, 1985/2002). In the Evangelical tradition others have brought similar ideas. See, for example, J.I. Packer, *Knowing God* (London: Hodder & Stoughton, 1973), R. Macaulay and J. Barrs, *Being Human: The nature of spiritual experience* (Downers Grove, IL: InterVarsity Press, 1978), S.J. Grenz, *Created for Community: Connecting Christian belief with Christian living* (Grand Rapids: Baker Books, 1996/2000), L. Keefauver, *Experiencing the Holy Spirit: Transformed by His Presence – A twelve week interactive workbook* (Nashville: Thomas Nelson, 1997) and T.M. Kelly, *Theology at the Void: The retrieval of experience* (Notre Dame: University of Notre Dame Press, 2002).

23 R.E. Whitson, *The Shakers: Two centuries of spiritual reflection* (London: SPCK, 1983).

24 For example, J. Butler, *The Works of Joseph Butler*, Volume 2, *Fifteen Sermons on Human Nature* (Oxford: Clarendon Press, 1922/1986) and E. Underhill, *The Mystics of the Church* (New York: Schocken Books, 1964).

25 T.F. Lull, *Martin Luther's Basic Theological Writings* (Minneapolis: Fortress Press, 1989), 165ff., 314ff.

26 T.F. Torrance, *Theology in Reconciliation* (London: Geoffrey Chapman, 1975).

27 T.F. Torrance, *The Christian Doctrine of God: One being three persons* (Edinburgh: T&T Clark, 1996), 262ff.

28 O. Skarsaune, *In the Shadow of the Temple: Jewish influences on early Christianity* (Downers Grove, IL: InterVarsity Press, 2002).

29 Skarsaune, *Shadow*, 267.

30 C.S. McCoy, *When Gods Change: Hope for theology* (Nashville: Abingdon Press, 1980), 29.

31 By Arian controversy I am referring to the fourth-century Christological heresy that in seeking to preserve the monotheism of God denied the deity of the Son.

32 J.D. Ehrlich, *Plato's Gift to Christianity: The Gentile preparation for and the making of the Christian faith* (San Diego: Academic Christian Press, 2001).

33 I might be labelled 'modernist' by J.W. Cooper in *Body Soul and Life Everlasting: Biblical anthropology and the monism-dualism debate* (Grand Rapids: Eerdmans, 1989/2000), and others, simply because I am holistic. But it is not that I am accusing substance dualism, or any other school, of subverting Christianity. Instead, I am suggesting that Early Hebrew thought was more holistic regarding human make-up, and today this concept is becoming more popular among the contemporary unchurched. Having said that, Hebrew thought also had its dualistic aspects, focused around the sacred and profane.

34 J.A. Gorman, *Community that is Christian: A handbook on small groups* (Wheaton, IL: Victor Books, 1993), 36ff., noted the difference between individualism: the self-sufficiency and independent separation of an autonomous person, the fruit of the Enlightenment, and individuality: being a unique person. C.N. Kraus, *The Authentic Witness: Credibility and authority* (Grand Rapids: Eerdmans, 1979), 84–85, like Gorman, saw individualism as a matter of alienation and pride, the essence of sin. I will be using these words in this sense.

35 Gunton, *Promise*, 33.

36 K. Giles, *The Trinity and Subordinationism: The doctrine of God and the contemporary gender debate* (Downers Grove, IL: InterVarsity Press, 2002), 32ff.

37 J.B. Cobb, *Reclaiming the Church: Where the mainline church went wrong and what to do about it* (Louisville: Westminster John Knox Press, 1997), 2ff.

38 See S. McKenna, *Introduction to Saint Augustine: The Trinity* (Washington DC: Catholic University of America Press, 1963) quoted in Gunton, *Promise*, 55, note 53.

39 Gunton, *Promise*, 33.

40 C. Schwobel and C.E. Gunton, *Persons, Divine and Human: Kings College essays in theological anthropology* (Edinburgh: T&T Clark, 1991), 145.

41 Gunton, *Promise*, 39.

42 Having said that, Augustine does seem to be blamed far too often, and I would not want to be one of those who discredit him. His intellectual contribution has been a lasting and invaluable theological legacy to the Western Church, both Catholic and Protestant.

43 Gunton, *Promise*, 48.

44 Gunton, *Promise*, 57, footnote 18.

45 McCoy, *Gods*, 32.

46 Gunton, *Promise*, 81.

[47] Holmes, *More Human*, 45ff.

[48] See J.Y. Lee, *The Theology of Change: A Christian concept of God in an Eastern perspective* (Maryknowle, NY: Orbis Books, 1979), 43. Not all Lee's arguments sit comfortably with me. For instance, I have a problem with his phrase, 'God must be the subject of this change', page 45, preferring myself to use a word like 'capacity' rather than 'subject'.

[49] Lee, *Theology*, 75.

[50] Little is heard in the Church of that part of God's nature that has the capacity to be excited about events in human life. Hull suggested that when a couple have a child, this is an event for God as well as for them. See J.M. Hull, *What Prevents Christian Adults from Learning?* (Philadelphia: Trinity Press International, 1991), 222ff. So in this sense, as we go through life, we delight God by our integrity and love for His Son, and so He, along with us, moves from knowledge to more knowledge about us. To learn is to change, for to be surprised is part of the phenomenology of spirit (223). Such a view of God appears to fly in the face of an 'omniscient' God.

[51] Lee, *Theology*, 115.

[52] T.E. Fretheim, *God and World in the Old Testament: A relational theology of creation* (Nashville, Tenn.: Abingdon Press, 2005), 272.

[53] I am not suggesting God needs to change, in the sense of evolve, but that He needs to be seen to be able to sympathetically respond, e.g., adapt to our ever-changing world, the Church, and individual prayer, etc. This approach honours the essence of relationships as Scripture portrays them.

[54] I am speaking of Europe, not necessarily North America, where the situation is different. But one wonders whether what has already happened in Europe will some time begin to happen in North America?

[55] Gunton, *Promise*, 10.

[56] Collins, *Trinitarian Theology*, 26ff., 96ff., etc.

2.

Recovering Cappadocian Theology

While noting Gunton's caution[1] that we should not romanticize the Eastern tradition, we must emphasize the significance of the achievement of the Cappadocian Fathers in the third century.[2] Basil the Great, Gregory of Nyssa[3] and Gregory Nazianzus achieved several steps in the development of a view of Trinity that until recently had largely been ignored. As we noted earlier, in Cappadocian thinking there is no 'being' of God except the dynamic of *persons in relation*. The two aspects, person and relation, are intimately connected. There can be no relationship without a response, even with God. The central emphasis of relationship in and with God prohibits a static view of Him. The consequence of this is that if 'becoming'[4] is more fundamental than 'being', then God must be the perfect instance of 'becoming'. As each person within the Trinity gives and receives, there is an ongoing 'becoming' at the heart of the Godhead. When I first began to study Cappadocian teaching, I found myself thinking that if God is Trinity by His nature, He is therefore also 'becoming' in His nature. Not changing or evolving, but becoming in His relationship with us. And I asked myself how this could be mirrored in human community.

The Cappadocians created a new conception of the being of God, seeing it to consist in personal relational communion.[5] God has no ontological content, no true being, apart from communion. God is 'a sort of continuous and indivisible community'.[6] Rather ironically, the Western Church now describes this idea of a social Trinity as a 'modern' doctrine of God: a communion of three persons – not individuals – in mutually constitutive relations with one another. The person (*hypostasis*) is both constituted by and constitutes the ontological category of communion.[7] Two people are a

relationship, three a community.[8] In thinking this through I began
to see that if God is relational, He cannot be static in an isolated
sense, but instead must be in constant harmonic response (*kinesis*)
with each other person of the Trinity, as well as the created world.
So in one sense, therefore, He is in permanent relational change,
being responsive in all relationships, whilst still remaining
unchangeable (immutable) both within Himself and toward His
covenant promises to us.

The Importance of Cappadocian Thought

The initial insight of the Cappadocians was to distinguish
between two ordinary Greek words that until then had been virtually synonymous: *ousia* (being) and *hypostasis* (*prosopon* or person). With their emphasis on being as relationship, rather than
being as isolated entity, they anticipated the postmodern idea of
the logical priority of persons. In Greek thinking, logical priority
emphasized the importance of the individual, whereas postmodern and Cappadocian thinking prioritizes persons in relationship. In modern times people such as Macmurray[9] and Strawson[10]
have developed these observations further.[11] We will be looking
at their ideas in due course.

When this combination of being and person is applied to the
Trinity, it is seen that each person is only what they are by virtue
of what all three give to and receive from each other. Yet
through these mutually constitutive relations each remains distinctive and particular.[12] Such a Trinitarian theology allows us to
develop an ontology of the personal, both for the Trinity and for
human nature with all of its relationships. The Cappadocians
saw that the way the Church views God is the way we view
everything else, including creation, human nature and redemption. God is a society of three beings in *perichoretic* relationship.
Bracken and Suchocki described *perichoresis* as the inter-anima-
tion in relations within the Godhead, a mutual co-inherence,[13]
while Gunton described it as a vital device ensuring that
Trinitarian language does not lapse into tri-theism.[14] I will be
enlarging on the term *perichoresis* later in this chapter (see pages
37ff).

The Cappadocians also saw God as Creator, Redeemer and Transfigurer (Sanctifier),[15] whereas most Western theology focuses primarily on the second, redemption. Largely ignoring the first and the third. The Cappadocians thought it essential that all three be seen as equally consistent in the persons and nature of God. Within the Church we are now beginning to see a literature emerging that helps redress this balance, especially in God's role as Creator. Fretheim's[16] book is particularly interesting on this theme since it suggests that God continues to 'create' in His role of seeking to restore relationships. This is a welcome recent development.

The legacy of the loss of the emphases on God as Creator and Transfigurer has been profound since these concepts carry key ideas that we now know we need in Western theology. For instance, we have until recently forgotten that we mirror the Creator in having the capacity for relationships. Likewise, as Christians many of us have abdicated our responsibility for continual positive change, despite the fact that this is promoted by Him. For example, transformative sanctification in becoming more Christ-like. We have also conveniently remained oblivious to the innate capacity in both God and ourselves to live theocentric community. These Cappadocian ideas suggest the need for a repositioning of soteriology within a larger framework of both Father Creator and (Holy Spirit?) Transfigurer. God is Redeemer, Creator and Sanctifier at the interface of continual positive change encircling the inter-relationships within the Godhead. I believe that in some measure this should be mirrored in human community.

Down through the centuries, some in the Western Church have managed to steer clear of an unbalanced, singular emphasis on redemption whilst still working within a more theologically traditional view of the Trinity. Wesley is a good example of successfully avoiding the forensic rationalism of Constantinian atonement. Achieving this by additionally emphasizing that 'regeneration and sanctification had to do with actual transformation'.[17] This process directly involved God as Creator and Sustainer, as well as calling upon the individual to take up personal responsibility. In the course of a conversation on social Trinity, John Harding reminded me that atonement is a Trinity relational covenant at the heart of God's nature. But Lee has noted that in general Western theology's failure was to stress God's redemptive aspects at the expense of His creative ones,[18] while largely ignoring altogether God as Sanctifier.

Interestingly, Barth agreed with the Cappadocians by acknowledging, as a central theme in his *Church Dogmatics*,[19] that the relationality of the Godhead is the basis for the divine relationship with the world.[20] Restoration of all human damage therefore involves redeeming all estrangement from God, which includes that with others and with creation. Barth, however, failed to develop the implications of these ideas. This is now needed and it is part of the Church's redemptive task to help facilitate this entire process by embracing Cappadocian ideas of social Trinity. Let me illustrate this with a closer look at the person and work of the Holy Spirit.

Pneumatology: A Personal Spirit?

Cappadocian social Trinity recognizes the unique contribution of each member of the Trinity. This has particular implications for the person of the Holy Spirit, illustrating how significant a social Trinitarian perspective can be for daily congregational life. In the past here in the Western Church the doctrine of the Holy Spirit has not been treated equally alongside other major doctrines, such as, say, the doctrine of the person and work of Christ. Berkhof's *Systematic Theology*[21] for instance, devotes over 100 pages to the person and work of Christ, but has no section specifically on the Holy Spirit. Likewise, Strong's *Systematic Theology*[22] devotes over 110 pages to Christ, but again has no specific section on the person and work of the Holy Spirit.

Gunton suggested that Augustine's treatment of Spirit was more in terms of substance than the personal and relational. He saw this as the Achilles' heel of Augustine's theology,[23] commenting, 'The overall result is that because the doctrine of the Spirit has inadequate economic hypostatic weight in Augustine, the father of Western theology also lacks the means to give personal distinctiveness to the being of the Spirit in the inner Trinity.'[24] Therefore, with no recognition of the role of the Holy Spirit co-inhering within the whole Godhead, it is difficult to conceive of the Spirit constituting and sustaining the Church dynamically.

Further, by placing great importance on salvation in the next life, the Church has inadvertently suggested that a limited *experience* is available of God and salvation/redemption here and now. Christianity becomes a religion where we have to wait until the next life before we can fully gain its benefit. This present life is merely the test of our faithfulness in consistently believing (intellectually) in something we cannot yet see or experience. If we are faithful in obeying all the rules, values and beliefs, we will eventually benefit (by dying). The Church has been aware of this failure, but rather than placing the blame on its own theological foundations, as it should, it blames sin, the Fall and our running from God for this breakdown in relations.[25] The message is clear: in this life as Christians we need merely to endure. Recent positive responses to this massive failure, like that of Fiddes,[26] are now beginning to emphasize relational Trinity and its power to form human community. These initiatives are extremely welcome.

But the Church's failure at a pastoral relational level, Gunton suggested, has given birth here in the Western Church to a seriously deficient view of the Holy Spirit's work and relationship with the Church/ecclesiology.[27] Cobb and Griffin have concurred in calling for a new ontology of the Church.[28] Collins, also, thinking along similar lines, describes the need for a new *ousia* (Greek, being or substance; in Latin, *essentia*, or *substantia*). The Greek concept of Trinity refers to the three divine persons sharing in the common substance (*ousia*), a structured, relational ontology.[29] In essence, these and numerous other authors have all acknowledged, one way or another, that a Spirit that is not active in Trinity and part of our world *now*, has no mandate or ability to create either a vibrant relational spirituality or authentic divine-human community. At best, we may be able to imagine and even experience the Holy Spirit assisting individuals with their private 'faith', but we cannot conceive of Him as a lived reality *now* of Trinity-in-humanity-birthing-community. The failure is, of course, not in the Holy Spirit's ability but in our understanding of the breadth of His ministry. It is our incapacity to conceive Him fulfilling His ministry of facilitating change and intentional community in both the Church and the world.

New theologies are now being written that help redress this imbalance.[30] What we are learning as a Church, with the help of Cappadocian ideas, is that within the Trinity it is the Spirit who effects change and conversion (Eph. 4:3–6) as both an event (conversion) and a journey (sanctification). Such an understanding suggests that the Spirit has the ability to connect with the deepest core of human interiority, as well as desiring to break down the barriers that prevent us living in more intimate and fulfilling relationships.

Lee developed this point:

> We are conditioned by God's Spirit in the valuational structures of our own spirit. We are transformed in our appetitive faculties to feel things accurately with the feelings of God, and to yearn for them. Put simply, God's Spirit is where God's deep story is. Our spirit is where our deep story is. Through the immanence of God's Spirit in the human spirit, the deep story that is intended for history is transmitted.[31]

When as a Church we do not have an informed model of the Holy Spirit *relating to us*, it is inevitable that we will also have an inadequate model of human spirit,[32] as well as an inability to see the Holy Spirit forming community beyond our traditional understanding of Church.

What Lee has suggested is that an inadequate Trinitarian pneumatology leads to an inadequate understanding of atonement and its transformative relationality both in Trinity itself and in humanity. It makes Christ's finished work private and individual, and separates the act of conversion from a *journey* of personal moral transformation.[33] Salvation is seen as the experience of a moment of enlightened faith and belief, together with a declared allegiance, but is not seen as a lifetime journey of growing in wholeness through a relational Trinity that moulds us into Christ.

Our understanding of Trinity therefore colours our expectations of spirituality, of transformative change and Christ-likeness. Professor Larry Shelton suggested to me that conversion is traditionally seen in Western dogma as a legal transaction, substitutionary in nature, whereas Paul, as a Rabbinic Jew, held more of

a covenantal view of law that emphasized maintenance of relationship, rather than a once-off forensic act.[34] The Cappadocian
covenantal and relational pneumatology lays a foundation for
deepening relationship with God as well as engaging with one's
own spirituality, both personally and relationally. Let me illustrate.

A relational God

> ♦ I have a great sense of God very much at work in my life;
> substantially, not exclusively, through the people of CCD.
> This sometimes thrills, sometimes terrifies, sometimes infu-
> riates ♦ The teaching to understand sin is most important ♦ I
> never thought of sin as a disease and thus of myself as sick,
> but I am! ♦ Discovering your baggage is vital, especially if
> you've been a Christian a long time – since it doesn't mean
> you have less baggage than others – often you have accumu-
> lated more! ♦ Emotion and human spirit made so much sense
> when I first heard about them; it means now that the whole
> of me is seeking to have a relationship with God ♦
> Repentance is beautiful! There's nothing ugly about it.
> Through repentance we see a huge side to God that has been
> hidden from us for so long ♦ Ordinary language cuts through
> the spiritual language that clouds reality

> ♦ Having hope that you can change, along with faith, releases
> God's power to change me ♦ Because if we know we are sin-
> ners with all the consequences of that state then we will begin
> to seek God for salvation, i.e. wholeness ♦ (knowing you can
> personally change) gives everyone the same opportunity to
> develop their gifts and callings in Christ for the good of the
> body of Christ and the world ♦ Delete 'become a Christian' –
> insert 'meet Christ in a new way' ♦ The emphasis of the jour-
> ney is about seeing Christ's perspective.

> ♦ I am more real with God. Whereas before I wouldn't
> express to God how I felt through fear of condemnation,
> now I realize God wants (me) to give Him my anger and
> pain etc. Also, I find that I meet God as a person and not
> a Biblical concept or idea, e.g. I experience God's love
> rather than believing it intellectually

The Church's Loss

The more we explore Cappadocian ideas, the more clearly we see the stark contrast with Augustine of Hippo. Augustine was writing near the beginning of the era when the Church was being conceived as an institution, mediating grace to the individual, rather than as a community formed on the analogy of the Trinity's interpersonal relationships with God and one another.[35] This process of institutionalization led to a number of changes at that time and to subsequent losses. From Constantine onwards the Church has no longer been envisaged as individual households or small communities of believers with a communal God. Tertullian (c. 160–c. 220) in his *De Pudicitia*[36] had earlier seen this danger, arguing that the Church should not consist of its clergy and its bishops, but of a Trinity, a community of faith and its free act of congregating.[37]

Augustine gave us little reason to believe in a God who can be known or experienced in this way, since his desire was to create structures of human intellectuality toward a singular Deity for whom community was epiphenomenal or secondary. It was a small step from there to a place where the structure of the institution became more important than the vibrancy of living relationships. It is now accepted that Augustine's Deity is less than fully personal, in part because He conceived Him as immutable. If something other than a relational Father is the ontological foundation of the being of God, then the world and everything in it derives from what is fundamentally impersonal.[38]

The combination in Augustine of the lack of appreciation of the subtlety and importance of Eastern Greek Cappadocian terminology, together with the predominant influence of Neoplatonism behind the intellectual structures of Augustine's thinking, meant that Western traditions have continued to see the question of 'being' in terms of core personal ego.[39] Such thinking does not promote the idea of a relational God and His power both to transform persons and create community. In traditional theology God is not perceived as promoting authentic relational spirituality that is able to restore and promote for us now the experience of fulfilling, life-giving, authentic community. In the past, therefore, faith communities like CCD struggled to find a theological framework to describe what they were seeking to do – in applying social Trinity relationality to human faith community.

Building on Cappadocian Thought

Zizioulas[40] noted that Augustine differed from the Cappadocians in two significant ways: he remained individualistic, following Greek categories, but he also denied that the being of God 'unfolds' within the relations of the divine persons. McFadyen suggested that we could not conceive of the relationality of God on our own as human beings. Instead, we needed the concept of God engaging His relationality as it is at the core of His being: 'As the (divine) Persons are what they are only through their relations with the others, it must also be the case that their identities are formed through the others and the way in which the others relate to them.'[41] In some ways McFadyen reflected Jüngel's teaching that 'God's self-relatedness is based on God's "Yes" to himself. In this "Yes" of God, God Himself sets Himself in relations to himself, in order to be who He is. In this sense being is in becoming.'[42]

Zizioulas, taking up the Cappadocians' ideas, suggested the idea of God as 'an event of communion' (an event of *koinonia*), as the essence of what the Cappadocian Fathers were describing: that is, a social Trinity.[43] Zizioulas argued that God *knows* through communion, and that *the event of communion* rests on the concept of divine relationality, divine self-knowledge and divine love. God knows by relational love. Likewise, God has no true being apart from communion,[44] for the being of God is identical with an act of communion.[45] This suggests that freedom lies in relationship, not isolated individuality. True being and its freedom therefore only come from a free person in relationship. Such a concept moves personhood into post-Enlightenment thinking, with echoes of both Idealism and Existentialism.[46] Zizioulas writes, 'The ground of God's ontological freedom lies not in His nature but in His personal existence, that is, in the "mode of existence" by which he subsists as divine nature. It is this that gives people, in spite of their different natures, hope of becoming authentic persons.'[47] Put another way, God's freedom is the freedom of the

Father who chooses in love to live as Trinity, a mutually constituted communion of three persons.

Zizioulas moved the Cappadocian idea of communion from person-in-being to event-of-relationship. Prestige noted that this 'new' way of thinking had implications for the way the Church needed to look at God: 'regarded from the point of view of internal analysis, as one object, but that, regarded from the point of view of external presentation, he is three objects . . . God + God + God = God'.[48] 'Object' is used here to describe the person of God. Using the same language, O'Donnell commented that God is one object in Himself, and three objects to Himself.[49]

Zizioulas noted that the Cappadocians developed an ontology of divine being by employing the Biblical rather than the Greek view,[50] focused on an ontology of love (relationship), rather than an ontology of *ousia* (being). As Richard of St Victor has exquisitely noted, if it is truly love, the two will seek a third in order to share their love: 'Shared love is properly said to exist when a third person is loved by two persons harmoniously and in community.'[51] Richard brought an approach to the doctrine of the Trinity that has great possibilities for developing a relational view of the human person. He developed the idea of the unity of the divine persons as *ex-sistentiae*, three persons being intrinsic to one another, continually emerging out of one another. His now famous definition of person is, '*persona est divinae naturae incommunicabilis existentia*': each divine person is essentially only out of, and in relation with the other person.[52] God is able to remain God's self in relational love, while also being available and desiring the capacity for dynamic loving relationship. The suggestion is, as C.S. Lewis has so ably noted, that God desires us to be both more fully human and to demonstrate a willingness to be loved by Him in order to learn love in relationship.[53]

Introducing *Perichoresis*

Not everything the Cappadocians developed is being eagerly accepted as the final word by the Western Church.[54] The implications of their theology are still evolving, and are yet to mature. But I believe that we have so far made enough ground to be able to distinguish between being and person, which then allows us to move further by adopting the Greek term *perichoresis*. As we saw earlier in this chapter, Bracken and Suchocki described this term as the life-giving relations within the Godhead, a mutual co-inherence,[55] and Gunton described it as a vital device ensuring that Trinitarian language does not lapse into tri-theism.[56] (By tri-theism, I mean the idea of three separate Gods.) The term *perichoresis* is used by the Cappadocians in two senses: first, that of reinforcing the unity of the Godhead, and, second, as the centre of consciousness in the Godhead, an interpenetrating of the persons wholly in one another. When thinking of social Trinity, a word is needed to describe how the persons of the Trinity intermingle within one another in an holistic way. This word is *perichoresis*. I quote Collins' commendation of Zizioulas for his part in reintroducing and applying this concept to us today: '[He] combines the radical outcome of the ontological revolution which is implicit in the Cappadocians' terminology, with a modern understanding of consciousness, *Dasein*, and freedom.'[57] In reaching this position, with our new understanding of social Trinity, we can now begin to apply some of these ideas.

Our Response in CCD

In reading the Cappadocians and authors such as Zizioulas, I felt I was personally moving toward a theology promoting relationality facilitated by the example of social Trinity. I began to see how we could build an ecclesiology more in keeping with our need to conceptualize a relational faith community helpful to postmodern people. The Cappadocians and Richard of St Victor gave me this platform. On this basis I concluded that the Church should be thinking in terms of the analogy of relation. What is really important is not something *in* a person but *between* persons, as it also is with God. It is not our ontic nature as such, but the process of our developing relationship with God.[58] Having the idea of the persons of the Trinity pouring life into one another permanently in divine loving harmony is extremely helpful when trying to imagine how a faith community can seek, by the way it lives, to mirror the divine nature. This idea applies to how as Christians we receive from the Lord; to our being able to perceive ourselves as relational beings; and to our capacity to honour one another. The concept of a dynamic *perichoresis* gives us a solution to the Constantinian problem of relations between God and the world. But the helpfulness does not end here. If we are formed in the image of Trinity along Cappadocian lines, then we are community-building beings. We have an innate, though damaged, drive toward living in relationships. Such a simple idea, as it is adopted, has a profound impact on one's outlook toward congregational life and practice. One can begin to conceive of a God who is promoting relational life, not just private individual faith. This understanding has particular implications for men. It dismantles the suggestion that at their best men are solitary, private beings. If men are in the image of God, then they should also be relational. They are given permission, even a duty, to explore deeper relationships.

When men adopt such a view it is not hard to see positive change in them as they tentatively begin to learn how to live deeper relationships with other men. One of the ways this has begun to mature in CCD is in the expectation that men should and will find community as attractive as women. Men are not the solitary creatures we have been taught they are. Instead, within CCD, we now accept that as they become more whole, men both develop the capacity and learn the value of being together. As a consequence, I have needed to change my views radically regarding how I see men, and now concede that they need community as much as women, though in a somewhat different way. Let some of the men in the community say it their way.

Being men

> ◆ Relationships with men in the church, in experiencing a level of intimacy and transparency that I have sought my whole life ◆ My troika (meetings of three men together) has brought male relationship with each other and God to new levels that I couldn't even of dreamed of a year ago

> ◆ I saw in Christ Church a number of men who were being given permission to be men, it caused enormous conflict in me. When I saw the number of men in Christ Church, even the physical number of men being able to freely and openly

talk to each other as a bloke, it was not something I had come across, not in my experience of anything, and that caused enormous conflict in me and it threatened me, and it actually for the first time I think it gave me hope . . . The other area for me that has been incredibly important but again has probably been the single most difficult thing, has been the whole emphasis on truth here. And I have found that really tough to cope with. And I think it is the combination of the two, having the hope of what I could become has given me the courage progressively to be able to face more and more truth about myself. I have hated that aspect of it. But it is probably the single thing that has actually kept me, and given me hope

• Your manhood isn't going to be ridiculed

• For me personally I didn't have a Christian background, I had never been to church in my life, I had no opinion on Christianity, on fellowship, community, church. All I knew was I was isolated and in much trauma, much pain, rejected by family, doing lots and lots of damage to myself because of what people had done to me. I was becoming quite ill, in isolation and really it is the men of the church, they are standing with me, that has enabled me along with the counselling, the finding out the truth about your damage, and why we are damaged, and why we do what we do to ourselves, that I am able to be here to be speaking about this tonight so openly. To be able to sit with other men and talking. I couldn't do this two years ago

• From a single guy's point of view that you are encouraged to go out, encouraged to date. Obviously we have responsibility for what we do and what we don't etc. But there is a freedom to say, yes, go out, explore, grow, learn. Whereas I couldn't before

Another application of Cappadocian ideas in a local congregational context is the suggestion that we are something special while we are together that we are not while we are alone. If

Zizioulas' ideas relating to social Trinity are valid, then private personal faith is not as merit-filled as many of us may have pretended it is. The solitary saint is part of the folklore of the Church, but is not endorsed by Cappadocian ideas. For instance, Christ promised to be among us where two or three of us are gathered together (Mt. 18:20). Does this teaching by Christ mirror social Trinity? One cannot deny that Scripture has a huge emphasis on being together – the Eucharist, prayer, anointing the sick, and going out in twos, for instance. Christ even said that we would be known as His in our love (the quality of our relationships) toward each other (Jn. 13:35).

It is likely that many of us in contemporary congregational life are involved in solitary tasks, especially when we know that we can do these jobs more quickly or more effectively on our own. Cappadocian teaching on the social Trinity, however, suggests that our actions are more in the image of God if they are done together, even where this takes more time and is less efficient. Being together needs to be more important than destination or outcome, and sharing responsibility in a team environment preferable to carrying it out privately or personally. In CCD, in seeking to mirror social Trinity, we have therefore experimented with the idea of doing things together, seeing this as an excuse for a get-together, or for making a job a relational event.

Another change in our own community was when we moved the worship band to the back of the congregation, requiring each person to proactively visualize worshipping Christ in relationship rather than continue to be passively 'led' in worship by the singers and musicians. This change has also allowed the singers and musicians to be more part of the body of worshippers (e.g. on the same level, rather than at the altar or on stage in front of everyone). It is an attempt to mirror social Trinity by a visual declaration of openness and relational oneness. This has not necessarily improved the quality of the worship time, or been helpful for everyone. Most of us in the congregation would agree that when it comes to sung worship together on Sundays, we still have a long way to go. But this idea has changed the focus and is one of the first things that visitors from other churches comment on. Helpful contributions to the idea of social Trinity and worship are now being made by others.[59]

Along similar lines, we have also removed most of the chairs so that we now have an open area for everyone to stand or dance. This creates more room for freedom of expression, be it movement, raising hands or foot-stamping in rhythm with the music, etc. (We are also fortunate in having in the hall we hire for our Sunday morning meeting a large sprung dance floor that helps facilitate this movement.) Doing away with a prescribed layout dictated by chairs or pews allows people to feel together, choosing where they stand and who they stand with during the opening block of sung worship. Each of us now has the potential to respond in our own way, yet as part of the Body of Christ. The children and teenagers often stay in for this part of our Sunday meeting and from time to time lead us with their banners, flags and lack of inhibition.

But we take this Sunday morning way of mirroring a social Trinity even further. As is common in a number of emerging churches, we have one Sunday each month when we do not meet for a formal Sunday meeting. On the last Sunday of every month we cancel Sunday church altogether. We do this to facilitate social relations in and outside the congregation. Groups meet option-ally for barbeques, some people visit friends and family, while others just sleep in and have a lazy day. This started by accident when a local theatre we were hiring had a Sunday market once a month, which meant that we could not meet on those Sundays, but it quickly became very popular, and is now part of our church culture. It allows our Sunday morning Bible study and worship meetings to be more special on the Sundays we do meet, helping to avoid them becoming stale and repetitive. As part of this change, we have a Eucharist on the first Sunday of each month as a special 'communion' together. Let me share with you some of the comments from members of the community.

Trinity in community

> ♦ The healing comes from God working through the members ♦ I have got a word – togetherness ♦ I have spent most of my Christian life talking to God, but not really waiting for a response ♦ It's about who I am – God's image, becoming who I was created to be – not a detached God ♦ Christianity . . . It's real and I can really have a relationship with Christ instead of imagining one ♦ It feels a bit like Christ Church is a place where you don't find God but in a sense God finds you, in that

you meet people around you who carry the Lord and you see the Lord ✦ The whole is greater than the sum of its parts

✦ If they come along to a service they have got it, they feel it, they walk in. You only have to be away for a week, two weeks and you come back into it and you feel it, the warmth of the congregation, the atmosphere, and the spirit and worship and it is just so tremendous. But we get so used to it, we lose sight of that, but when people walk into it, it is quite spectacular for them

✦ Because it is all an aspect of my own personality which is being exposed, in that relationship that wouldn't be exposed otherwise. Therefore it is another part of myself, another part of God which I am meeting because of the range of people that we have got here

Notes

1 Gunton, *Promise*, viii.
2 F.M. Young, *From Nicaea to Chalcedon: A guide to the literature and its background* (London: SCM Press, 1983), 92ff.
3 Coakley, 'Rethinking Gregory of Nyssa: Introduction – Gender, trinitarian analogies and the pedagogy of "The Song"', *Modern Theology* 18 (4) 431–444 (2002).
4 L. Ford, 'Contingent trinitarianism' in J.A. Bracken and M.H. Suchocki (eds.), *Trinity in Process: A relational theology of God* (New York: Continuum, 1997) 41–68, 56.
5 Zizioulas, *Being*, 17.
6 See Basil of Caesarea, 'Letter 38 4 MPG 32 332a and 333d5–333el, ET' in M. Wiles and M. Santer (eds.), *Documents in Early Christian Thought* (Cambridge: Cambridge University Press, 1975), 34–35 quoted in Gunton, Promise, 9.
7 Zizioulas, *Being*, 18.
8 See Grenz, *Created* and S.J. Grenz, *Theology for the Community of God* (Grand Rapids: Eerdmans, 2000).
9 See J. Macmurray, *The Self as Agent* (New Jersey: Humanities Press, 1957/1991) and J. Macmurray, *Persons in Relation* (London: Faber & Faber, 1961).

10 P.F. Strawson, *Individuals: An essay in descriptive metaphysics* (London: Methuen, 1959).

11 Gunton, *Promise*, 96.

12 Gunton, *Promise*, 11.

13 J.A. Bracken and M.H. Suchocki, 'Concluding remarks' in J.A. Bracken and M.H. Suchocki (eds.), *Trinity in Process: A relational theology of God* (New York: Continuum, 1997), 215–224, 221.

14 Gunton, *Promise*, 167.

15 Cobb, *Reclaiming*, 4.

16 Fretheim, *God and World in the Old Testament; A Relational Theology of Creation* (Nashville, Abington Press), 2005.

17 K.J. Collins, *The Scriptural Way of Salvation: The heart of John Wesley's theology* (Nashville: Abingdon Press, 1997), 16.

18 Lee, *Theology*, 80.

19 K. Barth, *Church Dogmatics – Doctrine of the Word of God*, G.W. Bromiley and T.F. Torrance (tr.) (Edinburgh: T&T Clark, 1956).

20 Collins, *Trinitarian Theology*, 11.

21 L. Berkhof, *Systematic Theology* (London: Banner of Truth, 1939/1963).

22 A.H. Strong, *Systematic Theology: Three volumes in one* (London: Pickering & Inglis, 1907/1962).

23 Gunton, *Promise*, 47.

24 Gunton, *Promise* 51.

25 L.L. Steele, *On the Way: A practical theology of Christian formation* (Grand Rapids: Baker Book House, 1990), 20.

26 P.S. Fiddes, *Participating in God: A pastoral doctrine of the Trinity* (Louisville: Westminster John Knox Press, 2000).

27 Gunton, *Promise*, 65.

28 J. Cobb and D. Griffin, *Process Theology: An introductory exposition* (Philadelphia: Westminster Press, 1976), 71ff.

29 Collins, *Trinitarian Theology*, 143.

30 See Grenz, *Created* and Grenz, *Theology*.

31 Lee, '"Other" Trinity', 195.

32 C. Schwobel, 'Introduction' in C. Schwobel and C.E. Gunton (eds.), *Persons, Divine and Human* (Edinburgh: T&T Clark, 1991), 1–29, 9.

33 See J. Vanier, *Community and Growth* (New York: Paulist Press, 1979) and M.V. Angrosino, 'L'Arche: The phenomenology of Christian counter-culturalism', Qualitative Inquiry 9 (2003), 6.934–954.

34 R.L. Shelton, *Divine Expectations: Interpreting the atonement for 21st century mission* (Waynesboro, GA: Paternoster, 2006).

[35] Gunton, *Promise*, 51.

[36] Tertullian, *La Pudicite* (De Pudicitia) (Paris: Cerf, 1993)

[37] Gunton, *Promise*, 63.

[38] Gunton, *Promise*, 54.

[39] Collins, *Trinitarian Theology*, 191.

[40] Zizioulas, *Being*.

[41] A.I. McFadyen, *The Call to Personhood: A Christian theory of the individual in social relationship* (Cambridge: Cambridge University Press, 1990), 28.

[42] E. Jungel, *The doctrine of the Trinity: God's being is in His becoming* (Edinburgh: Scottish Academic Press, 1976), 102–103.

[43] Zizioulas, *Being*, 18.

[44] Zizioulas, *Being*, 17.

[45] Zizioulas, *Being*, 44.

[46] Collins, *Trinitarian Theology*, 179.

[47] Zizioulas, *Being*, 43.

[48] G.L. Prestige, *God in Patristic Thought* (London: SPCK, 1936/1952), 169.

[49] J.J. O'Donnell, *Trinity and Temporality: The Christian doctrine of God in the light of process theology and the theology of hope* (Oxford: Oxford University Press, 1983), 41.

[50] J.D. Zizioulas, 'On being a person: Toward an ontology of personhood' in C. Schwobel and C. Gunton (eds.), *Persons, Divine and Human* (Edinburgh: T&T Clark, 1991), 33–45, 40.

[51] Richard of St Victor, *De trinitate* (Paris: Les Editions du Cerf, 1959), 7–9, quoted in Gunton, *Promise*, 92.

[52] R. Faber, 'Trinity, analogy and coherence' in J.A. Bracken and M.H. Suchocki (eds.), *Trinity in Process: A relational theology of God* (New York: Continuum, 1997), 147–171, 150.

[53] C.S. Lewis, *Reflections on the Psalms* (New York: Harcourt Brace Jovanovich, 1958), 71–74.

[54] D. Tuggy, 'The unfinished business of Trinitarian theorising', *Religious Studies* 39 (2003), 2.165–183.

[55] Bracken and Suchocki, 'Concluding remarks', 221.

[56] Gunton, *Promise*, 167.

[57] Collins, *Trinitarian Theology*, 144.

[58] Lee, *Theology*, 55.

[59] R. Parry, *Worshipping Trinity: Coming back to the heart of worship* (Milton Keynes: Paternoster, 2005).

3.

My Personal Problem with the Idea of 'Community'

People tend to talk more about a thing when it is going wrong than when it is okay. So in Western society today people are talking a lot about community. We are told that we are losing traditional communities through urbanization and mass migration, or we hear about the forming of contemporary 'virtual' communities through the web. A felt response to this loss could be the huge popularity of the TV programme 'Cheers: where everyone knows your name', an echo of the wish of many of us. Likewise, we can note the remarkable popularity of 'Friends', 'Heartbeat' or 'Last of the summer wine', which are all focused around small communities and deep relationships. This yearning for community seems to echo the truth that relationality is at the heart of social Trinity, and is also at the core of human need both in and outside the Church.

None the less, in seeking community we are having to redefine it for our postmodern age. Although its loss is being noted by many, this is only part of the story. Other forces are also at work. Part of our contemporary problem is that we are creating a culture of observers rather than a participatory culture. This only adds to our sense of isolation. A good example is the proliferation of the television soaps, all based around micro communities. We sit and watch the characters living out their lives. This came to me very strongly recently while sitting with a frail grandmother who was talking in animated and anxious terms about a court trial and its outcome in her favourite soap. Looking at her, I realized that these daily events on television were helping to keep her alive, as from day to day she was anxiously waiting for the next episode. She is part of an observer society that is vicariously living off the adventures and relationships of make-believe others.

Clarke Pinnock[1] cited the existence of community within congregations as one of the best reasons for a person to consider Christianity. In the past I would have unthinkingly agreed with him, assuming that by merely meeting as a local congregation church somehow mystically and automatically became community. It was as if little more effort was needed. So for the first thirty-five years or more of my Christian life I was happy to believe that by 'doing church', *koinonia*, by the warmth of fellowship together, we were also living community, and nothing more needed to be done. But I have now come to the conclusion that for the Church to offer community, especially the kind of community that is rooted in social Trinity, both a redefining of community and a range of changes must take place amongst us.

It had never really occurred to me that congregational life could or should be more than a series of regular meetings, and that 'fellowship' as I was practising it was actually not *authentic* community. I am surprised now that I could have held on to these ideas even though I saw that churches were emptying and in spite of the fact that for the rest of my working life, week in and week out, I was kept busy pursuing a huge range of 'things', many of which were unconnected with congregational life. Some were church-related ministry or teaching, but few related to faith 'community'. Still I did not make the connection that the failure of church, on the one hand, and the growing interest in community and its redefining, on the other, all suggested a failure of church as community. For me congregational life was never seen as the pouring of love into one another revealed in social Trinity.

In exploring these matters more deeply, I realized that the situation was actually much worse than I had at first thought. I actually had deep personal prejudices against ideas of 'community'. For instance, I believed that 'community' was only a term that described a way of meeting the needs of the weak and vulnerable, the sick and frail. *They* needed community. It never occurred to me that this should be a priority and focus for the whole Church. It is both hard and embarrassing for me to confess, but to my shame I did not believe that 'community' as I now understand it, was essential for growing churches full of 'strong Christians' living 'successfully'. I genuinely believed that we did not need community, or even relationality, beyond the traditional meetings of 'faith community'. My flawed assumption was that being Church is community, and nothing needed to change or be taken further.

All of this thinking was turned radically upside down in 1998 when we planted Christ Church Deal here in Kent, UK, and its members began to teach me some essential wisdom in this area. I have always been aware theologically that the whole Church worldwide, in any form, is *koinonia* (Heb. 12:22–23), defined as a natural bond of fellowship in the Holy Spirit (Eph. 4:3). But Christ Church has drawn my attention to the principle that the spiritual reality of *koinonia* does not in itself make community of the type many of us desire today. I began to see that the model of faith 'community' that much of the Church has been living with was not what the majority of (relatively healthy) unchurched people wanted as they sought community. They did not want meetings, but they did want relationships.

I also had to confess that I had an arrogant male gender issue to work through. My perception was that women preferred attachment (e.g. community and relationships) just as Carol Gilligan suggests.[2] This I was very willing to accept, but I (proudly) interpreted this as a sign of their weakness. In contrast, when it came to men and issues like wholeness and maturity, independence was my perceived healthy norm. After all, had I not grown up in a Christian culture where for man to be man he must be strong, successful and *independent*? He needs, I thought, to be able to stand alone, just as Beowolf did, having a fearsome power to protect, but requiring few relationships to sustain him.

In the Church such ideas translated for me into the 'solitary saint' of Church history as portrayed in thousands of Christian biographies and autobiographies, from John of the Cross, Luther, Tyndale through to John Bunyan, Hudson Taylor, Sadhu Sundar Singh, Thomas Merton, Corrie Ten Boom, Kagawa and Nate Saint. Most of these writings seem to focus on the journey and successes of the individual. My recent experience in CCD has turned all of this well-established prejudice and arrogance upside down. While not wanting to discredit either the lives or remark-able achievements of these men (and women), I have now come to regard much of this type of thinking on solitariness as unhelp-ful baggage.

Having to admit that I was wrong on all counts has been a long and humbling road to take. My recent conclusion is that faith community as Christians have lived it in the past is not commu-nity of the type that many, both inside and outside the Church, are seeking today. Also, it is not community as articulated in ideas of social Trinity. Were we to live a dynamic *perichoretic union* with a mutual pouring of life into one another, faith community would become something very different from that we have known. When any one of us even admits that this is God's norm for healthy human nature, we have, as Christians, a duty to change to building community and relationality. On this basis both male and female are *imago Dei*, in the image of God, meaning that men are also social beings, so need relational community as much as women do, only in a different way.

In placing such emphasis on community and its relationality, I am not denying that each person must decide for themselves whether God and His word are trustworthy, and whether salva-tion is for them.[3] This remains a given for me. Also, I would not wish to use the excuse of the mutual support of community to deflect from the place of personal responsibility. Social Trinity both suggests and requires the full participation of each individ-ual member. I would therefore agree with Oden that the Church must reflect the individual in the Spirit's work in bringing faith communities into being in response to grace.[4] I accept all these basic ideas regarding the balance between the individual and the social group. But this, on reflection, does not change the fact that I carried an unhelpful prejudice against the idea of community, and this prejudice kept me from seeing that many outside of the Church were seeking a type of community that I was not willing to consider. Similarly, many even inside the Church were want-ing to change in a positive way, but my prejudices stood in the way of helping this happen.

Regardless of the compelling evidence both from my own intellectual journey and my member teachers in CCD, I instinc-tively and stubbornly held on to the old ways, redoubling my efforts rather than taking the risk of changing my thinking. What I had to admit was that reproducing traditional institutional Church is always much easier for me. After all, I had had over thirty-five years of doing it this way. The task of seeking to create a new model of congregation as community was far too daunting to undertake. So it was only over time as part of the Leadership Team in CCD that I slowly began to accept that people were changing in positive ways as a result of sharing their lives together, men as well as women. Together they were demonstrating to me the type of community they wanted and needed. I have now come to accept, as Clark needed to, that groups of believers, and the environment they create, are the essence of church life and the most effective agents of change[5] for both men and women.

On reflection, the main reason why these new ideas hit me so hard was that they were so different from anything I had witnessed before in the wide range of churches I had been part of. At their core these differences focused around the *expectations* of those in CCD. Like most of the post-war generation, I had chosen independence (individualism) over community.[6] But within our faith community we were creating a womb for personal positive change that equated to a wholeness journey toward Christ-like-ness. I found myself describing this process as salugenic (whole-ness-giving) discipleship. I was witnessing before me a living discipleship model that, while having the individual at its heart, was facilitated by the salugenic social processes of the group as a whole.

I began to realize that when they had joined many in our community had been unwell – with a wide range of disorders – so they had a driven need to get well. This healing journey they did together, creating a type of therapeutic community within a faith setting. I began to see that at the core of each relationship there was a dynamic *perichoresis* that released a supernatural capacity to bring healing and wholeness through a deepening relationship with Christ. The radical nature of this process only dawned on me after the first couple of years of being part of CCD. But it set me out on the journey of putting into a historical and relational social context what was happening before my very eyes. In one sense we were recovering community, but in another sense we were

creating a type of therapeutic rela
realized was possible.

Stages in the Loss of Community

In no area of contemporary culture do people
communities they want. Maybe this is a natural
by every generation is brought to the position of
community for themselves. As I have looked more
this subject, I have been forced to conclude that it is
complex an issue to be resolved by one or two simple ans
Few of us can, for example, return to the villages of the 18
Most of us probably realize that the ideal, as we see it, of tha
sort of community life is now gone for ever – if it ever even
existed. Some, like Winter,[7] suggest that society is not seeing a
total loss of community, just a time of change with the emerging of a new, deepening communal sensibility and interdependence. The diverse range of opinions about the loss of
community has been a caution to me not to be all knowing
about the subject. Instead, I have conceded that what many of
us are looking for today in being part of a community within
our contemporary culture does not yet exist. Society still needs
to invent it.

The word 'community' in its modern sense was probably first
introduced by the German Ferdinand Tönnies. He described
Gemeinschaft as a way of life typical of that of the German peas-
ant in the countryside.[8] In English, the term came to prominence
in the nineteenth century through a cluster of authors and their
growing awareness of the appalling impact on the poor of aspects
of the hideous, soulless, industrial revolution, which had led to
the working classes giving up rural communities. As a result,
they had a desperate need to recover lost relationship. Before that
time the word 'community' had not had great meaning, probably
because community had not been seen as something that was
dying or being lost.

Kirkpatrick identified three systems that, since the Middle
Ages, have contributed toward constructing modern thought
regarding community.

individual atoms in
k philosophers, was
. the political social
Pilgrim Fathers, and
;tablish reductionist
1monwealth.[9] These
social model that is
term is used in the
trade, thereby pre-
d supremely cere-
1is modern person.
:ontrast to the val-
·er. In some ways

with the Idea of 'Community'

tional community that I had not

51

seem to have the
process where-
reinventing
closely at
far too
wers.
00s.

......on to the working
·~ auuress the loss of community that it
·~u~ca.

2. Organic functionalism

The contractarian model was followed by the organic functional model (Hegel, Burke, Marx, socialism, then Whitehead, Pols and others).[11] These thinkers responded to earlier models by seeking to make the social whole take precedence over the individual parts, suggesting an organic metaphor of 'society'. Such imagery of 'a society' is now almost universally accepted by social theorists. According to this theory, society as a whole is more important than the individuals in it. Hegel epitomized this viewpoint by suggesting that reality is fulfilled only in and through the whole, not in and through the parts alone.[12] The absolute, or spirit, is the whole of reality. Community is the embodiment of Geist or spirit. Society is community, and people make it up.

Such thinking sowed the seeds of Marxist totalitarianism, because when you push the notion of society as an organism too far, as Marx did, the organic whole takes precedence and all its subsidiary parts must be subservient to it.[13] The consequence of such thinking is a functionalism that discards all that is not useful. In Marx's case,[14] this meant the revolutionary purging of a pathologically diseased society. In the twentieth century this model was little challenged, except by thinkers such as

Whitehead with his comprehensive metaphysics.[15] Seeking to redress some of the fragmentation of our culture, Whitehead suggested an organic model of community through his concept of 'occasion'.

3. Mutual personal model
Kirkpatrick noted that the organic functional model created a number of problems, including one central problem: how to reconcile our Western liberal insistence on the freedom of the individual with our desire to enter into interpersonal relations with others.[16] The answer, his third model, is the mutual personal emphasis. Kirkpatrick began with Buber, who, he suggested, has, through the influence of Feuerbach,[17] done more than anyone else to establish the essential nature of human relationship.[18] Only in relations, Buber argued, is the self fulfilled, for 'the primary word *I-Thou* can only be spoken with the whole being'.[19]

For Buber, unity with God and community among creatures both belong together[20] (a model entirely compatible with Cappadocian ideas of social Trinity, mirrored in Buber's Jewish tradition). Communities arise through persons

> first, taking their stand in living mutual relation with a living Centre, and, second, by their being in living mutual relation with one another. The second has its source in the first, but is not given when the first alone is given . . . The community is built up out of living mutual relations, but the builder is the living effective Centre.[21]

But we are getting ahead of ourselves. Before considering this third model, let us look more carefully at the impact of the individualism of atomistic contractarianism upon the Church and then at its impact in a more recent social context.

The Toll of Enlightenment Ideas on the Church

With hindsight, it seems ironic that the 'Enlightenment', which birthed individualism, should have led to the Marxist system, which in many ways denied individuality. Both in different ways have contributed to a dismantling of community. To this we must also add the industrial revolution that from the 1700s onwards wove its way through these, denying the individual authentic identity and expression. Part of the reaction to these constraints and losses was the conceiving of a range of counter endeavours from the arts and crafts movement, with its return to individual style, to communes searching for community. The communitarian movement was also birthed at this time, together with a whole range of intentional communities from commercial to therapeutic. All these sought community in the face of a growing individualism with its dark side that undermined community.

'Enlightenment' thinking went much further than merely making human personhood individual. It also birthed Deism and Scepticism, giving people permission not to believe in Christianity or any other absolute values. Instead, rather than continuing to believe what they had been taught, individuals could set their own beliefs relative to themselves. One of the outcomes was that what remained of nominal Christian values and community was absorbed by 'secularization', with people no longer trusting in the values and beliefs taught by others but finding their own values. The drive had begun toward what is now being called 'selfism', in which people make themselves the centre of their own worlds. The Church, as one of the victims of the Enlightenment, would never be the same again. As Banks observed, in response to these changing values Catholicism followed the cultic path of structure and control, seeking to hold on to ideas of community, while Protestantism followed the path taken by the synagogue and worshipped a book.[22] The Bible, or, rather, bibliolatry, with all its need to learn laws and rules, was in danger of taking the place of worship and the intimacy of relationship with Christ, both personally and communally. I am not saying that respect for the Bible is wrong, only that it can be when the Bible becomes a substitute for intimacy with Christ, and applying rules and values becomes more important than the person.

The Protestant Church's new position was illustrated in the winter semester of 1899 to 1900 at the University of Berlin when Adolf von Harnack delivered his 16 lectures entitled *The Essence of Christianity*.[23] 'The kingdom of God,' he said, 'comes by coming to individuals, making entrance into their souls, and being grasped by them. The kingdom of God is indeed God's rule – but it is the rule of a holy God in individuals' hearts.'[24] Such thinking had become firmly rooted in Western Protestant thought. Under the heat of the Enlightenment, ideas of community had evaporated. Individualism now ruled.

One of the post-Reformation tendencies was to 'spiritualize' and 'internalize' faith, a process that became even easier as everyone gained personal access to a Bible. Faith and the Christian's relationship with Christ became more private, personal and 'spiritual'. Protestantism did in some ways allow people to be more free, but also resulted in their being more alone.[25] Lindbeck described this as a 'Marcionite tendency'.[26] This has taken its toll on the quest of faith communities for a relational faith. Individual faith becomes more important than relational faith. Comments Robinson: 'Christians should be the last people to be found clinging to the wrecks of an atomistic individualism which has no foundation in the Bible.'[27]

In society generally from the 1960s there has been a growing awareness of the loss of community.[28] Only recently, however, has the Church echoed this awareness. Etzioni,[29] for instance, with his Jewish roots and his training under Buber, argued that society is beginning to ride a wave that is returning community to us. But he suggested it needed to have both a social, political and a personal agenda if it is to be beneficial. Bellah[30] likewise called for a renewed understanding of the crucial role of community in constructing personal identity. Rapport summarized the beginnings of this growing awareness, commenting: 'Recent decades have seen an upsurge in "community consciousness", "community development and rebuilding" and "values and works".'[31] Let the CCD community speak for themselves regarding the need for a move away from such individualism.

Our changing view on the need for privacy

* The more you become vulnerable to others in a healthy way, and allow others to draw near, the more capacity you have for relationships * I am having to learn to let go of my privacy (my way of staying in control) and choose to move into relationships. It is a real battle * I seem at last to be able to relate to myself, and to see how I have made it impossible for others to relate to me. Privacy may now be valued as chosen rather than

self-imposed ◆ Now I can no longer work on my own for long
– I so hate the isolation of it that I am seeking to rectify it. The
depth of relationships is far deeper than before because we all
share the same journey, we're learning together as well as cry-
ing and laughing together ◆ There doesn't seem to be any point
in being private because our story can help others, and we are
encouraged to gossip what God has done for us ◆ Sense of privacy – why keep it private if it can be shared? I've found this
aspect difficult, having been very closed and private ◆ I feel that
my life is not my own any more. I'm beginning to enjoy the
honesty and transparency, but still find it hard as I'm pathetic at
relationships ◆ Privacy has become less and less important.
Much more keen to allow others to share my private world ◆
I'm very grateful for being encouraged to open the doors of our
home and live in community. I don't have so much privacy any
more, but I don't resent that. As long as I have a room I can go
to and close the door when the need arises

Within the Church, as in wider society, I believe Enlightenment
individualism still holds far too much ground. Yet the tight-knit
rural community of our distant pasts is not what society is seeking today. The car and global travel, the media, the mobile phone
and internet, together with the loss of absolutes and the rela-
tivization of one belief to another belief have brought this to a
close. So I do not believe that we should talk about the 'recovery'
of community within the Church. What has worked in the past is
clearly not succeeding now. I have therefore been forced to conclude that the Church needs to embrace a range of fundamental
ideas regarding community, many of which Church and society
have either forgotten, or never known. We must harness all of
these ideas to help construct a new type of faith community for
ourselves in our century. But to achieve this, society will first need
to address one of the newest enemies of relationality – selfism.

Individualism Leading to the Cult of Selfism

In our present Western culture what has been called 'rugged individualism' has led to what Vitz described as 'selfism'.[32] The cult

of self is now the foundation of many of our Western values: phrases like 'what is best for me', 'it must fit me', 'they no longer give me anything' are just some of the often-heard echoes of self-ism. It is the idea that the world must revolve around 'me', that 'my' needs are paramount, that it is essential I begin looking after 'myself' as no one else will. For large numbers of people today this attitude is the driving force behind their thinking and behaviour. Selfism rules.

When we look at the demise of community, we should not ignore the impact of selfism. Contemporary values are such that the quest for community has become far less important than this commitment to self. Values focused around selfism, because of their selfish self-centredness, stand against the possibility of our being able to contribute in any selfless way to the building of community. My observation is that those who commit whole-heartedly to the process of selfism often end up with very little. For instance, winning at the expense of others can bring a deep loneliness. Many in our own community have tried this route and paid the price emotionally. It seems there is something intrinsic to the process of seeking rich rewards for the self that can lead us down a path of constant failure and defeat, ending in despair and illness.

People become increasingly fragmented and embittered by the persistent effort and failure they experience in seeking self. Of course, some of us do not fail. We succeed. But the more we own, the fewer friends we have to enjoy it with. Especially tiresome are all the other selfish people who require that we share our 'success' with them. Selfish people are not pleasant company for each other. So the fruit of selfism can either be a broken despair – the high cost of trying to please self but failing – or, at the other extreme, success at the expense of others resulting in our finding ourselves alone and despised.

Selfism reveals itself in a range of ways. For instance, gambling to gain, like trying to win the lottery (and not doing so), is part of our culture. Likewise, success in the media is the dream of numerous teenagers, who are seeking to be discovered, wor-shipped, given loads of money, the chance to buy fast cars, and, finally, a tropical island that allows them the *solitary* space to 'be themselves'. It is all about self. But it is about a damaged and selfish self that has become less by being at the centre increasingly less able to live life in a relational way.

Society has progressively seen more selfism over the last few generations. In a journey toward making ourselves the centre of our world, we are less and less willing to give to others. For many, material success goes hand in hand with the urge to be alone and in control. This is another area that prevents us from being able to live community in any meaningful way. Those caught up into the values of materialism find it difficult to see what they are doing wrong. The commitment to live selfism has the capacity to blind us to any other values, for instance, to the idea that God has created us, and that, like Himself, we are community-building people. This blindness excludes all other ways of living. It is important to the Lord that we live in love with one another, so inevitably it becomes important to our dark side that we live for ourselves. This decision to put one's self first thus makes us unfit for either fulfilling relationships or supportive community.

From the Enlightenment onwards there has therefore been, both inside and outside the Church, a deconstruction of the idea of community, together with its valued relationality. As a result, most Westerners today are able to choose their values without the sometimes uncomfortable constraints of a religious culture that has a tendency to direct people into what to believe and how to live. What I have been learning is that one of the ways the Church could therefore respond to the postmodern search for meaning is to offer authentic community.

Notes

1 C.H. Pinnock, *Reason Enough: The case for the Christian faith* (Exeter: Paternoster Press, 1980), 93ff.

2 C. Gilligan, *In a Different Voice* (Massachusetts: Harvard University Press, 1982/1993), *passim*.

3 T.C. Oden, *Systematic Theology*, Volume 3, *Life in the Spirit* (Peabody, MA: Harper Collins Paperback, 1994/1998), 282.

4 Oden, *Life in the Spirit*, 280.

5 S.B. Clark, *Building Christian Communities: Strategy for renewing the church* (Notre Dame: Ave Maria Press, 1972), 23.

6 L. Crabb, *The Safest Place on Earth: Where people connect and are for ever changed* (Nashville: Word Publishing, 1999), 180.

7 G. Winter, *Community and Spiritual Transformation: Religion and politics in the communal age* (New York: Crossroads Books, 1989).

8 F. Tönnies, *Community and Association*, C.P. Loomis (tr.) (London: Routledge & Kegan Paul, 1887/1955).

9 F.G. Kirkpatrick, *Community: A Trinity of models* (Washington: Georgetown University Press, 1986), 13–61.

10 Kirkpatrick, *Community*, 19ff.

11 Kirkpatrick, *Community*, 62–98.

12 Kirkpatrick, *Community*, 67.

13 Kirkpatrick, *Community*, 83.

14 K. Marx, *Selected Writings in Sociology and Social Philosophy* (London: Penguin, 1963).

15 A.N. Whitehead, *Process and Reality: An essay on cosmology* (New York: Free Press, 1929/1947).

16 Kirkpatrick, *Community*, 137.

17 L. Feuerbach, *The Essence of Christianity* (New York: Harper & Row, 1841/1956).

18 Kirkpatrick, *Community*, 141.

19 M. Buber, *I and Thou*, W. Kaufman (tr.) (New York: Touchstone, 1958/1996), 54.

20 M. Buber, *The Way of Response: Martin Buber, selections from his writings* (New York: Schocken Books, 1966), 158.

21 Buber, *I and Thou*, 94.

22 R. Banks, *Paul's Idea of Community: The early house churches in their historical setting* (Grand Rapids: Eerdmans, 1980/1988), 112.

23 A. von Harnack, *The essence of Christianity* (Das Wesen des Christentums) (Leipzig 1900).

24 Cited in G. Lohfink, *Jesus and Community*, J.P. Galvin (tr.) (London: SPCK, 1985), 1–3.

25 R.C. Walton, *The Gathered Community* (London: Carey Press, 1946), 108.

26 G.A. Lindbeck, 'Confession and community: an Israel-like view of the church', *The Christian Century* (1990), 492–496, 493.

27 J.A.T. Robinson, The Body: A study in Pauline theology (London: SCM Press, 1952), 9.

28 D.W. Minar and S. Greer, *The Concept of Community: Readings with interpretations* (Chicago: Aldine, 1969).

[29] See A. Etzioni, *The Spirit of Community: The reinvention of American society* (New York: Touchstone, 1992) and A. Etzioni, *The Spirit of Community: Rights, responsibilities and the communitarian agenda* (London: Fontana Press, 1993/1995).

[30] R.N. Bellah, *et al*, *Habits of the Heart: Individualism and commitment in American life* (New York: Harper & Row, 1985).

[31] N. Rapport, '"Community" in current use' in A. Barnard and J. Spencer (eds.), *Encyclopedia of Social and Cultural Anthropology* (London: Routledge, 1996/2000), 136–143, 116ff.

[32] P.E. Vitz, *Psychology as Religion: The cult of self-worship* (Carlisle: Paternoster, 1977/1994), 57.

4.

Macmurray and Human Damage

With the breakdown of traditional small communities, people liv-ing in urban areas have become more and more dislocated with-in themselves, and estranged from others. This process leads to increased isolation. Most of us are saved from total isolation by what is sometimes described as the 'communal urge', which is a sort of biological imperative intrinsic to human nature that may be described as the desire and need to live in fulfilling human relationships. We live with the tension caused by needing some private space, while retaining a deep desire to spend time with others. If we remain healthy, and are self-supporting, most of the time for most of us, relationships, one way or another, will pre-vail. Community, being together, is constitutive of selfhood. It is in community that we realize our potential of 'fleshing out' the portrait of the self.[1] By being together we are more able to learn about ourselves. It is tragic that the more damaged we are, the less able we are to enjoy relationships with others. There are numerous reasons why we fail to commit ourselves to deep rela-tionships. But before considering this further, let us explore Kirkpatrick's third and final model of *mutual personal* as a foun-dation for community.

In contrast to atomistic contractarianism and the organic func-tional model, in the mutual personal system relationships are at the core of all we value. This model recognizes the place of the individual while also having relationality at its core. Kirkpatrick observed that – not unlike Hegel – Buber, because of his ambiva-lent use of organic language and symbols, left the way open for a philosophy of persons that preserves the uniqueness of person-hood. John Macmurray took up this opportunity and challenge, preferring personhood, and, more specifically, relationship, to Cartesian individualism (the latter being the idea that human personhood is no more than mind and body). Macmurray's mutual personal model, drawing also on Hebraic traditions, creates the possibility of unique Holy Spirit/human spirit unity in community.

Enter John Macmurray

John Macmurray is one of the few major philosophers of our time to place the category of 'persons in community' at the centre of his metaphysical system. In questioning the emphasis on individuality that resulted from Enlightenment ideas, Macmurray began to develop a relational foundation for community. His philosophical system starts from and returns to the centrality of person in relation. As we will be noting later, his ideas sit comfortably alongside Cappadocian thought. Macmurray suggested that if we hold to the dualism of Cartesian man, we make it impossible to argue for personal knowledge of another because such knowledge is not in what we *think* (Cartesian) as people, but, instead, in what we *do* in relation to other agents.[2] Macmurray therefore moved from the idea of the Cartesian individual private self to a view of personhood as relational.

Macmurray suggested that knowing I am in relation to another person must be the 'starting point of all knowledge'.[3] To be a person is to be in communication with 'the Other', meaning that knowledge of the Other should be the presupposition of all knowledge.[4] But instead of using the term 'the Other' in a contemporary negatively construed sense, Macmurray was adopting a positive construct. He invested fresh meaning in the term, suggesting that instead of describing an enemy, or 'the other' who is seeking to exploit us, 'the Other' is an equal who also has the capability of relationship with us – a positive mutuality. Therefore, Macmurray denied the possibility of isolated personhood.

Also, by making the self the primary agent, Macmurray rendered unnecessary traditional Cartesian dualistic thought and practice. Action, and therefore *becoming*, rather than *being*, is the basis of self. This in turn allows the personal self to be understood as a unified whole.[5] This concept, whereby personhood is constituted by relation to the Other, Macmurray called the personal model.[6] Put another way, he argued that we all have our being, not in our individual existence, but in our being-in-relationship, and this relationship is by its very nature personal (i.e., communal).[7] Macmurray saw our human nature as always lying beyond us as a goal to be reached out to and sought after. So freedom, for him, is not in our isolation from others, but in our being realized in and through fellowship or community. He saw this process as a journey toward a complete realization of the self through a complete self-transcendence.[8]

But Macmurray also took one further step, locating his 'principle of relations' in God's love, which then flowed into church life. In doing this, he anticipated the *perichoretic* principle of 'mutual co-inherence'. Full realization of person in relations requires the power of God. I support Macmurray's emphasis on the importance of recovering a Hebrew model of theocentric community.[9] He claimed that Jesus must be understood in Hebraic terms, not in the categories of Greek Platonic or Aristotelian philosophy and argued that in the Hebrew Bible the heart of monotheism lies in the conviction that the union of humankind into one community is the ultimate intention of God (1 Sa. 25:29; cf. 1 Cor. 3:16; Eph. 2:13–14; 4:13), making it the necessary end of the historic process.[10] Yahweh adopted Israel and sought to shape it as an example of divine-human community. The coming of Christ changed this. Macmurray understood Christianity to be a religion that superseded Judaism, taking over Judaism's task of preparing the universal community. Such a goal, however, is not possible unless human nature wills it, for the structure of all human relationships is the expression of human intention.[11] Only life in intentional community can fully reflect human nature.[12] This idea is echoed by Levinas: 'The human accomplishing its destiny of being human . . . merits the name *spirit*. It is with the other man that this spirit rises up in being.'[13]

Kirkpatrick conceded that some of Macmurray's thinking is now considered quaint.[14] But he argued that Macmurray is still relevant since most of us now live in a rootless culture, and need to relearn relationships. Drawing on Macmurray, Kirkpatrick has called on the Church for a new reality of theocentric Christianity. This call gives us two helpful aspects to the concept of community: first, a move away from individual selfism, and, second, the suggestion that the Church should urgently wake up from its continuing slumber under Enlightenment thinking. Grenz, in suggesting that culturally society is already moving into a 'post-individual' age,[15] would support his move.

What is being suggested by these men is actually far more radical than first appears. On the basis of authors like Macmurray, Kirkpatrick and Grenz, any definition of spiritual personhood or activity must now include a relational community aspect. As Pingleton sadly noted,[16] Christians are not yet doing this instinctively. For instance, Benner, a therapist and Christian leader, defined spirituality as the 'human response to God's gracious call to a relationship with Him'.[17] There is no mention of other human relationships or community, especially not as a *felt* experience. In fact, much of the time, the idea is absent in Christian writing. Buber, Macmurray and Kirkpatrick are unusual in their questioning of individualism and their emphasis on the importance of relationality and its community.

Applying Macmurray's Thinking

We noted earlier that society today seems to embrace values that resist relationality, unless they are self-serving. We have also noted that some parts of the Protestant Church (using the term in its widest sense) have been both victims and passive supporters of this process. They have continued to hold on to traditional practices and values that are unable to counter the ongoing fragmentation of our Western culture. The evidence seems to suggest that history and past practice are not enough to reverse the desertion of people from some parts of the Church. Like MacLaren, I am suggesting that some denominations and congregations will need to reinvent themselves with a deeper appreciation of community if they are to have a credible response to this deteriorating situation.[18]

I am not suggesting that the Church has been ignorant of this. In fact, there is a substantial literature on, for instance, the theme of building church community through cells.[19] Of course, the number of book titles may actually be evidence of how badly things are going wrong, while not being evidence of successfully helping to correct the problem. But I particularly like Gorman's *Community as Christian*, which notes that since the Enlightenment there has been a subversive undermining of community to such an extent that she sees little true community in either society or the Church today. For Gorman, true community is that which looks out for others in love, and is not, as in many small groups today, consumed by self-centredness, a cultural cult of narcissism,[20] or, to put it in the language of this book, selfism. Also helpful here is Rasmussen,[21] who focuses on the moral ethical relational aspects of the loss of community, with guidance on how the Church might respond.

Given the serious state of parts of the Church today, the implications of Macmurray's ideas are far-reaching. He anticipated the contemporary emphasis on social Trinity and the renewed postmodern interest in relationships. If we apply his approach and move away from individualism and selfism, thinking in terms of the priority of relations as the foundation of human values, we do come closer to the contemporary interest in both relationality and intentional community that is found outside the Church. Sadly for Macmurray, his own thinking made it increasingly difficult for him to be part of the Church as it was, and in his latter years his ideas increasingly isolated him from the wider body of the Church.

Building on Macmurray and Cappadocian ideas, we can begin to argue that much in individualism and selfism stands against the values we could be helpfully adopting in local congregational life. Generally most church meetings and relationships have a lot of self (selfism) in them. They need much more of Christ and 'the Other'. While accepting that responsibility rests with each individual, we maintain that relationship with the Lord and one another should be the central core of what we do as Christians. Each person in a local church becomes a God-given 'Other', in the positive way we are defining it here, to be loved in mutual personhood (Mt. 5:43ff.).

Activities and programmes within the congregation should therefore be measured by their success in building relationships rather than by the more traditional measure of attendance figures and income. Likewise, 'success' in wholeness and maturity should be measured by the growing capacity of members to give love to one another, and their choosing to write a positive community history together. Maturity would then no longer be epitomized by the isolated, solitary Christian saint but instead, by our increasing capacity for deepening relational personhood. This new and growing capacity to receive and give love facilitates 'the Other', giving us the freedom to become ourselves. The local church would become an intentional community dedicated to 'social Trinity relationality' as the basis of knowing God, others and ourselves.

One of the ways we have sought to adopt Macmurray's thinking in CCD is to develop a 'social calendar', and, in addition to the planned events, to encourage a whole range of spontaneous, informal social activities that are intended to do no more than allow people to be together. Many of these events have nothing directly to do with 'religion' or 'evangelism'. In fact, at the initiative of some of the participants, any talk about 'homework', the journey and personal maturing are all strictly banned. So not every meeting or get-together is for discipleship, teaching and training, or for 'evangelism' in any sense. Since we are spiritual beings, football may be just as spiritual as a prayer meeting, but spirituality is not its focus. Such get-togethers, whether for quilting, abseiling, watercolour painting, watching a good DVD, or just for coffee or a meal, have no ulterior religious motives. Held at the initiative of individual members, they simply facilitate relationship. Unapologetically, some meetings are just for men, or for women only. Others are mixed. We have found that in certain respects men and women practise community in quite different ways. For instance, women are frequently content just to meet and chat, whereas men want to 'do things' when they meet. Times for each and both are essential.

However, while at a group level we as Christians need to be a lot more laid-back about goals for meetings, at a personal level we probably need to be more focused. Adopting the view that successfully doing relationships together is more important than achieving goals will both revolutionize and moderate our personal actions and behaviour. When we as Christians realize that we can participate in accomplishing the destiny of being human in the life of another, each interaction becomes a unique opportunity. So we need to stop for a moment before we make a call, or meet someone, and ask ourselves what the Lord would want to leave with that person by the end of the meeting or phone call.

As followers of Christ, we need to move from what we want to get out of a relationship to what the Lord might want to achieve. This will often mean that we do not say what we want to say, as this becomes less important than what the Lord wants to say. For instance, instead of achieving what we want to achieve, we seek to communicate that the other person is loved by the Lord and by us in a deep and significant way. It means making acceptance more of a priority than accomplishing a purpose. By the time we say goodbye to the people we have met, they know that we have *their* needs at the centre of *our* values. Such lived, relational love helps build theocentric community. I am not talking here about a slavish pietism, or our duty to practise unconditional love, but our desire to be more real and more able to give and receive.

Macmurray suggested that relationships should form the foundation of human personhood. But as we move from the relationship of two, to a full community philosophy, Macmurray has little further to say to us. What he does propose is that when two people learn to live relationship together, we have the basic building blocks of community. Successful relationships are contagious, and they quickly reproduce themselves. Where two people are living in love, they will want others to share what they have.

Our Personal Damage Making Us Unfit for Community

Macmurray's message is an exciting one for the Church today. But the fact that authentic or successful community requires healthy relationships is not helpful for most of us. For in addition to Enlightenment rationality, individualism, and the selfism most of us have inherited, we also bring a legacy of damaged relationships. Although levels of such damage and breakdown vary from person to person, most of us are more damaged than we are willing to admit. Divorce, bereavement, betrayal, abuse and disappointment – these and many other experiences build a history that most of us bring into any relationship we wish to explore. Any previous toxic experiences will caution us against further commitment, and any type of significant abuse will teach us not to be vulnerable ever again.

Yet regardless of our bad and difficult pasts, because it is relationships that have deeply hurt us, it must now be relationships that help heal and make us whole. For this process to begin to happen, we need to put ourselves in the path of healthful relationships, instead of following our instinct either to avoid all relationships or seek to be in control. To damaged, broken people, being part of a community can seem unrealistic or like a nightmare. Who would want to be that close to others? Why tempt fate yet again, and get more hurt and abused? 'I'm out of here' is a common refrain as people run from such intimacy and vulnerability. Even if our instinct is not to flee, then it is certainly to hold people at arm's length and hide ourselves rather than give ourselves. But how have so many of us become like this?

Most damage in us comes from three main areas: first, our heredity, by which I mean all those good and bad characteristics that we inherit in all areas of our lives from our biological parents; second, the damage that others do to us, that is, all the pain and trauma we pick up throughout life by others' abuse of us; and, third, what we do with the damage done against us, that is, the ways we choose to protect ourselves from the pain of what others have done. Most clinical self-harm or unrighteous hate of ourselves would fit into this last category, described in our ministry as 'sin against ourselves'. These three make up the main sources of damage to us seen from a human perspective. From God's perspective, however, it is far less complicated. He looks beneath the surface of our lives into the underlying profound damage at the core of our beings. This baggage focuses around the desire toward darkness that every one of us has, that is, our wilfulness in being more likely to harm ourselves than help ourselves. Our natural instinct is to see the negative rather than the positive. God is very aware of the deep (and sometimes hidden) drive in us all to find the bad more alluring than the good.

When people join our community, we accept them as they are, but this is not how the Lord would see them. Instead, He has very harsh words to say to us all about how He sees us, 'All the people on earth had corrupted their ways'; 'Every inclination of his heart is evil from childhood' (Gn. 6:12; 8:21; cf. Mt. 15:19). In saying this, God is focusing on our natural tendency not only to fail to do what is right, but also to self-harm. By this I mean that outwardly most of us think more highly of ourselves than we should, while inwardly we are darker than we are willing to admit. This self-deceit is the basis of all of our self-harm. The implications are serious. The principle of social Trinity suggests that we are all naturally able to live healthy relationships. But the damage in us, from God's perspective, means that we are more likely to ruin a good friendship than deepen it.

What God suggests is that we all suffer in varying degrees from this damage. We carry a darkness in us that self-deceives. But because we keep it 'below the waterline' of our consciousness, we can all allow it to remain in place and go unchallenged. We live life consciously believing that we are a certain type of person, mostly good and Christian, while God sees in us numerous levels of self-deceit. Christ made similar observations, which, though addressed to the Pharisees, illustrate well our darkest selves (e.g. Mk. 7:1ff.). In this sense, all of us are Pharisees. We are so blinded by religious rules that we are unable even to see the King of glory. Likewise, Christ was very open and aware of the darkness and deceit in human nature (Mk. 2:8). It therefore does not surprise God that most of us find authentic community, or even a desire to be in community, too much of a challenge to be endured. It is so much easier for us to believe in our goodness or our holiness when we are on our own than when we are in relationships, for then the truth will always surface! For instance, for many of us it is so often preferable to leave immediately after the Sunday service, than linger and attempt to form relationships with people who we find irritating or inadequate.

The problem is that many of us are so disordered emotionally that even if we were to be rid of our drives to self-deceit, we would not find it easy to live successful relationships. Some of us may carry organic damage from birth that puts us at a disadvantage in relationships, that is, we may have either physical disability or learning disorders that make normal relationships difficult. But for most of us, our incompetence in relationships will be the consequence of early abuse or neglect.

What is shocking is that one in four of us, merely by living our 'ordinary' adult lives, will experience a 'breakdown' of our ordinary routines and for a season, often many months, will be incapable of 'normal relationships'. Shenker has suggested that alienated people are those who accept the need for a stable identity provided by society, but because of personal circumstances either reject or are unable to internalize these criteria.[22] For increasing numbers in our Western society, the forces of individualization work with the pathological forces of broken personhood to produce toxic loneliness and a fragmentation of our personal and relational environment. While more and more are needing the support of community, many of us are increasingly unfit to be part of it. Here are some of the ways CCD members describe this damage.

The damage of toxic emotion

• I was frightened most of each day. So I could not be sure if or when it would get very bad, so if I went out I would get very drunk to overcome that fear. Or I would stay inside and be very demanding emotionally on others around me

• Grief, pain, shame, anger/revenge, hate of self, hate of others, guilt fear, hopelessness. All of the above at different moments: the result was that I was lonely, angry, and unapproachable inside, all my relationships were made in sickness

• An inability to identify or express emotion. Fear – debilitating, dominated my life so at times I was incapable of functioning – paralysed. I became more and more incapable of relationship and isolated myself more – I had become more self-absorbed. I was incapable of knowing the impact I had on others

• I felt very angry and the person who suffered most was my husband. I took it out on him by physically, emotionally and spiritually beating him up. It made me very depressed, as I felt powerless to do anything about it

• I defended the pain I felt by being angry with everyone around, and myself. I didn't know before CCD that I was angry, but it became very clear and it kept me in complete isolation

♦ Shame – didn't feel I deserved any better and this hindered change. Helped maintain my self-hate and rejection of myself; which meant I wouldn't draw near to other people

I have also frequently observed deeper and more sinister layers to this breakdown of people and community. Most of us are in the habit of harming ourselves as a direct result of the damage done to us by others. By seeking to manage and control the ways others have hurt us, we seek to deny the pain and trauma we are carrying. We tend to put in place a whole range of coping mechanisms to prevent us ever again being abused in this way. This 'sin against ourselves' will drive us to inner fragmentation and isolation. Let me give you a personal example.

In my late childhood an old man whom I loved and trusted tried to sexually abuse me. He sought to do this on several different occasions. At the time I laughed it off, denying the seriousness of the situation. But in my early twenties I began to admit to myself that I had been sexually abused. My recognition of this abuse opened my eyes to its consequences in my life. I now had the explanation, for example, of my unnatural dislike of old men. By the time I owned the abuse, my denial had had a profound negative impact on my relationship with mature male adults. The abuse against me was bad, but what I had done in denying it while at the same time trying to avoid it ever happening again was far more damaging to me a decade later. If I had not admitted this abuse, I would have been incapable of enjoying the spontaneous relationships that community brings.

What I am suggesting is that our Western society and its Enlightenment values have done much to break down both human community and the value of relationships. But I am also suggesting that we have personally added to this damage by what we have done to others and ourselves. As we become more damaged, we are less able to live relationally, yet are more in need of the support of community. So although most of us have lost community as a result of social forces outside our control, we have also been either active or passive contributors to this process. As a consequence, until we have let go of the damage in our pasts, none of us is capable of building the type of community we would like to be part of. This is a trap from which, as we find ourselves with ever more damage in our lives, we find it increasingly difficult to escape since the steps we need to take to resolve the damage are less and less accessible.

One of the ways in which most of us seek to prevent others' damage intruding, and our damage toxically contaminating even more relationships, is by our use of formulae, guidelines, patterns, or rules in our relationships. In reflecting why it is that people slip into rules, I have begun to see that these rules allow us to control the way we live relationships. They often take the form of what psychologists call 'scripts'.

We all live by these scripts, and many of them, like making a cup of tea or driving a car, are essential to our well-being. Which one of us would want to learn from scratch how to make a cup of tea each time we are thirsty! But the dark side of our nature, the part we deny in ourselves and pretend God cannot see, also writes scripts. As a consequence, we judge others, learn to think in 'superior' ways, and have a higher opinion of ourselves than we ought to have. We write these scripts instinctively to avoid others hurting us, and also to avoid the truth about ourselves and others.

Such attitudes and behaviour mean that we are far from being ideal raw material for building communities of the type we would like. Also, in our arrogance, we certainly consider others around us to be particularly unsuitable! Much in our character has a tendency to do exactly the opposite of what is required of us for building long positive histories together, as clearly observed by God in Scripture. Instead, on the basis of our dark side and its scripts, we are all likely to contribute to the breakdown of trust in relationships. To illustrate this ongoing damage in our own lives, most of us have only to ask what is the longest friendship outside of the family that we have held on to. Our darkness and self-deceit allows all of us to do what we like, but without the responsibility of accountability.

On this basis, that is, with most of us still having a bias toward damaging relationships rather than developing them, it seems unrealistic for leaders or followers in the Church to expect people to build community. We may be able to survive the formality of a church meeting, but many of us will need a season of healing and deeper wholeness before we can achieve more and be the people others need us to be in this adventure of creating community. It has been a very hard lesson for me to accept that it takes great maturity to live as a long-term giver in authentic community. For instance, it is so much easier to blame other people for us not getting well. Or tell them to 'pull themselves together', than to continue to support them for an extended period as they uncover layer after layer and give the baggage to Christ.

Few of us have the capacity to love people naturally and proactively in this way without burning out. W need to grow up and mature a little, for only then can we be people who are capable of contributing to the type of community many of us want (and need) to belong to. Instead, what usually happens is that in our damaged state we try for a while, then get hurt, either by our own or others' baggage, and quietly leave, moving on to the next congregation or group. It is a cyclic trap that refuses to release us from our own personal damage, while also increasingly isolating us from those people we want or need. Alternately, we take our place in a hierarchy that allows us to maintain a safe sense of control of our boundaries so that our damage can remain contained.

Three Unhelpful Ways of Managing Damage in Relationship

Over the years I have compiled a long list of reasons why we find it such a challenge to live in close relationship with others. Most of us have a number of traits that soon emerge when we seek to cope with the damage that we and others carry. We will focus here on three challenges that we typically face in a Christian setting: judging others, being right and intellectual dogmatism.

Judging others

From a Biblical perspective, every human being is damaged at the core of their being, spiritual, emotional and mental. One expression of this damage is the tendency we all have to judge everyone and everything. From the core of our being there comes a continual flow of judgements. These may be as 'innocent' as criticism of the clothes other people are wearing, or the way they pray, or as 'perceptive' as noting a flaw in their theology. Such judging gives us the feeling of being 'above' others, and from this superior position we judge whether they are right or wrong, 'sound' Biblically, and useful or a nuisance to us. By such judging and its outcomes, we fragment our world, dividing everything into 'us' and 'them'.

In the course of judging others, and in order that we may better categorize and label them, we put every person and every situation into separate 'boxes'. We do this because we do not believe that we can make a relationship safe unless we can control it. Having compartmentalized people in this way, we feel able to respond to them according to the scripts we are comfortable with. Thus, by judging people and situations, we believe we have some control over them.

In our first wave of research in Christ Church some years ago, a significant proportion of the congregation specifically said that one of the most amazing things they experienced at CCD, in comparison with previous experiences (school, church, family, work, etc.), was that they were not judged. Listen to what members said about the benefits of being part of such a culture.

Not judged

> I am free to be me, I am not judged, not looked down upon, not condemned by anyone, that there is a freedom

> ◆ People can go for a year and say well 'I don't believe in Christ yet and I don't believe in it all', but they are not rejected from the church because they don't believe. They are given that permission to have space ◆ That is what makes a difference, a complete acceptance of everybody, no matter how sick, damaged, how bad their life has been, how bad their life is, the phrase is that the life itself is what matters

> ◆ There is no pressure at all on people to become Christians. I think we have seen lots of people come in who aren't Christians ◆ They don't feel under pressure to become a Christian

> ◆ We do not suffer religious crap (sorry). They can feel the warmth of Christ without ever hearing His name or being put under pressure. They can, however, hear peoples' stories

♦ I was talking to a Christian leader, I am thinking of a Christian leader in the church I was in before. If they asked me anything I would always feel I know it is wrong. I was very on guard

♦ For me I think it is the fact that you can be honest about how you really are and people still care about you anyway

♦ The idea of being welcomed into the community that doesn't have this hierarchy or cliques, that you can't get into, that everybody is welcome, there are no levels of 'I have been here longer than you'

♦ I went thro' a period of drinking a lot when I first came, but to be honest, it was not this major thing that I let go of, it was that I am just bored with waking up with a headache. It gets like that, everybody so doesn't judge you about it so in the end it was 'I don't need to do this to myself anymore'

♦ I made a mistake and I am still here, and it is OK

♦ Emotional freedom and well-being, mutual honour, honesty about feelings, sharing in the sufferings of others. Christ is a reality, and it's an honour, and touches us like nothing else can. To stand with others in their pain, and see them come through. Not judging/condoning them

When talking earlier about the idea of a social Trinity, I suggested that God puts relationships first. Let me illustrate. On several occasions Christ clearly put the needs of the person ahead of rules, even God-given ones. For instance, He healed people on the Sabbath (Lk. 6:9–11), allowed lenience when His disciples' behaviour was judged (Lk. 6:1–5), and challenged religious leaders where they had lost touch with God's perspective (the widow's mite, Mk. 12:42ff.). What comes across from Christ's lifestyle and teaching is that rules are intended to help guide us, but cannot be justified where they threaten relationships or our responsibility to honour and help a person.

This need to judge others and live by rules is illustrated in a contention I had with the Lord a number of years ago. A couple came to see me who, though not married, had been together for a number of years and had two children. As part of the leadership of a local congregation, I had been taught that if such people wanted to be part of our congregation, they would need to separate until we, as Christian leaders, thought they were ready to marry. What the Lord said to me, however, was the opposite of that. He required that I 'absorb the evil' of this situation, if evil it was, and honour them both by coaching them gently toward the possibility of regularizing their relationship by a 'celebration' of marriage when they felt this to be appropriate. This I did, and now, some years later, they are married and part of the Leadership Team of CCD.

My initial judgemental instinct, based on the rules I had been taught, was the opposite of what the couple needed and the Lord wanted. The 'absorbing of the evil' was a choice to tolerate the position in the short term in order to earn the right to the couple's trust and be given an opportunity to lead them to a loving God. Theologically, I am using the idea of Dennis Martin,[23] who suggested that in Christ we are able to give to the Lord the sin and misbehaviour of others and its impact on those associated with it, yet without requiring the person to change. We live alongside them, rather than demanding immediate change from them. We wait for the Lord to convict and help them out of their chosen way of life.

Church life based on these principles means choosing to lay aside rules and judgement of others in favour of loving the individual. This requires that we absorb the evil, an act of intercession whereby you love the person while they are in the midst of the sin, yet without condoning the sin. The congregation carries the hurt and shame of the damage, bringing it to the cross, while seeking to enable the individual or individuals to remain in relationship, loved and included instead of judged and excluded. It is a difficult balance to achieve since ongoing sin damages the congregation and should not be tolerated. In CCD we have not got the balance right yet, but we are proud to be a community of second chances.

We see this value system illustrated in Christ's overwhelming emphasis on love, even love of enemies (Lk. 6:27ff.), no doubt in the hope of making friends of them. Christ lived and taught both a life of forgiveness, in which we lay down our right of revenge, and an intent always to put people first. Such values are essential if we as Christians are to maintain long-term friendships. In Christ we see a life lived out as social Trinity, extending into His relationships with all those who wished to receive His help, guidance and blessing on their lives. But, sadly, because of our inclination to darkness and our baggage, few of us have either the desire or the capacity to live consistently in this way. Instead, our penchant – a disease of human nature and its institutions – is to judge everyone and everything, and to turn such scripts into rules.

Needing to be right
My second observation is related. It is the annoying and incessant need for human beings to always be right. I have observed, and been drawn into numerous arguments where two or more parties are seeking to prove that they are right and the others are wrong. Our *rights,* and our *being right* is something we will fight for, even if it means that a relationship will be damaged or even die. We all have a tendency to put our rights ahead of friendships and by standing up for these rights, as we see them, we all inflict considerable damage on friendships. In many of these situations I have admitted to seeing value in both opinions, but this is rarely a satisfactory outcome for those involved. One well-known example of this need is the 'downgrade controversy' that consumed the later life of Charles Haddon Spurgeon, sucking life from him as he endlessly debated with the Arminians. Knowing he was right, he sought to correct his fellow Christian, and it weakened his latter ministry.

Our need to always be right gives us a value system different from that of God, in our perspective of reality, our relationships and our behaviour. The message of a social Trinity clearly puts relationships first. But our judging and our drive to be right separates us from others, like a prince or princess looking down on the world from a strong tower. Very rarely will others see things the way we do. In some ways, being sure of our point of view may be positive in affirming our unique personhood. But a dark side lurks in the wings. We will often push too hard to make our point, to the detriment of the relationship. This can be much more of a problem for men than for women. Many women will be more cautious about expressing opinions that will cause friction or division. They choose a more subtle way, perhaps communicating their confidence in their perspective by a look, or gesture, or by telling a third party. But the sad truth remains that many of us would rather be right than be in relationship. For some of us, being right and alone is more satisfying than having friends.

What I am suggesting is that behind most 'I'm right – you're wrong' attitudes is something much more unhelpful, even sinister. Even though Christ forbids such judging (Lk. 6:37–38), in our pride we insist on maintaining our stance. From there we go on to judge that all others are wrong and we *alone* are right. This, of course, feeds our sense of superiority. We cannot accept that those with a different opinion may be equally 'right', when looked at from their perspective. Our arrogance denies us the possibility that we might be wrong! So we are never wrong, and look upon all other (sad) mortals as somewhat pathetic and ill informed. No one is more dangerous than a self-righteous person (Pr. 8:13; 16:18–19; 21:24, etc.).

Intellectual dogmatism
A third trait that obstructs our being able to contribute positively to authentic community is that our head consistently overrides and dismisses our heart. We have already noted that to prove a point we will often seek to force on others what we believe, thereby putting the relationship under threat. Our intellectual conviction that we are right is so strong that we refuse to see the damage it might be doing both to us and to those around us, and this in spite of the fact that Scripture suggests that we are all too damaged to be free to believe in our own righteousness. Time and time again I have been saddened by the arrogant stubbornness of a person who refuses to acknowledge that the other person may have a helpful point. Being critical toward others, often in a superior way, is endemic in some parts of the Church. Some people in congregational life see it as their duty, and a continuation of the Old Testament 'prophetic tradition', to point out to others their mistakes and faults. To illustrate this point, we need only look at abuse in the Church and the proliferation of denominations. Community has little defence against self-righteousness.

When we are driven by our head and not our heart, we are dangerous to others and ourselves. Most of us are not willing to see that our striving hard to protect our rights can cause others a great deal of pain. Because rights are more to do with our head, and friendships with our heart, the head and its cognitive powers will prevail much of the time. What we see before our eyes (e.g. friends being hurt by us, and broken relationships) is rarely enough to make us change our minds, or drive us to feel the need to say a 'sorry' that will help to restore the relationship. I have met numerous people who have not talked to relatives and friends for decades simply because they think that the other person has a duty to contact them. Or they know that the other person is holding a grudge, but do not think that they have a responsibility to do anything about it. They cognitively justify ignoring what has happened, instead of emotionally grieving over the damage to the relationship.

Such situations are especially (sadly) true between Christians. Paul the apostle suffered this scenario with Barnabas over John Mark (Acts 15:36–41). I suspect that they disagreed about whether John Mark should be part of the team. It is sad that they could not resolve this disagreement at the time. Similarly, after a long and fruitful relationship of many years, Karl Barth had a dispute with Emil Brunner over a matter of pastoral theology and for the remaining years of their lives they let the matter divide them. One wonders what would have happened if in both cases the person and the relationship had been put first. This is an important issue for many emerging churches and independent groups, who feel they have points to score against more traditional congregations rooted in Constantinian thinking.

As we have already noted, when we are driven by our heads, we are likely to do and say things that will hurt ourselves and others. The welcoming and maturing of our healed feelings is a key contributor to building faith community, for then our emotional life will help temper the more toxic pride of our head. For instance, when we develop the ability to read how people are responding to what we say, when, that is, we can read their body language, we have the EQ (emotional intelligence) to interpret what they are 'saying' as a whole person. Such skills are essential if we as Christians are to facilitate the communities that we are proud of. It is much harder to be hurtful to people when we can see they are struggling badly with what we are saying, than when we are blind to how they are feeling. Likewise, when we can see that a point is not being received, then we know that it is unhelpful to press it.

Within life in CCD this is an area we have looked at long and hard. As a consequence, we do not encourage a 'thus saith the Lord' type of dogmatism. Over the years we have adopted a range of guidance that suggest that none of us has the right to tell others off, not until, that is, the Lord Himself begins to put this issue or area on our agenda. The conviction of sin by the Lord, or a telling off by Him about values and behaviour, must be the first step. It is only after people have begun to see the sin or disorder in their lives, that we have the right to take the matter up with them. It is *the Lord* who spoke through the prophets to the people, not the prophet or people to the people. We have always felt that outside of exceptional circumstances, it is the Lord alone who has the right to tell people off in this direct and chastening way. We do not have that right, especially not from the pulpit or the giddy heights of leadership.

The prophets and Christ spoke to the nation, the monarchy or the leaders, religious and governmental. But we see in Scripture little evidence of such 'telling off' being directed to the individual, to the poor, or sick, the downtrodden farmer or rural villager. As Knut Heim suggests,[24] we have a duty to comfort the afflicted, and afflict the comfortable! In CCD we find it especially important to be cautious when speaking 'truth' into people's lives where one is seeking to help those who are vulnerable, emotionally damaged or from an unchurched background.

Taken to extremes, of course, this principle can become a problem. When people carry damage, they will invariably hurt those who are seeking to love them and support them. We must all be mindful of our responsibility to keep the congregation a 'safe place'.[25] In CCD finding ways of maintaining a healthy accountability to each other without slipping into judgement or exclusion, is an area we are working on at the moment.

An Alternative Way of Life

In CCD we work on the basis that division in relationships is never helpful. To facilitate the process of loving each other despite different opinions, we seek to celebrate diversity within unity of relationships. We do this on the basis that building relationships and sustaining them is one of the Church's basic responsibilities.

As noted earlier, speaking negatively to people, or pointing out to them all their faults, is surely the Lord's task, not ours. We do not feel that it is our mission to keep other people humble and on the right path by making it clear to them when they err. We seek to practise the simple truth that we do not have the right to say to people what we think about them, especially not in the name of Christ. 'Walking in the light' is being in the light of Christ together, not having the right to abuse others. We are not called to hurt or dismantle one another, but to build each other up. We have a duty to see Christ formed in us and in one another, but this is best done by encouraging one another, not by putting one another down. Bringing a 'Biblical' brokenness to a person is exclusively the work of God. It is rarely ours to manipulate or engineer. It is holy ground that the Lord will in time open up with the person, and at its heart is the person's recognition that this situation, bad as it is, has been the work of the Lord, and has not been in any way humanly initiated. God Himself has numerous ways of keeping us humble and bringing us to our knees.

Seeking to live such values, placing the building of positive relationships at the centre of our lives, removes one of the causes of tension in congregational life. Many church leaders feel the need to speak and direct the lives of people 'in the name of the Lord'. Some do not seem to stop and consider the impact this may have on members in their care. Approaching others as a leader, and speaking to them with the authority of office, can be very abusive. A typical example of such abuse occurs when members tell a leader that they have decided to leave the congregation. What can follow is a flood of interrogative questions, such as, 'Have you heard this from the Lord?', 'What Scriptural support do you have for this decision?', and, 'You do know, don't you, that such a move will hurt you and the church?' Such questioning seems intended to intimidate people and bully them into not leaving. It is not the basis for building trusting community. The pastor may achieve what he or she sets out to do, but at what cost to the individuals?

In CCD we seek to live with a different value system, in which we follow as a golden rule the principle that we will support anyone in anything they wish to do, providing that it is not illegal, clearly self-harming or harmful to others. I may sometimes have reservations about the decisions people make, such as a choice to come off medication, or to begin a challenging academic degree without first testing their ability, and I may ask them the basic questions commensurate with pastoral care, but this will be done within a framework of being positive and supportive. Being directive can be manipulative. Our encouragement will extend even to supporting those who wish to leave the community, or decide to take a six-month break from Sunday church. At one time or another, all of us need to make important decisions about our lives. If it later goes wrong, that is still fine, and should not be used as evidence that we fell from the tightrope of God's will as Christian's sometimes see it. It is always helpful to do a post-mortem, but not in a climate of 'I told you so'.

Affirming community, relationship and initiative should be the underlying motive in our pastoral care. Putting the person's needs ahead of rules or our own best interests is essential if the Church is to survive in the twenty-first century. As Christian leaders we must shape 'church' around the needs of people, not, as so often in the past, requiring people to conform. Let the members of CCD comment on some aspects of this.

Life in CCD

> ✦ Without community we would not have church ✦ For the first time in my life I feel like I have a family around me. A group of people who genuinely love and care about me ✦ We are still in the process of becoming a community ✦ People all pulling together ✦ I now have mums, dads, grandmas, granddads, uncles, etc., coming out my ears, and I love it ✦ It's not very church like ✦ To me it's my home ✦ It portrays the closeness and support of one another that we pertain to, without giving the impression of being a cult (community) or a dead church ✦ It means to me, togetherness, 'warts and all' ✦ It describes what we are ✦ If we are a church in the way God wants us to be, then family and

community will follow ♦ CCD appears to be operating more as a community, i.e. revolving around people, rather than as a church structure ♦ Extended family ♦ Community is bigger than family and less exclusive. Community conveys a more real meaning of who we are than church does to non-Christians ♦ A place to be respected and honoured and encouraged, to make mistakes ♦ It reflects the diversity of our make up and that we live in and out of each other's pockets ♦ It accommodates all types of people and having a multiple personality disorder I have found it has coped with all of mine! ♦ A church to be proud of

Facing up to the truth about the three characteristics of human nature and its behaviour to which I referred above – judging, the need to be right, and intellectual dogmatism – could mean recognizing that our tendency to hurt ourselves and others is more dominant than most of us are prepared to admit. We do what is right for us, or what we think is best for others, but do so out of our baggage and our habit of hurting ourselves and others. Our belief and its judging separates us from others, while feeding our sense of superiority. This in turn drains us of the ability to receive and give love, and to put others first. Most of us believe that if we make a mistake, admit to it and say sorry, others will take the opportunity to abuse us. Because of all this, together with a range of other values that we do not consciously admit, such as our dislike of ourselves and others, we are unable to live the values of social Trinity. These characteristics, common to all of us, ill fit us for authentic faith community. They steal from us the capacity to mirror aspects of the mutual giving and receiving of social Trinity. Even if we were to find an ideal community where none of this occurred, we would be well advised not to join it, as we would surely do it damage with our own baggage! But God anticipated this problem, and responded during the Early Hebrew period with an answer that fits all of us if we want it. Let me explain.

Notes

[1] C.O. Schrag, *The Self After Postmodernity* (Newhaven: Yale University Press, 1997), 78.

[2] Macmurray, *Self, passim.*
[3] Macmurray, *Persons*, 76.
[4] Macmurray, *Persons*, 77.
[5] Macmurray, *Self*, 86.
[6] Kirkpatrick, *Community*, 146.
[7] Macmurray, *Persons*, 17.
[8] J. Macmurray, *Conditions of Freedom* (London: Faber & Faber, 1950), 16.
[9] Kirkpatrick, *Community*, 198 and J. Macmurray, *The Philosophy of Jesus* (London: Friends Home Service Committee, 1973), *passim.*
[10] Macmurray, *Persons*, 60–61.
[11] J. Macmurray, *The Clue to History* (London: SCM Press, 1938), 100.
[12] J. Macmurray, *The Nature of Religion, St Asaph Conference* (London: SCM Auxiliary, 1938), 9.
[13] Levinas, cited in J. Robbins (ed.), *Is it Righteous to Be? Interviews with Emmanuel Levinas* (Stanford, CA: Stanford University Press, 2001), 112–113.
[14] Kirkpatrick, *Community*, 137.
[15] S.J. Grenz, *A Primer on Postmodernism* (Grand Rapids: Eerdmans, 1996), 167.
[16] J.P. Pingleton, 'A model of relational maturity' in L. Aden, *et al.* (eds.), *Christian Perspectives on Human Development* (Grand Rapids: Baker Book House, 1992), 101–113.
[17] D.G. Benner, 'Spirituality in personality and psychotherapy' in L. Aden, *et al.* (eds.), *Christian Perspectives on Human Development* (Grand Rapids: Baker Book House, 1992), 171–186, 173.
[18] Maclaren, *Mission*, 103–104.
[19] The following are some examples: H.J. Clinebell, *The People Dynamic: Changing self and society through growth groups* (New York: Harper & Row, 1972), J. O'Halloran, *Living Cells: Developing small Christian community* (Dublin: Dominican Publications, 1984), R. Wuthnow, *Sharing the Journey: Support groups and America's new quest for community* (New York: The Free Press, 1994), G. Bilezikian, *Community 101: Reclaiming the local church as community of oneness* (Grand Rapids: Zondervan, 1997) and G. Martin and G. McIntosh, *Creating Community: Deeper fellowship through small group ministry* (Nashville: Broadman & Holman, 1997).
[20] Gorman, *Community*, 13.
[21] L.L. Rasmussen, *Moral Fragments and Moral Community: A proposal for church in society* (Minneapolis: Fortress Press, 1993).

[22] B. Shenker, *Intentional Communities: Ideology and alienation in communal societies* (London: Routledge & Kegan Paul, 1986), 25.

[23] D.V. Martin, *Adventure in Psychiatry: Social change in a mental hospital* (London: Bruno Cassirer Publications, 1962).

[24] From a personal conversation while talking about the draft of this book.

[25] We have just completed the first draft of a new book that draws some of these principles together. We have tentatively entitled it '*Making the Church a safer place, and some of the reasons why it isn't*'.

[26] One of the initiatives we have under way in the community at the moment is to try to find helpful ways to support people when they choose to leave the church. People leave for a range of reasons: because they would like a break, because they want to go to another church, or because they are moving to new jobs, etc.

5.

Introducing the *Rapha* Principle

Verses 25 to 26 of Exodus 15 close with the phrase, 'I am the Lord, who heals you.' This is a passage that always has been, and still is, very popular in some parts of the Church. Some love to quote these verses when they pray for anyone with a physical illness, as if reminding the Lord that it is His duty to heal this person. However, even though these verses continue to be used by Christians in this way, they seem to play scarcely any part in Biblical and academic surveys of Old Testament theology.[1] In the course of researching these verses and their context over several years, I have read more than forty commentaries, but, like Lohfink, have found very few references to these texts. But in spite of the fact that few commentators treat these verses in any depth, I believe that they are central and core to all that follows in Israel's journeying, through to the Sinai covenant and beyond.

This absence of in-depth commentary surprised me because I see these verses as a unique self-description of Yahweh as 'physician of Israel',[2] the one who cares for Israel's health.[3] Luther,[4] Lohfink, and Preuss[5] translate the phrase as 'I am the Lord your physician' (*Ich bin der Herr, dein Arzt*).[6] Like Lohfink, I see this encounter as more than just a single passing incident in Israel's unfolding history. Rather, these verses are a profound declaration of the type of God Yahweh wanted to be to His people. Traditionally, within a Hebrew context, sickness and efforts at healing and recovery primarily took place within the family. Yet this passage moves healing beyond even the traditional role of diagnosis of disease by the priest (e.g. Lv. 14:1ff.) into the sphere of Israel's national religion.[7] While not dismissing the role of the priest, the passage suggests that Yahweh wants to be a physician and diagnostician, and share this with *all* the people. These statements were not spoken to an individual, but instead to a group of people whom Yahweh was encouraging to trust Him more fully.

One can only speculate on the reasons why the Church has not taken up these verses and stressed the importance of this exchange between Yahweh and His people. As a student of Scripture who is not a Hebrew scholar, I am not well placed to comment. But I see the theme of a God who reveals Himself as healer and protector to have been subsequently fulfilled in the incarnation and ministry of Christ. His power to heal, for instance, was part of His messianic authority, a declaration of who He was. This He lived out before a doubting Pharisaic leadership. Exodus 15:25–26 speaks of Yahweh's wishes, anticipating Christ's power to teach, heal and live in deep intimacy with His disciples. This passage documents this capacity and wish, anticipating the fuller revelation of social Trinity still to be given. One reason why these verses have not had a more formative role in the Church as a whole may be that traditional interest in the Old Testament story focused around Sinai and the covenant of Yahweh with His people. In the light of those momentous events, most interest in other aspects of the Exodus story paled.

But I feel that this passage is important for another reason, and I appeal here to what theologians call 'the germinant principle'. This is the idea that a passage, or even a book of Scripture, may be relevant in different ways, and have different applications, at different times and in different places. A further suggestion in this idea is that a passage may have different meanings for different contemporary situations. I am suggesting, therefore, that in some ways this passage could extend its truth into our times, to this moment, in a special or significant way, and that what it can say to us now could be both helpful and very timely. Let me illustrate why I believe this.

Exodus 15 begins with a hymn of praise (vv. 1–18) for the deliverance of the Israelites from Egypt. It signifies a way of putting the slavery of Egypt behind them, ending this part of their history. At Marah we see a whole new drama unfolding that puts Israel to the test.[8] Yahweh wants to turn the bitterness of the waters into the sweet water of healing relationship with Him. These verses are pivotal. They mark the beginning of a new phase of Israel's life with a 'test' that is to be fundamental to Israel's future success or failure. Yahweh is laying out for His people a way of doing relationship with Him, and they can either learn this, or suffer the consequences of refusing. Note that Moses is the speaker, but the passage slips into the voice of Yahweh.[9] Verses 25–26 read:

> He said,
> If you will listen: Listen to the voice of the Lord your God,
> and do what is right in His sight,
> and give heed to His commandments
> and keep all His statutes –
> of the diseases that I inflicted in Egypt,
> none will I lay upon you.
> For I am the Lord, the one who heals you (is your physician).[10]

Yahweh is imposing on Israel the rule of His social will, but is also promising that if the people live by His will, He will not inflict on them the kind of sickness He had inflicted on their oppressors (as recorded in the plague narratives of Ex. 7 – 12). The assumption is that if they do not obey, the people will suffer these diseases. The Hebrew is in the language of high historic prose, a style used when a conditional promise of blessing is founded on a divine self-presentation.[11] Yahweh is promising to Israel that they can be 'healthy', free from these diseases, if they learn to listen to His voice, obey Him, and begin living as He suggests.

So what kind of healing is Yahweh offering Israel (and us)? In Exodus 15:26 the Hebrew semantic field of 'heal', *rapa*, or *rp'*, is normally translated 'heal', 'cure' or 'physician': 'The use of the word *rp'* is explained by the fact that sin was regarded as a spiritual disease, so that *rp'* is to be understood as healing of the soul (as in Ps. 41:4) or the transgression (Ho. 14:5; Je. 3:22).'[12] Lohfink found 80 references in the Hebrew Scriptures to the root *rp'*, excluding the divine name. Of these, 42 belong to the category of Yahweh the healer/physician.[13]

The Hebrew root *rp'* originally meant 'to patch or sew together, to unite or make whole', usually explained as mending or stitching together pieces of torn cloth,[14] a meaning it also had in Akkadian, Old Aramaic and (more recently) Ethiopic. Walking round the streets of Maadi, in Cairo, in 2006, I noticed the word *'rapha'* over a shop. Going in, I saw that those inside were menders of clothes. In modern Arabic this is still a word for people who repair things. In Hebrew, *rp'*, meaning of 'repair', came to be used as a metaphor for healing or being made whole. This interpretation, rather than our contemporary understanding of instant healing by God, is consistent with other Old Testament uses of *rp'* (Lv. 14:48; 1 Ki. 18:30; 2 Ki 2:21–22; Ps. 103:3–5; Je. 19:11, etc.).

Here at the beginning of the wilderness journey one sees a new phase of Israel's history, where Yahweh is seeking to begin building a unique relationship with His people, following their release from slavery. This relationship is focused on a promise of freedom from disease and damage through healing and positive change, initiated by obedience to Him: 'In the Old Testament, the usage of *rp'* is decidedly holistic (cf. the similar usage of *sozo*) where the range of meanings includes deliverance from sickness, demons, death, and sin, sometimes within two chapters of the same book (cf. Lk. 7:50; 8:36,48,50).'[15] Yahweh will help His people toward wholeness of personhood, a spiritual psycho-synthesis.[16] I am suggesting that Yahweh is saying that He is able to help restore us in the way a piece of torn cloth is mended and restored. He offers to tell the Israelites personally what they have to do to become free and then remain free from the judgement of sickness.

But this Exodus 15 promise of healing is subject to several preconditions. If God's people are to be 'repaired', to be free as Yahweh intended, they must first learn to listen to His voice and then act on it by doing what is right from His perspective. They are expected to live in obedience to His Law (submitting to it) and keep the spirit of the Law as they learn it. On this basis, no one is promised instant physical healing, but, instead must undergo a journey with Yahweh that sews their fragmented selves back together. This 'sewing' is both in themselves, into one another and into Yahweh. Body-spirit unity is restored by divine voice in divine-human relationship. God's initiative, not theirs, is the start and finish of this process, but their positive response is crucial to the healing journey. Yahweh clearly sees this process as ongoing. This transformation, as well as physical protection and wholeness, are experienced as the people allow God to draw them to Himself, a process that exposes their own fragmented view of reality, showing them their sin, which is seen by Yahweh as disease. Therefore, my own contemporary translation of the *Rapha* promise reads like this:

> 'I am the mender, the one who sews you together, into Christ'
> (Ex. 15:26).

What I am suggesting is that the Egyptians suffered disease from the Lord in part because of their chosen role as oppressors. Likewise, we are all under threat of becoming oppressors, that is, of becoming those who judge and believe they are right, having unrighteous power over the lives of others. Instead, we must become woven into Christ, living His values in two ways. The first is that we must recognize the risk of becoming an oppressor, and instead align ourselves with the poor, sick and oppressed, associating with the victim and the abused, not with the victimizer and abuser. We must actively seek to live in relationships of equality and mutuality.

But, secondly, and more directly from the text, as well as learning relational healing, we must choose to be woven back together within ourselves. What is assumed is a surrender to the will and words of Christ as we listen and act on what He tells us (Ex. 15:26), so we can begin to enjoy wholeness.[17] This process will be a bringing of wholeness to our inner selves, along with all of our relationships, including our relationship with Christ. Such a result is in keeping with both Cappadocian and contemporary ideas of a social Trinity.

This passage therefore raises for all of us today the question of whether as Christians we are willing to hear His voice and seek to live His way, or choose, instead, to live for ourselves (e.g. be oppressors). It is a message that is very relevant for our times as this willingness to let Yahweh restore relationship by bringing wholeness to our fragmented selves is an essential precondition for our ability to live in and contribute to theocentric community.

Hearing God's Voice

At the core of Yahweh's invitation to wholeness is relationship – listening to Him and responding. Throughout the Old Testament there is a sense that one hears the voice of Yahweh by reading His words: 'However, if you do not obey the LORD your God and do not carefully follow all his commands and decrees I am giving you today, all these curses will come upon you and overtake you' (Dt. 28:15, cf. 28:45, etc.). Passages like these are a reminder of what Yahweh originally said to Israel as they began their journey with Him, as well as speaking of the consequences of not obeying. But what I would like to suggest is something more radical.

Alongside the traditional view of hearing Yahweh's voice by reading Scripture, I also see the possibility from Exodus 15:26 that the Lord wishes to talk to us individually so that we can either remove or avoid sickness, fragmentation and damage in our lives. If social Trinity is to become a wholeness reality for any or all of us, then we need much more help than we are presently receiving in incorporating this relationality into our daily lives. I believe the promise of this passage is that the Lord will help us to live the way He requires. He wants to lead us while being with us in just as tangible a way as He was with the Israelites in their wilderness journeys.

This understanding is reinforced by the teachings and example of Christ with His disciples, illustrated in His final Passover meal (Jn. 13 – 17). As followers of Christ, all believers can personally be taught by Him about what it means to be sewn together, both within ourselves, into one another and also into Him. In CCD and *Rapha* workshops we have taken up this suggestion by the Lord and have begun allowing Him to talk to us in this way. As we have done so, remarkable things have happened. We have found that He wants to give us very specific knowledge and understanding about how and why we become sick and damaged. This becomes the key to unlocking healing. Those who in the past would have relied on someone more experienced to hear from God for them have discovered that God speaks directly to them in unique but unmistakable ways. The supernatural becomes almost natural when God is invited to be part of conversation and relationship. It would seem that the Lord is more willing to speak to us than we are willing to allow. When we give Him an attentive ear, and let Him talk to us about our damage and how to let Him heal us, He has no shortage of things to say!

It is important to note that this promise of Exodus 15:26 is not a personal, private message in the contemporary 'selfism' tradition. For Yahweh was speaking to the *whole* nation that He was adopting. So as Christians we need to see a corporate dimension to this process, following social Trinity reality in human relationality. God will frequently give part of an understanding to one and the rest to another, reinforcing our need for each other in wholeness. Again, although Yahweh addressed the individual, He did so within the nation as a whole. As we learn later in Scripture – see, for example, the story of Achan in Joshua 7:1ff. – God's perspective is clearly that the lifestyle of the individual can impact the whole nation. So hearing God's voice not only brings wholeness to us individually, but also contributes to the well-being (or detriment, if we refuse to listen) of the whole community.

What we have discovered in CCD is that seeking to live in faith community has a tendency to bring to the surface much of the damage that we have incurred in our personal lives. For instance, if we have had an abusive father, we will find it difficult to trust our heavenly Father. Or if we have not known trust in our early lives, we will be unlikely to trust others, even though we are 'in fellowship' with them. What we find when in close relationship with others is that we do not naturally have the capacity to live in mutual giving and receiving with others, even when the community is Christ-centred.

Most of us have a tendency to be takers rather than givers, and need to receive more help than we are able to give back. But no community can prosper, or even survive, where everyone is a taker. When, however, we introduce a wholeness dimension to congregational life, in which we know that others are also choosing to let the Lord talk to them about their damage or baggage, a shared commitment to support each other begins. We are all on the same journey. By openly declaring that we need to change, and need help as we do this, we allow others to support us. Simultaneously, we offer to give help to others. Each person acts as both giver and taker. In this way, a mutual giving begins, so that on this journey together we see a deepening relationship with Christ, others and ourselves. Relationality becomes a strategic part of growing maturity and wholeness, with God speaking to us as its enabler.

Numerous support structures have evolved in CCD as we have learned together as a community. Examples include mentoring, whereby one person, by sharing from their experience of hearing the Lord, offers support to another who has been on the journey for a shorter time; and discipleship groups, which provide opportunities to hear the Lord together, both for one's self and for each other. We also encourage people to share aspects of their story with each other – not from years ago when they were converted, but more recent experiences of how God has told them something about their damage and how He wants them to change. Such a way of living is called a 'narrative culture'. One can visit Christ Church and say to almost anyone, 'Can you tell me your story?' and the person is likely to reply, 'What part of my story do you want to know about?' This daily engaging with the community of God's people in a manifest way is a living out of social Trinity.

The most common response we receive when people first encounter the idea of 'hearing God's voice' is that they as Christians have been seeking God's help in this way for years, but have not yet been helped by Him. But this *Rapha* model as we now practise it suggests that God may well have been talking to them, but they have not yet tuned into His wavelength. We frequently suggest, therefore, that they need to learn how to hear and then how to interpret and apply what God is saying. They must learn to recognize the ways that He may be speaking to them. Most of us only have the capacity to hear what we want to hear. Learning to hear what God is saying, from His perspective, when it is the opposite of what we expect or are accustomed to, takes faith, much practice and an openness to new ideas that few of us find natural. What we do not expect we will often not hear, even if it is from God. So we all need companions we can trust, who by their example will encourage us to step into this unknown territory.

I am suggesting that hearing God's voice in a new way is something more easily caught than taught. To help this process, I have written a Bible Note, one of numerous Bible Notes that I have prepared, that looks at 30 ways in which the Lord talks to us, as revealed in the Bible. For instance, through nature, teaching, prophecy, other people and circumstances. In talking about 'hearing God's voice', I am thus suggesting that there are a wide range of ways of doing this. I encourage each person to explore the ways in which God talks to them, be it through dreams, other people, meditation, Scripture, circumstances, etc.

Here I am beginning to speak in contextual language from a culture with which I am familiar in CCD and *Rapha*, but this may be unfamiliar to many others. In talking in this way, I am placing myself firmly in enthusiast, Pentecostal and Charismatic traditions, but I find that people from all backgrounds can find ways of hearing God's voice that suit them. Those with no Christian background do, however, sometimes struggle with the whole idea of hearing God's voice as a means of pursuing wholeness. To these we speak in the language of psychology, and talk about an 'inner voice'. Much of the time I treat the two as similar, suggesting, as Scripture does, that one of the main ways in which God speaks is by His direct voice, or the 'inner voice'. I am not speaking here of 'voices in our heads', often a sign of illness, but voices that come from the core of our being, from our 'heart'. So, as we do in CCD, from now on I will be using these two concepts of God's voice and our inner voice interchangeably. Community life has a positive tendency to sort out whether it is the Lord talking, or merely personal self-indulgence.

But a word of caution. The process of hearing God's voice can easily lead to what Middlemiss described as a 'degradation of reason'.[18] Christians see listening to God as a noble task, but it can lead to a dependence on supposed 'immediate revelation' that can fuel a departure from reason. As Christians, we do not always get it right when we 'hear the Lord' talking to us. So to help avoid any unwise misunderstanding, it is very important that we invite the wisdom of other people in talking through what we are hearing (cf. Pr. 15:22; 24:6). Also, some of us have a tendency to get arrogant as we begin successfully to hear the Lord's voice. To counter pride, and prevent people lording it over one another, we encourage questioning and intellectual debate. This we do in a number of different ways, such as questioning things we may have believed that now may not fit, or admitting that we have been living with rules at the expense of relationships. For some this can be a contentious area, for they may have been taught to believe a certain set of values and have been told that these must not be questioned because they are 'Biblical'. But in CCD we seek to maintain a perspective that holds that God's truth can withstand intellectual rigour and exploration, and we need not fear the change that it brings.

Celebrating Unity Within Diversity

When we planted CCD, a number of us came with the idea of all needing to believe the same 'Biblical' truth. This is the idea that there is a fixed block of 'Biblical' knowledge that we must all believe. This inevitably means that instead of new believers being taught to hear God's voice for themselves, they are told to turn to those who have greater understanding and experience. But over the years we have sensed the Lord wanting us to learn how to celebrate diversity in unique personhood and in beliefs, rather than clinging to a type of conformity that is intended to keep all of us believing the same 'Biblical' truths.

So two things have happened. Increasingly, as a leadership team we have tried to listen more to what both the Holy Spirit and members have been saying, and to take this on board as positive learning for change. We have not always done this well. We are still learning. We have also sought to let go of much of the thinking that suggests that we all need to believe the same thing in order to prove that we are all 'Biblical'. The Holy Spirit seems to be saying something different to us: He seems to be inviting us to learn how to celebrate diversity. This allows us to expect God to speak through unchurched newcomers and to value their contribution to community life.

Some teaching in Scripture cannot be questioned. This includes the teaching on the person and work of Christ, the atonement and the place of the Church. Likewise, we must not let go of some core beliefs, such as those expressed in the Apostles', Athanasian and Nicene Creeds, and also the statement of faith of the local faith community. Other aspects of teaching, however, can be open to interpretation, for instance, the date of the second coming of the Lord, and the place of the gift of tongues in a believer's life. Like our personal opinions, our views on these can be as diverse as we wish. Some of us are in danger of seeking to construct a whole intellectual theological framework for every contingency in life when much can very easily be left up to individuals to decide for themselves. Admitting that you do not have answers can be very liberating and levelling for yourself and others. It is unfortunate that some feel a need to have an answer for everything, while expecting everyone else to believe what they believe. For these people, conformity becomes more important than the liberating freedom and maturity of differing opinions.

We recognize that it is sometimes difficult to express a differing view without sounding critical or arrogant. But in CCD we do still encourage the voicing of contrary opinions. For instance, in our Leadership Team meetings we often disagree and put forward opposing views, both Biblical and personal, but after discussion – and voting, if necessary – we seek to all stand together to support the final decision, regardless of what was expressed by individuals. Unity is to be treasured, but finding unity in diversity is a challenge.

Behind such practice is the idea that we are allowed to disagree, even with and within the leadership. But as we question, we must also learn grace. Differences must be expressed in a spirit of love, with a desire to honour each other rather than to criticize and undermine. Authentic community must be able to exist in a climate of different opinions. My reason for mentioning this is the problem of hearing the Lord's voice, expressing it and then discovering that 'the Lord' is saying something quite different, or even contradictory, through another person. Surprisingly, little of this happens here in CCD, but in community life we all need the grace to be able to admit that we might be wrong. It is easier to hold on to our hard-earned and publicly declared view than to go back and rethink the issue from a new perspective. I have personally made numerous mistakes since we planted CCD, and have had to say sorry on many occasions.

Within the community and *Rapha* we encourage people to bring apparently conflicting or contradictory views into the open so that these may become sources of positive change. Again, this is something we are still learning how to do, and do not do very well at times. For instance, because our community is so psychologically aware, if someone raises a criticism, it is all too easy to look behind the 'complaint' to seek to identify the 'baggage' that is driving it. So we turn the comment back on the one complaining, putting ourselves in danger of ignoring the validity of the criticism being made. Finding a balance in this takes a great deal of maturity. We accept that since we are all different, we should no longer see the need to all believe the same things in order to live as faith community. We remind people that none of us has sufficient knowledge, or a theology comprehensive enough, to 'judge' whether anyone else is right or wrong. We are all mortal, and fallible. Each of us is responsible to the Lord for our own understanding and behaviour. This is a very steep learning curve.

Another way we seek to encourage diversity is by holding seminar programmes with visiting national and international speakers.[19] These teachers bring a range of new concepts to the community, and help people learn new ideas that for many would not have been possible or even desirable in the past. Expanding our horizons in this way increases our capacity to hear new ideas and truth from other perspectives, including God's. We also encourage people to further their academic life if they wish, taking a career break if necessary. This brings greater richness to community life and stimulates personal growth.

The ideas I am putting forward here are not unique to CCD or *Rapha*. Other modern authors have taken up the suggestion that Hebrew therapeutic ideas were not about healing but about hearing God's voice and acting on it.[20] But a word of caution. When talking about hearing God's voice, I would not want to advocate an exclusivist approach that uses God's voice to shut out all others. For instance, Middlemiss talked of the bifurcation in the Western Church of existentialism versus rationalism, experience versus theology, subjective truth versus objective, knowing a person rather than knowing about a person, or I-thou opposing I-it.[21] But the 'either/or' is far too simplistic, and causes dogmatism. Instead, I believe we all need to strive as Christians for a more mature middle ground that allows us to openly live our theology and opinions, diverse though they may be, in healthy relationship, rather than in separate (private) lives.

'Sin' and the *Rapha* Journey

The other key issue for me emanating from Exodus 15, alongside
hearing God's voice, is the use of the word 'disease', and its theological connection with the idea of sin. The suggestion in this
passage is that disease is the consequence of disobedience, and
disobedience is sin against Yahweh, ourselves and one another.
The word 'sin' is a controversial word, but Dallas Willard gives
us some help with it. He sees sin as distinct from the person, and
suggests that it is the incapacity of the soul to coordinate the
whole person, internally and externally. By spiritual disciplines,
Willard proposed, we are able to progress toward wholeness, an
integrating of the person by God's Spirit and the person's own
spirit.[22]

Put another way, 'Man is a sin-sickness bearer.'[23] Benner,
among others, has made the same point,[24] while Adams called
sin-engendered sickness *hamartiagenic*.[25] In returning to Exodus
15 and reading here one of the earliest stories that shaped life in
Israel, we see Yahweh making a direct connection between obedience to Him and the issue of disease and sickness. For Him it is
a stark choice: live in obedience to the way He tells us to live, or
suffer the consequences of the sicknesses of sin. As Nicola Jane
Soen, who is from our community, reminded me, God loves us,
but needs our obedience in order to heal us.

Three thousand years after the events of Exodus 15, some med-
ical experts are beginning to agree with Yahweh, so that today we
hear talk of the 'psychophysiology of illness'. The idea is that a
person's emotional and spiritual life impacts the physical body,
and the body's sick condition can adversely impact the spirit and
emotion. This is a growing field in modern medicine.[26] Yahweh is
making the connection between the way we all live and the
'lifestyle diseases' that we all compulsively feed, from caffeine
and street drugs, to medication, through to numerous other
addictive disorders, ranging from abuse of credit cards to self-
harm. Such behaviour will in time damage our physical state as
well as weaken our spirit.

Viewing ourselves as fragmented and damaged by a disease
called sin has a number of positive benefits. It implies that this is
our 'normal' state, the starting place for all of us, even after

conversion. Christ's blood may cover our sin, so that we are no longer held to account for it by God, but the fullness of salvation lies in the wholeness of transformed relationships, with God, others and ourselves. It is in this transformation that we know freedom from the damage done to us by our wrong, sinful living. The *Rapha* promise means that God wants to show us how to live, and how to recover wholeness in all areas of our lives, including living in a more healthy way. He invites our chosen response, our *becoming*, a journey of positive discipleship change. But the suggestion also is that as members of the Body of Christ, we can only do this as a group. No one person has either the will or the capacity to do this privately. To possess such wholeness, following social Trinity, we need both the Lord and others to free us from our sin.

Taking up Willard's idea of sin, and drawing on the Cappadocian dynamic of *perichoresis*, I want to propose a new and different definition of sin, based on both the context of the *Rapha* promise and more contemporary definitions. We are beginning to note that living the *Rapha* journey and its promises requires continual personal positive change. Gotz suggested that all material reality is static, while spiritual reality is in a permanent state of change.[27] The Cappadocians suggested that even at the heart of God there is continual relational becoming, a dynamic *perichoresis*. God dwells mainly in this spiritual reality and, therefore, if we are to harmonize with Him, we also must be willing to move personally into change through engaging both His wishes and spiritual reality. To *be* is to resist change, while to *become* is a personal, *spiritual* posture of permanent maturing change.

On this basis, if we do not seek to change positively in terms of wholeness, we will be unable to grow in Christ-likeness. Personal change is essential in order to become more like Christ. Christ-likeness means that we begin to display in our lives the qualities that we see in Christ. These include His ability to live unconditional love, a power to heal, and a capacity to put other people first without becoming enslaved to them. Such qualities are all unnatural to us; they require a way of life that we do not naturally live. They have to be learned, coached into us by Christ through our choice to be positively changing in relationship with others.

Therefore, resisting changes that God wishes us to make, as presented in this *Rapha* passage, becomes sin to us. If we remain unchanged, we are in a place of sin. Such a concept of sin is not new. Christ expected substantial change from all His followers (Mt. 18:3). This is a perspective that members of CCD have found very helpful.

Sin

♦ I always knew that I had decided to follow Christ, but now see the hope of sins forgiven and being free, as the Bible had always said I could be, yet I knew I'd never experienced. I now see that I'd never really known God, although I knew all about Him, and the Bible

♦ Seeing the unreality of my relationship with God against the backdrop of my hate/anger towards men, women and God. How my sin (seen for what it really was and its vastness) stood between me and God, and yet finding love and not judgement or condemnation. Realizing the spiritual world and all its reality made being a Christian or choosing Christ seem less of an intellectual exercise than a life-style choice

♦ I've moved away from the traditional evangelical idea that when we become a Christian and repent of our sins, we're born again and move into a life of freedom from sin. I now see my sin and recognize that dealing with my sin is a daily process. I also recognize the importance to God of a life of brokenness, rather than triumphalism

♦ I never saw the sin in my life that I needed to repent deeply over. I thought making a simple prayer of asking Jesus into your life made you a Christian, and hearing the Word of God changed you. Now I realize that emotions need to be healed, and what's in our spirit cleaned in order to be able to become in a place where you can even try to follow Christ, because before you wouldn't know Him at all. So, Christian to me now means following Christ, being like Him, but firstly asking Him to show us baggage in order to see where we may be able to go, and how we may be able to be

 ⋆ I have grown up believing that everything I did was sin, and so I became affected by the word. I now use it to understand the dark areas and drives within me that stand against God, causing damage to myself and others

At this point I confess to being in a quandary. On the one hand, I feel uncomfortable saying that a church or congregation that resists change is necessarily in a place of sin; on the other hand, I am more comfortable saying that individuals within the church could be. How the Lord sees it I am not sure, though what I am clear about is that the expectation of the Christian life should be for positive change. As Christians we all need to change to be both more like Christ, and to develop greater capacity for relationality. I believe that an unwillingness to seek this change reduces our capacity to be in harmony with ourselves, one another and God's nature and wishes.

For some, becoming Christian is seen as a *moment of change* called conversion, but this Exodus passage suggests that it means a life lived in a spirit of ongoing positive change, led by the voice of the Lord. Though many in CCD and *Rapha* see becoming Christian as a journey, most would still experience a moment of first 'meeting Jesus'. The Hebrew words *nacham* (to lament, grieve, be sorry, change one's mind), and *shub* (to turn back, to return) both describe this moment of turning away from a lifestyle of sin.[28] Christ took up this key theme at the beginning of His ministry (Mt. 4:17), and was still emphasizing it toward the end of His life (Lk. 24:46–47). But the Hebrew idea of sin as resisting change also suggests the need for a life of positive change. Thinking along similar lines, Reid saw sanctification as a journey of becoming free from sin(s), and the process of eliminating personal evil dispositions and practices.[29] Both of these are key aspects of the *Rapha* journey and essential for the shared relationality of faith community.

The concept of a spiritual journey has a long history, going back to Old Testament times. Paul speaks of this journey in terms of becoming like Christ, a journey of sanctification. I will expand on this later. The birth of Protestantism saw an increased focus on conversion and the atonement, rather than a journey toward Christ-likeness. We do see exceptions to this, as in John Wesley's class and band meetings, but overall the idea of a journey was largely lost, with the emphasis on a moment of conversion and on the atoning 'finished work of Christ'. In this, apart from our committing ourselves to Christ, little more is required of us. For instance, there is no place for our 'works', and if God does not 'heal' us or make us whole there is little we can do about it. Such a way of thinking has prevailed in our Protestant traditions to this day. This has not proved the case in Catholic tradition, however, and any dictionary of Catholic practical theology or spirituality will have a section on life as a journey or pilgrimage.

In summary, I am suggesting that the *Rapha* promise takes us out of the realm of faith as only personal and private, into a realm of relational positive change. Also this type of change allows us to become whole, while also giving us an increasing capacity to live more healthfully in relationships. Finally, this approach, with its emphasis on a journey into Christ-likeness, allows the Lord to show us our sin and to teach us how to live more freely from it.

Rapha: An Empowering Intrinsic Spirituality

In Exodus 15:26 Yahweh offers a model of change that contemporary people in CCD find conceptually attractive, whether or not they have a personal belief in Jesus Christ. Listening to the voice of God (or their inner voice) gives them an intuitive way to begin exploring their personal spirituality. As they do, both their own and others' spirituality begins to live to them. It therefore comes as no surprise to them to find that they are living in a fragmented way, and that God wants to offer them an alternative if they wish to seek it out. People learn to welcome God's perspective, for the *Rapha* promise is both atonement and a journey of sanctification. As a retired pastor friend of mine helpfully reminded me, *Rapha* is a promise of a total provision for maintenance of the person's well-being throughout life, which includes a transforming Holy Spirit relationship.

As we have noted, a traditional interpretation of these verses is that God should be expected to heal a person instantly. What we are seeing is that this is not the only way to interpret this passage. Instead, I am suggesting that healing by God is conditional upon our living a certain way, and obeying both the Spirit and the word of God. I am not denying that instant healing can and does take place in the contemporary Church. We have experienced it personally in our congregation and ministry. However, these particular verses, looked at in their context, promise something much more profound and broad-based. The promise is more specific, and, in my view, even more remarkable than instant healing.

'Signs and wonders' are welcome, of course, but I am concerned that some people chase these experiences. ('Have you had a miracle today?'). This approach also communicates the impression that God is required to sort out the problem, rather than each person needing to take personal responsibility for their damaged, sinful and baggage-ridden states. Power evangelism and healings clearly have a place in the Church, but over the years I have observed that for some people this expectation is not enough. In order to be whole and well, they need much more than just the spontaneous 'miracle'. People need help finding a way out of the maze of their intransigent sicknesses and spiritual failure. For this they must begin a journey with Christ, not just seek a miracle or take up the latest spiritual fad. This is why we talk about the *Rapha* 'journey'.

The *Rapha* promise is described as a learning journey of hearing God's voice and then acting on it. This idea is key to all our thinking. I also describe it as a *salugenic* (wholeness-inducing) discipleship journey toward becoming more like Christ. In teaching this journey, I have found it helpful to see it as God giving us the opportunity of working with Him on the healing process. This gives us both the wholeness we are looking for and the deeper knowledge and intimacy with Christ that many of us desire. It was a significant moment for me when some years ago I began to see these two needs merging in my ministry. I was describing a journey that we can all make, and need to make, of personally becoming more whole and more like Christ, while at the same time I was also finding myself helping people clear the ground of all of the psychic, emotional and spiritual debris that stood in the path of their possessing deeper intimacy with Christ and with others. But Yahweh does not say that this new way of living is available only to those who are or get ill. I believe, instead, that in this passage He gave His people a vision of wholeness that all of them could possess, just as we can today.

Wholeness journey

The community is like a hugely extended mirror – showing up clearly one's own attitudes towards oneself and God. It enables us to see the best and worst in ourselves and each other – what more incentive could we have to change!

♦ Right at the start and very quickly, within 2 minutes of sitting on the sofa, I know this is going to be the place where I am going to find the answers

♦ The emphasis on discipleship and the fact that our journey into maturity in Christ is a journey and it is not just an event. And that has been one of the most important things for me. Because in all the other churches I think that I have been part of, there has been no emphasis on that at all and I used to feel very frustrated that I had kind of, might reach a plateau

♦ There is a real emphasis on discipleship and on our relationship with Christ being something that grows and develops, and it is a journey and that we are really encouraged to be honest when we first arrive at the church as to where we are. And then decide with other people's help how we are just going to start the journey

♦ I said I was part of a therapeutic community. If you say that people don't put all the barriers up that you are part of a church. And then I said it was like a journey, in three parts, three stages, to start off with you have to learn to honour yourself, and when you start to do that you can start to honour other people, and when you do that you can start to honour God and then you start to become a bit more mature

This salugenic discipleship journey, I believe, is a message that the contemporary unchurched are open to because the integration of spirituality into health and healing is now on the postmodern agenda.[30] Similarly, within the Church healing as a

spiritual discipline is for some a key to new possibilities in reliev-
ing suffering.[31] But few outside the Church, in exploring these
new ideas, are looking to the Church for help. This was emphasized to me by Dr Mark Sutherland at the conference, *Key Issues
in Pastoral Care*, held at the University of Birmingham on 31
March 2001: 'Pastoral care must seek to revive the connection of
deep spiritual reality we all actually live in.'

In CCD we encourage people to begin consciously grasping
their own spiritual nature within themselves. This also gives the
Lord permission to talk to them about themselves, especially
about those areas of their lives that do not please Him. Because of
the *Rapha* promise, we know that this is something He will be
pleased to do. He wishes to reveal to us all the 'drives' that run
contrary to our being able to live relationally with Him and others. I use the term 'drives' to summarize what we have been talking about so far regarding the damage in our lives. A drive is an
inner propulsion, a basic urge, an impulse. Some drives are good,
some toxic to us. But I use the term slightly differently from its
original Freudian use to describe libido (sex) energies. Instead, I
mean it to include all those psychic and spiritual energies that are
our nature. Toxic drives are formed by the build-up of the negative human experience and emotion that accumulate in all of us
over the years.[32]

I suggest to people that these drives or energies are among the
principal causes of much emotional and psychophysiological disorder. It is only as we allow the Lord to talk to us about these that
we can admit and emotionally connect with them ourselves, giving them into the cross. Many of these drives have contributed
over the years to our inability or unwillingness to change. But
God is able, by His Spirit, to bring to our consciousness what
would otherwise be hidden to us by us (Ps. 25:4–9,14; 119:99). It
is both Christ's promise, and the *Rapha* promise, that the Holy
Spirit will release the truth of the unrighteous drives hidden
within us (Jn. 16:13; 1 Tim. 2:4). This wholeness also becomes the
release of the empowering we need to both live in and enjoy relationship.

A fundamental part of the *Rapha* journey is the dismantling of
these drives and the toxic emotion we have accumulated
through the years by a process of catharsis, which functions as

an integrating of the various parts of our human make-up, enabling us to release the damage affectively as well as cognitively. To live with wholeness we must be capable of embracing the righteous emotion that is part of who God created us to be.

The benefit of righteous emotion

• Before CCD I had little awareness of any of my emotions. Now I'm beginning to find them, I realize they may be sickly, but at least they're there! Improving my emotional health is an area I'm currently working on

• The teaching to honour oneself/love oneself, I found very helpful, also because it taught me to look past the self-hate and dare to believe that I could change

• I have always been prone to depression. These days I immediately recognize it as inverted anger. So instead of just spiralling down into more depression I have begun to deal with the anger that it really is

• I am more emotional. I am more at peace with my emotion. So I guess more emotionally healthy!

• Becoming aware of my emotions was a big step, and learning how to listen to them every day has really helped me to understand why some days I don't feel great, and knowing that I have the tools to know what to do about it

• The 'make peace with my emotions' made sense and explained a lot

• I have been letting out emotion as and when rather than every 20 years

• Frees us to be real with who we are

• I am more together and consistent than ever before, even though I appear to be on a spiritual and emotional roller coaster

♦ I am more real with God. Whereas before I wouldn't express to God how I felt through fear of condemnation, now I realize God wants (me) to give Him my anger and pain etc. Also, I find that I meet God as a person and not just a Biblical concept or idea, e.g., I experience God's love rather than believing it intellectually

♦ In most charismatic churches people do tend to operate in their emotions, but at the same time deny them

What Yahweh is inviting in Exodus 15 is a 'spiritual' relationship with a 'spiritual' God, but lived in our world now. By allowing God to engage with us in this way, we begin to see spiritual and material reality as two aspects of the one reality. The two worlds co-mingle, and we begin to live in both realities, both within ourselves and in all human relationships. We develop a spiritual consciousness of God and His perspective that helps build faith community here and now for all of us.

This alternative way of looking at these verses in Exodus 15 has resolved for me what Volf has called social dissonance.[33] This phrase describes the irreconcilable gulf between what one sees in the Church regarding discipleship, wholeness and Christ-likeness, and what we see from Scripture that God promises to give all of us. Yahweh, speaking to the Hebrew Assembly, seemed to have assumed that every one needed this lifestyle change and its healing ongoing protection.

Notes

[1] N. Lohfink, *The Theology of the Pentateuch: Themes of the priestly narrative and Deuteronomy* (Edinburgh: T&T Clark, 1994), 37.

[2] Lohfink, *Pentateuch*, 61.

[3] Lohfink, *Pentateuch*, 36.

[4] See J. Hempel, *Theologische Literaturzeitung*, W.A. Lambert and H.J. Grim (tr.) (Philadelphia: Muhlenberg Press, 1957), 809–826, cited in Lohfink, *Pentateuch*, 37.

[5] H.D. Preuss, *Old Testament Theology*, Volume 2 (Edinburgh: T&T Clark, 1996), 144.

[6] Lohfink, *Pentateuch*, 37.

[7] Lohfink, *Pentateuch*, 70.

[8] Lohfink, *Pentateuch*, 41ff.

[9] B.S. Childs, *Exodus: A commentary* (London: SCM Press, 1974), 267.

[10] Lohfink, *Pentateuch*, 44.

[11] Lohfink, *Pentateuch*, 45.

[12] See C.F. Keil, *Commentary on II Chronicles* (Edinburgh: ET Publishers, 1872), 465, cited in W.T. Brown, *Israel's Divine Healer* (Carlisle: Paternoster Press, 1995), 331.

[13] Lohfink, *Pentateuch*, 69.

[14] See F. Brown, *et al.*, *A Hebrew and English Lexicon of the Old Testament with an Appendix Containing the Biblical Aramaic* (Oxford: Clarendon Press, 1907/1962), 950, and Brown, *Divine Healer*, 26ff.

[15] A.K.Y. Chan, *et al.*, *rp'*, 'Healing' in W.A. van Gemeren (ed.), *The New International Dictionary of Old Testament Theology and Exegesis,* Volume 3 (Carlisle: Paternoster, 1996), 1162–1173, 1165.

[16] S. Grof and C. Grof (eds.), *Spiritual Emergency: When personal transformation becomes a crisis* (New York: Penguin Putnam, 1989), 47.

[17] See W. Erland, 'Shalom and wholeness', *Brethren Life and Thought* 29 (1984), 145–151 and C.R. Wells, 'Hebrew wisdom as a quest for wholeness and holiness', *Journal of Psychology and Christianity* 15 (1996), 1.58–69.

[18] D. Middlemiss, *Interpreting Charismatic Experience* (London: SCM Press, 1996), 21.

[19] For example, seminars have been led by Professor Clarence Joldersma (USA – Philosophy), Professor Elisabeth Donaldson (Canada – Education), Dr Viv Thomas (UK – Leadership and Spirituality), Professor Richard Flory (USA – Sociology), Dr Martin Stringer (University of Birmingham – Theology) and Dr Kenneth Wilson (Westminster College, Oxford and Queen's Foundation, Birmingham – Philosophy and Theology).

[20] See J.H. Thompson, *Spiritual Considerations in the Prevention, Treatment and Cure of Disease* (Stockfield, Northumberland: Oriel Press, 1984), 33, and G. Fitzpatrick, *How to Recognize God's Voice* (Fairy Meadows, NSW, Australia: Spiritual Growth Books, 1984/1987).

[21] Middlemiss, *Charismatic Experience*, 61.

[22] D. Willard, *The Divine Conspiracy, Rediscovering our hidden life in God* (San Francisco: Harper, 1998), 35–59.

[23] See R.A. Lambourne, *Community, Church and Healing* (London: Darton, Longman & Todd, 1963), 58. I am not suggesting that sin is the cause of all sickness, or that getting healed is merely a case of confessing sin. Human nature is far too complex for such a simplistic approach. Also, as a ministry, we do not focus on physical healing, there are others far more gifted at this than we are. What I am suggesting is that sin has penetrated every area of our lives so that we are damaged in all areas of our being.

[24] D.G. Benner, *Care of Souls: Revisioning Christian nurture and counsel* (Grand Rapids: Baker Books, 1998), 159.

[25] J.E. Adams, *Competent to Counsel* (Grand Rapids: Baker Book House, 1970), 105.

[26] J.L. Andreassi, *Psychophysiology: Human behavior and physiological response* (London: Lawrence Erlbaum, 2000).

[27] I.L. Gotz, 'On spirituality and teaching', *Philosophy of Education* (1997, Online). Available from http://www.ed.uiuc.edu/EPS/PES-Yearbook/97_docs/gotz.html (accessed 13 January 2003).

[28] P.D. Woodbridge, 'Repentance' in D.J. Atkinson and D.H. Field (eds.), *New Dictionary of Christian Ethics & Pastoral Theology* (Leicester: IVP, 1995), 730–731, 730.

[29] M.A. Reid, 'Sanctification' in D.J. Atkinson and D.H. Field (eds.), *New Dictionary of Christian Ethics & Pastoral Theology* (Leicester: IVP, 1995), 756–757, 756.

[30] J.P. Miller, *Education and the Soul: Toward a spiritual curriculum* (Albany: State University of New York Press, 2000).

[31] See, for example, D.S. Becvar, *Soul Healing: The spiritual orientation in counselling and therapy* (New York: Purseus Books, 1997), C.K. Brown, 'The integration of healing and spirituality into health care', *Journal of Interprofessional Care* 12 (1998), 4.373–381, W.R. Miller, 'Spirituality: The silent dimension in addiction research. The 1990 Leonard Ball Oration', *Drug and Alcohol Review* 9 (1990), 259–266 and W.R. Miller (ed.), *Integrating Spirituality into Treatment: Resources for practitioners* (Washington DC: American Psychological Assocation, 1999).

[32] J. Lampel-de Groot, 'The theory of instinctual drives' in J. Lampel-de Groot (ed.), *Man and Mind: Collected papers of Jeanne Lampel-de Groot* (New York: International Universities Press, 1985), 175–182.

[33] M. Volf, *After Our Likeness: The church as the image of the Trinity* (Grand Rapids: Eerdmans, 1998), 18.

6.

Introducing Theocentric Faith Community

Back in the 1980s Gleick spoke of the 'butterfly effect', the notion that a butterfly stirring the air today in Peking can transform storm systems next month in New York.[1] His idea, which embraces concepts from quantum physics, suggests that any act in any form impacts the whole. What is being suggested is that within material reality there is no such thing as a 'discrete' act. Every one of us is part of the same closed system where everything has a ripple effect on everything else around it.[2] Some of these ideas are now being taken up by the contemporary Church.[3]

This view that every action and interaction has an impact on everything around them is entirely consistent with the relational dynamic of *perichoresis* in social Trinity. Macmurray's perspective of personhood and wholeness similarly suggests this quantum principle. The action of the one impacts the whole. Our understanding of the way in which we live in relationship with each other is crucial for both our journey of wholeness and our life in Christ. We need to recognize how we have been and are affected by all those around us, and how our lives and choices will impact them. It should be no surprise, therefore, that when God first introduced Himself as Jehovah *Rapha*, a living and relational God, He also suggested ways of being together in community. Christ became the living example of this way of life.

Israel had struggled to survive first Egypt, then the Exodus, which in turn led them into the wilderness experiences. The central Palestinian hill country was rugged and inhospitable. From these tough beginnings Hebrew faith and relations were forged during the Settlement period of the Judges. In these hill country settlements life was centred around the extended family, creating an egalitarian culture where all were treated equally. Yet we also see the beginnings of a unique relational identity, family solidarity and a model of community growth toward maturity.

Most social scholars who study the Ancient Near East would say that what I am describing – for instance, the corporate identity, village solidarity – was typical of all cultures of that day. But I would like to suggest that because of its focus on Yahwistic kinship and its theocentricity, there was something distinct about Israel that set it apart. I use the word 'kinship' to describe a family relationality that may not exist biologically for us, but that, as we get drawn into it, will increasingly allow us to be part of 'family' and kin in the way God wants it to be for us. By His nature God is able to love us by drawing us into a family in which He is the head and kin.

Johnson noted that the historic period of the Early Settlement by Israel in the central highlands of Palestine was dominated by the concept of kinship.[4] Here Yahweh sought to create a people with several distinct features, and these, I believe, could be of relevance to us today. The formation of community seems to have been Yahweh's central act.[5] From the time of the Exodus He emphasized *'theocentric* community', that is, He Himself as kinsman in their midst (Ex. 34:4–7; 40:34, etc.), 'a society without rulers'.[6] Israel's population was to have a special 'kinship' with Yahweh.

Our review of this period begins with the Early Settlement era (around 1200 BCE), because I believe that Yahweh had a definite intent with Israel. He desired to shape their lives around Him, wishing to teach them about both Himself and the type of community that best reflected His values. He initiated this process with the Exodus from Egypt, leading into the Early Settlement period. This brief period ended with the birth of monarchy, though the concept of theocentric community extended into the history of Israel and is seen throughout the Old Testament. So although I will focus more especially on the Early Hebrew period, I will not be limiting myself to this time, since the whole of Scripture extends and unpacks what began with Yahweh's adoption of Israel.

Yahweh spoke to Israel, communicating His wishes. Scripture suggests that He talked directly to people (Ex. 14:1; Nu. 12:3,8; 14:26, etc.), and that in His pre-incarnate theophanies Christ Himself also visited people (Gn. 3:8ff.; 18:1ff., etc.). Wheeler Robinson is helpful here in describing how this process may have taken place.[7] The prophets and spiritual leaders heard Yahweh's voice. We do not know how Yahweh transmitted His perspective, but it is clear, both from viewing the surface evidence in Scripture, and interpreting it in the light of subsequent recorded events, that Yahweh did successfully communicate His wishes to Israel.

The name Yahweh can mean 'I will be God for you',[8] but Yahweh could only authentically achieve such a claim through fellowship with His people. He Himself gave them the means to fulfil His requirements (e.g. Je. 31:33–34; Ezk. 11:19ff.).[9] Such an attempt by a deity to 'rule by fellowship' seems to have been unique among these ancient peoples. Most other ethnic groups around Israel had gods that typically ruled by fear and conniving. Bright suggested that Israel's notion of God was entirely unique, Yahweh having been brought with them from the desert.[10] Both Mendenhall,[11] and Gottwald,[12] emphasized the equality of social life in these Israelite communities. Although this interpretation has been challenged,[13] what is clear is that from the Exodus onwards Yahweh sought to promote a unique type of community, with Himself being present, in fellowship, through the *mishpachah*, to all His people. Many of these extended families are to be found in clusters, making up small villages. Kohler,[14] for instance, suggests that some 40 local regions were occupied during this Early Settlement period.[15]

The word *mishpachah*, a Biblical term, describes the extended Hebrew family or small community that Israel adopted as its way of life. But I am not suggesting that Hebrew scholars fully understand what is meant by the term.[16] Much research is still needed. What we do know is that it describes clusters of houses, built in this region during the Iron Age I period, which accommodated hitherto unusual extended 'families'. A word of caution is necessary, however, because this 'household' is not the 'family' as we know it today. What made these households unique was not only their extended nature, with several generations living together, but also the distinctive 'four-roomed (pillared) houses' they lived in that helped promote the fulfilling of the Law as well as cohesive relationships. This is in marked contrast to society today where one-person homes and 'living apart together' are the trend.[17]

Bietak found these unique types of dwellings as far away as Syria and Egypt,[18] while Buminovitz and Faust suggested that they were exclusive to Israel, even when found outside this region,[19] a view that had earlier been suggested by Shiloh.[20] The layout of these clusters of houses was shaped by the ceremonial demands of Jewish purity law. Each room could be entered from a central space, without passing through other rooms, therefore purity could be strictly maintained, even where a ritually impure person resided in the dwelling. Men were thus able to avoid menstruating women.[21] What is evident is that commitment to Yahwhistic theocentricity and community could even influence the architectural design of the home one lived in, such was the comprehensive influence of Yahweh's wishes in helping construct the type of community He desired. An exquisite example of this home is described by Ottoson,[22] while a broader archaeological perspective is given by Finkelstein.[23]

Gottwald characterized Israel as a 'socially revolutionary movement primarily of peasants'.[24] The focus of the disclosure of Yahweh was among the settlement households, where He was active.[25] What united the tribes, what made them a unified people, was a strong sense of communal solidarity, co-inhered by the will of Yahweh toward them.[26] With this concept of theocentricity, the eternal will of Yahweh was given visible form among the people in extended family, ritual and the architectural layout of their homes. These were an expression of redeeming divine grace, a triadic notion of community that sought to incorporate social righteousness (e.g. the Law), compassion and love (e.g. in relationship) and localized worship (e.g. through the Eldership of the extended family, through the shrines and later through the Temple).[27]

Yahweh Promoting Kinship Community

Yahweh's desire to be King of Israel, to live in relationship within His adopted community, was reinforced by His giving the

Law Code at Sinai (Ex. 19 – Nu. 10:10), which followed the encounter that gave the *Rapha* principle. Thus Yahweh's social will was expressed not only in the people's physical surroundings but also in their value system and the way they dealt with breakdown when it occurred in relationships. It is through the Book of the Covenant (Ex. 20:1 – 23:19), argued Hanson,[28] that Yahweh set forth a pattern of behaviour in keeping with His nature, seeking just harmony both between and within families. This was a type of mutuality. By this divine-human relationship Yahweh helped shape household behaviour, structured the economy, blessed reproduction and was nurtured as creator and redeemer. He was the teacher, warrior, lawgiver, judge, head of the household, mother, *go'el* (redeemer-kinsman), and giver of freedom to Israel's slaves, while also being Israel's husband.[29]

Yahweh emphasized the righteous and just expression of the Law, so when righteousness was injured, the orderliness of mutuality and community life was disturbed. The righteousness of Yahweh the Lawgiver and His Law should be the guarantor of peace, and therefore of deepening kinship and successful community. This was encapsulated in the idea of the local Assembly, where the community under its Eldership met to resolve local problems, apply the justice of the Law, and maintain the righteousness of the community. Without social rules of righteousness no community can exist long term. It breaks down into anarchy. The righteous person is the one who carries out justly all the demands of community life, embodying and reflecting the nature of Yahweh. The impression one gets is that each community interpreted the Law as they felt best for themselves. But as the prophets later noted, the idea of mutuality, solidarity and corporate responsibility (Is. 1:17) was not always realized (Je. 7:5–7; 22:1–5, etc.).

What I am suggesting is that we see in these passages an outline of the type of community that Yahweh desired, a community that shaped kinship, mutuality and loyalty to Yahweh and one another. Justice was brought to bear on relationships, mirrored in the treatment of both the slave and the foreigner. But these values were to be tested, for, on the one hand Yahweh was strengthening His requirements on Israel, while, on the other hand there was an erosion of some of these early values. By the time of the monarchy, with its more central government, Temple and loyalty claims, we are beginning to see the breaking down of the *mish-pachah*.

For instance, although Yahweh elected the dynasty of Saul and David (1 Sa. 16:9ff.; 16:1ff.; Ps. 89), monarchy brought many unique features of a negative as well as a positive nature. On the positive side, these included endorsing the nomadic value system that all men were brothers, not slaves, as other contemporary monarchs often saw their subjects.[30] But we also see the beginnings of the emphasis on the responsibility of the individual, in that liability for one another was categorically rejected.[31] An illustration of this is that blood revenge was constrained by the right of sanctuary (Ex. 21:12–14; Nu. 35:13–29; Jos. 20, etc.). Finding the balance between the needs of the community as a whole and individual responsibility and rights was as much a problem for the early Hebrew as it is for us today. We may even see a hint of this tension in that Yahweh was initially strongly resistant to the shift to monarchy (1 Sa. 8:6ff.; 12:12ff.,17b; 15:11, etc.).

Along with the seeking of a balance between community and individual rights came a range of difficult challenges. For instance, we see piety gradually undergoing a transformation of the greatest consequence, a transformation that turned the religion of Yahweh into a religion of observance.[32] Israel gradually ceased to be a kinship relationship, becoming instead a *kingship* community. For the monarch, as the divinized representative head, was not capable of providing a single unified framework for all the diversity of life as it was being lived at its roots within a strong sense of community.[33] As an example, Yahweh claimed to be omnipresent, whereas the king was not. Some of the stronger focuses of theocentric community, however, never really left centre stage, reappearing as they did in post-exilic desires (Ezr. 3:8ff.; Ne. 8 – 9, etc.). For example, there was an instinct to return to Temple worship and when this faltered, a subsequent emergence of the local, independent synagogue. Likewise, a number of the Early Hebrew ideas noted in this book did survive one way or another into post-exilic times. But one gets the impression that few of these ideas seem to have matured in the way Yahweh had wished. The imbalance between the rights of community and the individual is an example of this.

In looking at the broader picture, we see that the Early Hebrew model of community placed relationship at the heart of both wholeness (e.g. having the mature capacity to live in community) and theocentric community. Individualism, with all its selfism as we know it today, would have been inconceivable. Relationships were focused around Yahweh, the community and one's self. These, reinforced by the just and righteous nature of Yahweh and His Law, all contributed to the welfare of the *mishpachah* or village community. Also, because Yahweh was at the heart of this process, all relationships became anointed with the holiness of Yahweh, illustrated in Decalogue No 1, 'Hear, O Israel: The LORD our God, the LORD is one. Love the LORD your God with all your heart and with all your soul and with all your strength' (Dt. 6:4–5). What we see is an evolving vision of a God-centred community with all the basic tools to live out social Trinity in human community.

Building Theocentric Kinship Community

What I am noting here is that in the Early Hebrew period the concept of the social unit was dominated by the idea of kinship.[34] Israel often understood itself as a community of clans and households (Je. 2:4–8; 31:1, etc.), where Yahweh was the Father, Israel the son, the wife, the foundling, slave and resident alien within each *mishpachah*. This strong sense of Yahwistic theocentric community dominated Israel's and early Judah's social and religious life,[35] shaping corporate identity and creating sustainable local communities: 'I will walk among you and be your God, and you will be my people' (Lv. 26:12). Yahweh was Himself the common cause, the cohesive centre. But this was tempered by a strong tribal or clan sense of independence, which resisted, especially in the Early Settlement period, any serious limitation of local independent tribal freedom.

One has the sense that the internal core of these *mishpachah* sustained each individual against all external forces. The internal culture, with its allegiance to Yahweh, was expected to be stronger than its hostile surroundings. Such a social system would exert decisive influences on the individuals as they learned to become givers to community, not takers. Life shared was the priority at both a local and a tribal level.

What I am saying is that Yahweh wanted a people for Himself, and went to great lengths to be their King. By the four-pillared house, the practice of worship, and the seeking of His will through interpreting the Law, local communities engaged with Him directly at all levels of their lives. He would be their protector, guide and friend, the centre and focus of daily life. In fact, He was conceived as having anthropomorphic qualities, an indefinable extension to His personality that enabled Him to exercise a mysterious influence on His people, the power to release blessings or curses.[36]

When covenant was broken with Yahweh, so, it seems, was also the motivation and power to *live* community.[37] Restoration of covenant was first needed through corporate obedience, releasing a renewed power and purpose to sustain theocentric community. Yahweh provided a God-centred intent to actively live theocentric community. It suggests the releasing of a synergy through righteousness, compassion and worship that is not otherwise accessible to any one of us alone. I believe the tough character building of the Exodus and wilderness, and then of the Settlement period, all helped promote a distinct *kinship theocentricity*, a relational kinship with both God and one another. For us in CCD this preparing of the individual to be a builder of community begins with an emphasis on the uniqueness of the individual. Let me illustrate the unfolding of some aspects of this process.

Group healing IQ/Someone already knows

♦ I think that is one of the most valuable things that I have found is that when you are talking to someone about their own situation, you can refer them on to several other fellas around that have hit the same, something similar or, let them talk to them. You can send them from one to the other, right across the community and I think that is a real value, real benefit that we talk so openly about where we have come from. And there is a real resource there, I have found

♦ It stands with and supports people that are showing the wear and tear of life. And they can empathise from experience

• In other words there will always probably be someone in Christ Church that has been through what you are needing to go through and understand

• There is a sense that the load is shared. If you have got a problem, we seem to collect people with problems, you can seek someone else to help you, a community of helping. I think a community can be three people if two are prepared to help the third

• People are buying into the principle of giving

• I think probably mentoring is one of the main ones for me, that you actually have someone who listens to you • if it is bad, it is going to be alright somehow, because someone else is with you

• Nothing you can say will stop me caring about you. You cannot shock me. Because a lot of people think that what I have done or how I have lived is so bad that surely there is no chance, and it is this idea that there is hope and concern and care

• Learning you can trust people again, and that you learn to love yourself when you haven't been able to. Because they love you first. And that who you think you are isn't who you are. So you have permission to dream . . . outrageous!

• We don't all live in the same house but yet we are net-worked

For Israel, one of these distinctives included a collective liability for the trespasses of the individual.[38] For instance, based on the *Rapha* promise, 'punishing the children for the sin of the fathers' is seen as an obvious expression of God's righteousness (Ex. 20:5–6; Nu. 14:18–19; Dt. 5:9–10, etc.). I see such promises as an opportunity for parents to shed themselves of their hereditary psychic, emotional and spiritual baggage. I do not see these passages as the curse that they are judged to be by some in the contemporary Church. Instead, I see them as God acting in His graciousness, through the fulfilling of the *Rapha* promise, in giving us all as parents a second chance to pass on to our children what they need in order to live life fully. Let me explain.

Most of us are cursed to relive the lives that our parents lived. Despite our very best efforts and intent, and even our prayers to God, many of us end up reproducing the toxic hereditary baggage of our forbears. For some of us the similarity is disturbing. But God, through the *Rapha* promise, and our listening to His voice and acting on it from His perspective, gives us a second chance to redeem what has been stolen.

In letting go of the toxic heredity that most of us have inherited, we can gift to our children the opportunity to begin where we have reached, rather than being cursed merely to reproduce who we have become. This reliving of our parents' failures and damage seems to be the pattern for most of us. But in both family and its extended community we are able to turn the curses that might have remained on us from the last several generations into blessings that can last for a thousand generations. Through our ministry, I have seen this process in both my own life, and the lives of endless people. This is the gracious act of a God who has a profound interest in what we pass on to the next generation, both good and bad. It offers the opportunity of an inheritance that, when possessed by us, will benefit all those around us in positive ways, as well as gift to our children all that they need to live life more fully. Although we did not specifically include this area in our research, here is what one mother mentioned as part of her description of the community:

Impact on children

> ◆ I look at the children playing together on a Sunday. How they are, the fact that we are as a community learning to accept and love each other and all the different values that Peter is encouraging us to work towards in our own lives. It feels like they feel the draught of that and they are learning because we are learning these same things, as far as I can see they are just getting on together, not judging each other, you see them playing across the ages and across the sex too, although there are still boys and girls, getting on together.

> Which in that kind of large group of kids . . . Obviously there
> are tensions, it is like life I think, but I can look and think it
> is amazing what is happening, developing that sense of com-
> munity for them that we just didn't have, like an expansion
> of what is going on with us

Ancient Israel saw its obligation as a requirement to keep itself holy, and this was a community responsibility.[39] The reasons for living in Yahweh's way were considered highly beneficial, but not in an individualistic sense. For, unlike today, people *belonged* to a family rather than *had* a family.[40] Yahweh had a certain 'common cause' with their best interests. These were a desire for common identity *within* the early Israelite *mishpachah* or village community, which facilitated a certain type of relationship with Yahweh, one that allowed the individual to see their life in community as worship. Like Christ's own coming and His gift of Himself to His disciples, this relationship with Yahweh promised that healing or wholeness could not only be part of individual human experience here and now, but also be of benefit to the whole community.

Put another way, Old Testament faith, especially in the Early Hebrew period, knew very little in any situation of a religious individualism that granted a private relationship with Yahweh unconnected with the community either in its roots, its realization or its goals. The idea of the godliness of the solitary saint that we have inherited from the Enlightenment would have been unrecognizable. Selfism would have rendered the *mishpachah* dysfunctional and unsustainable. Instead, we see an attempt by Yahweh to initiate a divine-centred society that gave relational meaning to divine demands, summoning the individual to live in permanent response to Him and all those around them. The household, or households, were, in their entirety, in a quantum sense, regarded as a psychical whole.[41] It was toward a perfected people of Yahweh that an individual's hope was directed,[42] not toward a private personal faith.

In reflecting on these ideas over a number of years, I have noticed what might be a pattern. It is God's heart to share His love with us all, and this suggests that we all have in us the potential for living a joy-filled life for others. But our damage, and the baggage of our forbears' history, frequently places a need on us, a self-survival instinct, to focus on ourselves in order to stay well. This self-interest, self-centredness, or, at its worst, self-ism, makes us unsuitable for the kind of community that many of us wish to belong to. Before we can contribute positively to community in the way we imagine we should, we need to let go of the toxic damage of our pasts. Yet we have become trapped in a cycle of sickness that isolates us from the very people we need to help us break free. For many of us this dark place in which we find ourselves can only be broken by a God who understands and wants to teach us to live relationally, experiencing some of the *perichoresis* that He lives.

But I am not suggesting that we return to the values and practices of the Early Settlement period. Instead, I believe that God has a clear vision and wish for a certain type of theocentric kinship community, the principles of which still have much to say to us today. It focuses, through the *Rapha* promise, on how we should live relationally in our contemporary world, for instance, in finding more balance between individuality and the demands of community. I am suggesting that from its inception the Hebrew community creatively assumed motherhood of the religious life of the individual, allowing later prophetic thought regarding community and individuality to begin living in fruitful interaction.[43] The vision of Yahweh suggests that our living in theocentric faith community has the potential of releasing a certain power to live ever more righteously, with a holiness that fills us all with the joy of life both in Christ and with one another.

Holiness as a Way of Life

Holiness in Hebrew daily life seems to have been a key factor in building community, one of the values Yahweh and His people had in common. Like a perfume, it permeated every relationship, acting as a type of binding agent on the building of both community and clan relations. What today we would call a practical honesty and integrity was required by everyone within the extended family. This was a transparency of relationships, a type of relationality where what you see is all there is, a practical, cohesive, transparent, relational holiness, a life of honest openness.

So what does it mean to be 'holy'? It is often taken to mean 'separate', but this is not how I read it in the Hebrew Scriptures, and not, for that matter, the way we see it in CCD. To be separate, in one sense, is the opposite of holiness. I do not see that Yahweh was teaching His people to live in an isolated way, withdrawn and private. Instead, holiness seems to be a melding together, a bonding of one with another, Yahweh with His people and one another. The traditional definition, which suggests 'coming apart from others', that many of us may have been taught, is not consistent with principles of wholeness relationality that we find in Hebrew thought.

Within our own community we see holiness as being whole or 'real' (e.g. authentic). It is by holiness that we contribute to the process of making all of us as human as we fully can be. God is holy and real to Himself and all of us. It was while I was talking one day with Dr Kenneth Wilson that it became clear to me that Yahweh wanted to be kin, with everyone focused around Him (a theocentricity). Holiness was both the distinctive medium and the outcome of a theocentric community. I now see holiness as the inevitable practical result of allowing Yahweh to dwell in our midst and integrate His perspective into all areas of our life. This holiness is an alluring, attractive, cohesive holiness to which people are drawn; it is the freedom to live in health-giving relationality. Let members of CCD speak of how they see and experience this for themselves.

Being real

> • I never knew how much I pretended it was working, because I thought if I pretended enough it would work eventually. You can argue one person's story but when 5 or 6 people tell you 'it has worked for me', it is not just a one off. It is not that it has worked for them but it is not going to work for me. It is like, it has worked for them and them, so there is a really good chance it is going to work for you

> • I would say that I have been open to people for a long time but it's the reasons for that that gives me the greater sense of

uncomfortability about intimacy . . . Because of this relationship(s) do tend to have a problem and I would say I have a low capacity for relationship

♦ I have never been so open about how I feel/felt etc. with people. I can reveal things that have been hidden for a long time – this has enabled me to be vulnerable and as a result has helped me help others

♦ I don't feel the need to hide my shame away inside me. As I bring out who I have become into the open, then I don't have to live in fear of people finding out my secrets because they aren't hidden any more. So it is easier to let people a bit closer

♦ I agree with you, I see it as relationship, but it is relationship in the family of community. And in this one you can be who you are

♦ I have a similar point. I have been able to sit with various people and be utterly and bitterly and deeply honest and frank about my feelings, and explore them and come out with a result, not just because they are genuinely interested, which I hadn't experienced before Christ Church, but also because they are trained, they know what they are doing. They have the experience and you can go into stuff with confidence

♦ I would say that it is a place where you can take your mask off and start to be honest about what you have really got. It is a place where you can, this is personally speaking, dare to let yourself out of the cage

♦ We are a church of emotionally troubled people, 99 per cent of whom are troubled to a greater or lesser extent. And the other one is lying

♦ Christ Church is the only church I have been to which I didn't feel I had to apologise for

+ There is an accountability with each other within the community

+ When you come out of a place of denial you need people to be real with you, but know they are not judging you at the same time

+ You won't be forced to deal with something you are not ready to accept, or even you don't see yet. That you are allowed to grow into the truth almost before it is exposed and spoken about. So there is a personal responsibility rather than a confrontation

To be honest, as a community we have struggled to live with the idea of this pragmatic holy God in our midst, even though we believe that without Him at the core of human community no one can be truly whole, 'real', holy or authentic. We accept that no one can become more fully human or able to know authentic internal wholeness without living in relationship with Him. Though we recognize that many move toward greater wholeness before being able to choose to know the God who is helping them find healing, we believe that the fullness of being authentically human is ultimately discovered in relationship with the Creator who is social Trinity. What we have come to accept is that God's holy authenticity calls us all to personal and corporate authenticity, and this state and process is itself a practical, cohesive, relational holiness.

I am therefore suggesting, somewhat paradoxically, that a holy person, household or nation is one that is most natural or real, in a profound sense. This is in contrast to the more traditional Christian understanding of someone who has successfully separated themselves from the ups and downs of life. I am suggesting, rather, that this holiness is achieved while connecting, engaging, giving and receiving in interdependence. This holiness is a willingness to positively change in a way that increasingly allows us to move toward deeper harmony with God's wish and intentions, both with ourselves and with others.

This understanding of holiness also suggests a new perspective on sin, which for human beings is a most *un*-natural state because it is so distinctively different from social Trinity. Through our sin we are both selfishly self-destructive and resistant to the relationships that help make all of us holy, more human and more transparent. To reach a place of personal harmony, of wholeness, within authentic community requires a journey by individuals who together are willing to change in accordance with God's *Rapha* theocentric wishes. To achieve this in Israel was the responsibility, within community, of every person as kinsman, whether Jew or stranger. Based on the early covenant requirements, everyone was expected to be holy, so that both life and community could be constructed in a real, authentic, holy way. Holiness as wholeness was learned and lived relationally, and this journey became holy in both moving toward Him and one another.

Living this Practical Holiness

The idea that holiness can be lived and created together could have far-reaching relevance for the twenty-first-century Church. Some Christian traditions suggest that we can all be holy on our own. This naturally leads to the idea that as Christians we need to separate from the 'world'. In one sense, the need for separation is valid, since we are all helped by keeping away from those things that would harm us. Likewise, to allow a growing holiness by our sanctification helps the process of our becoming more separate from the sin(s) of our past lives. But in contemporary society, over-emphasizing such a separation is not entirely helpful. Instead, we should be seeking a holiness that keeps us *in* the world, in the most natural sense. To be more human we must, in a range of righteous ways, be more immersed in the values and lifestyle of our contemporary culture, enjoying what is whole and righteous, rather than fearing its contamination.

Such a stance, in which we carry Christ with us in a relational, relevant way, helps make each of us a far more convincing Christian in the eyes of postmodern society. What also becomes obvious to us as we begin to think in this way is that we cannot realistically live holiness as solitary individuals. We need others to help us become more holy. We cannot be either holy, or in community in isolation, but only in mutual relationship as part of the wider world around us.

I am not saying that in CCD we are all 'super holy' types of people who are successfully living sanctified lives. If you think that, come and meet some of us! We are all very much at the beginning of this journey. But the idea that holiness should be a practical, hands-on, relational experience, in which we know the sweetness of Christ among us, is of real practical importance. Let me give you three examples from our own experience.

One of our members, a gifted five-string bass-player, has played in bands all his life. He is a regular contributor to our Sunday worship music, and is also a member of a blues band that does regular gigs both around Kent and overseas. He is the only churchgoer in this band. We encourage this involvement, enjoying it with him, and encourage people in the community to go along to the pubs he is playing at to support him. He, along with others of the community, will naturally carry the aroma of Christ into these settings.

Again, several of us with a business background run a business school in the community, and have accreditation to teach and award a range of qualifications in management, business and training. As people grow in their journeys, a desire for such learning grows naturally along with new energy to channel into new ventures. We encourage business initiatives, giving support to those who have a good idea, or a growing interest or expertise in some field that is marketable or commercial.

Likewise, in our teaching we encourage people to recover the lost years by returning to formal education, choosing subjects for which psychometric assessment helps them to understand they are naturally gifted. Where people are naturally skilled, and are then given an opportunity to use that skill, they will usually excel. Only one member of our community is studying theology, as we normally encourage people to pursue academic qualifications that lead to a job and professional income. Recent examples are the probation service, an MBA, neural biology and social science research. In every case, what these people have learned on their personal journeys, and the positive changes it has brought to their lives, has released them to go into further study, professional life and long-term relationships. This is practical holiness, the power to love and give taken into normal daily life.

We all need to become more involved in our culture, not by accepting its values and lifestyle, but by seeing, understanding and relating to people where they are. To be more human is to be an ambassador of Christ, meeting people where they feel most comfortable for us to meet them. As Christians, to be more holy, we need to be more relevant and accessible. We need to be encouraging social involvement in the culture around us so that in an experiential way others find Christ in the marketplace, pub and lecture theatre. Most people realize that to engage success-fully with these wider relationships they first need a significant measure of healing from Jehovah *Rapha*.

A Life of Faith as a Way of Life

As we have already noted, the 'four-pillared house' suggests that religious belief and its practice even influenced the architecture of Israel's homes. The design of the dwelling along ritual lines extended the worship of Yahweh into the daily lives of everyone living in such a dwelling. Life became worship as families lived and related day after day in an environment that expressed ongo-ing allegiance to God.

Behind this idea is something deeply important – the concept that faith in God is lived out with a 24/7 lifestyle. Faith is not just a Sunday morning meeting occasion. When faith is no longer rel-evant to our daily lives, it is replaced by things that we feel are more important. Peter Brierley, the Church statistician, noted that issues like unfulfilled expectation, changes in lifestyle, and loss of faith have all contributed to the collapse in UK congregational attendance.[44] Behind these shifts is the message that Church is no longer relevant to our business, personal or relational life *outside of the church setting*. The link between faith and life is broken. This suggests to the Church that we need to find ways of living rela-tionship with Christ that infectiously influence every area of our lives. Practising faith community helps restore the overall rele-vance of our faith. At a practical level it helps make faith and life in Christ more relevant to what we do.

People today are still looking for a spirituality that makes demands on them in a whole range of ways. Many people both inside and outside the Church are seeking a meaningful and significant lifestyle that requires both relationship and ongoing personal change. But much of our contemporary culture, with its emphasis on individual selfism, does very little to meet these needs. While people are looking in a post-individual way for lasting relationships, they are also still carrying personal baggage and toxic history that militate against this ever happening. Borrowing ideas from the Early Hebrew Settlement of Palestine, I have been describing a Christ-centred, theocentric kinship community spirituality that undergirds all aspects of our lives. This spirituality and its outworking in relationships is not static. It is a vibrant, every moment type of belief and practice that enriches all aspects of our lives and helps us to deal with our personal baggage and sin. This is a spirituality that speaks to people today at a time when, though the Church is failing, interest in spirituality and a spiritual lifestyle is rapidly growing.[45]

Responding to the Implications of Hebrew Kinship Community

The kinship community model of spirituality in the Hebrew period suggests a number of practical ideas for our Christian communities today, such as a flatter, extended family structure with an elder at the head. In the time of the Judges, this flat organization was reflected in the absence of a king, leadership instead being offered by a diverse range of judges and prophets. The concept of extended family as community meant that faith and life walked together for everyone. This model also suggests a range of other ideas, such as the corporate concept of God's presence, meaning that He is present with the many in a way that he may not be with the one. Also, we see from Yahweh's perspective a deeper relational accountability to community, while holiness is a group matter that all participate in and contribute to. All of these ideas, along with many others, could be of help to us if we were willing to ask how we might apply them.

But one idea is central, and that is the corporate idea of faith as a way of life from day to day, rather than just being focused around a few meetings a week. For these Israelite highlanders, Yahweh and His ways were woven into the warp and weft of daily life. Yahweh was part of the daily toil of life in the home, and expressive of the faithfulness of the seasons outdoors. Yahweh was the benefactor and leader, the one who helped make life what it was. He was not seen as an appendage to a secular life, but instead was at the core of how the Hebrew people believed and lived. This perspective may sound romantic and far-fetched, but was clearly the ideal that Yahweh was seeking, as we have already noted in the Exodus 15 passage. He wanted to lead His people, and bring them health and wholeness by talking to them, mentoring them personally and relationally in how they might live.

Combining the Exodus passage and its journey with the idea of a kinship community suggests the possibility that we should put God first, then honour people as the basis of a type of faith community that many of us are looking for. These values, when drawn together, help create a mutual honouring of one another and an increasing capacity to live as part of such a community, with the Lord's help. Social Trinity and faith community help make us all a little more human.

But one other matter stands out. It is the fact that living such values would significantly change our over-emphasis on the importance of the individual. Instead of thinking of ourselves all the time, we would begin to think in terms of the importance of our role in the community as a whole, and begin to place our values at the helm of the community, not at the feet of self-interest.

Here in CCD we have not yet got this right, but we are trying. We see most folk who have started on their personal *Rapha* journey going through several stages as they seek to learn how to join and contribute to such a community. Because it has to be learned, it is not for everyone. Some people are not ready to make such a commitment. Once on the journey and part of the community, everyone reaches a point when they realize that they have done enough 'homework' to allow them to live independently of the community. They are able to support themselves in their growing wholeness. Some leave temporarily, mostly coming back in due course. This is more often the case with men, who find it helpful to rejoin from a place of emotional 'strength' that allows them to offer support to others and explore friendships of depth and equality. Others remain and go on to the next stage of moving from dependence to independence. This is more often the case with women, who, rather than stop, to begin again later with a fresh start, want relationships to evolve into something more mutual. The community values a mature *interdependence*. Neither independence nor dependence is the goal, but for most people each is a season on the journey to wholeness.

By interdependence, we mean people finding their wholeness, desiring the ongoing giving and receiving of relationship. They know that this way of life in community is now their free choice, rather than a self-centred desperation. For both genders there comes a point where one decides to commit to the community and begin giving back. It is when we do not need community in order to survive, but instead choose to be part of community, that we can begin to make our most significant contribution.

Reflecting on What We Have Learned So Far

In thinking of Hebrew community and the contemporary renewed interest in community, I have come to the conclusion that we are not faced with an either/or of community or individuality. Instead, I share with Johnson the need to see in the text of Hebrew Scriptures an 'oscillation' between the one and the many. This we see illustrated in a range of areas, such as kinship and community, king and people, nation and individual, and Yahweh Himself and the 'angel' or 'messenger'.[46] But I would not wish to romanticize Israel and its relationship with Yahweh. From what we know of Yahweh's ambitions, they were far from fulfilled, since Hebrew recorded history illustrates a process of continual recidivism, an ebbing and flowing of buying into and then quitting commitment to Yahweh. For instance, the sin of humankind lessens the productive possibilities of the earth, so that the heavens proclaim the glory of God with less clarity on a smoggy day than on other days.[47]

We see from Scripture that all unity, through gracious divine revelation, is created and maintained by God Himself, so that when one breaks covenant law one also breaks the grounds of one's own unity.[48] Exodus 15 and a range of other passages show that a social pathology of disease is a normative assumption in the Old Testament. Its final aetiological factor is Adam's, 'man's' sin.[49] We see from the beginning of Genesis the intention of God to create human beings in relationship, just as He is. This in turn leads us to a view of the Christian 'soul' as a communally constituted self of relationality that finds personal full identity by the indwelling Spirit.[50]

But for Israel, the monarchy, then the Temple ritual, followed by the Babylonian Exile (Ezk. 5:15) all contributed to the breakdown of theocentric community. A life of worship gave way to more formal religion. A remnant returned and sought to develop a community around the Temple (Mal. 3.16–18) but this new community focused more on the Torah, and led to the formation of the synagogue as the depository of the written Law and Prophets.[51] Yahweh seems to have become more and more transcendent, rather than theocentrically living among His people. Despite the best efforts of Ezra, Nehemiah and others, theocentric community as I have been describing it seems to have stalled. What little remained came under even greater threat from Hellenization. When Christ came offering a return to theocentric community, embracing the potential of *perichoresis*, His invitation began a recovery of Yahweh's intentions for Israel.

Notes

[1] J. Gleick, *Chaos: Making a new science* (London: Sphere Books, 1987), 76.

[2] J.E. Lovelock, *Gaia: A new look at life on earth* (Oxford: Oxford University Press, 1979/87).

[3] See D. O'Murchu, *Quantum Theology* (New York: Crossroads, 1997).

[4] A.R. Johnson, *The One and the Many in the Israelite Conception of God* (Cardiff: University of Wales Press, 1942), 11.

[5] G. Ernest Wright, *The Biblical Doctrine of Man in Society* (London: SCM Press, 1954), 19.

[6] D. Fiensy, 'Using the Neur culture of Africa in understanding the Old Testament: An evaluation' in D.J. Chalcraft (ed.), *Social Scientific Old Testament Criticism* (Sheffield: Sheffield Academic Press, 1997), 43–52.

[7] H. Wheeler Robinson, *The Religious Ideas of the Old Testament* (London: Duckworth, 1913), 102ff.

[8] T.E. Fretheim, 'Yahweh' in W.A. van Gemeren (ed.), *The New International Dictionary of Old Testament Theology and Exegesis* (Carlisle: Paternoster, 1996), 1295–1300, 1296.

[9] Wheeler Robinson, *Religious Ideas*, 86.

[10] J. Bright, *History of Israel* (London: SCM Press, 1960), 132.

[11] G. Mendenhall, 'The Hebrew conquest of Palestine', *Biblical Archaeologist* 25 (1962), 66–87.

[12] N.K. Gottwald, *The Tribes of Yahweh: A sociology of the religion of liberated Israel – 1250–1050 BCE* (London: SCM Press, 1975/1979).

[13] See Mendenhall, 'Hebrew conquest', 66–87, Gottwald, *Tribes*, N.P. Lemche, *Ancient Israel: A new history of Israelite society* (Sheffield: Sheffield Academic Press, 1988), 163, and N.P. Lemche, *The Canaanites and Their Land: The tradition of the Canaanites* (Sheffield: Sheffield Academic Press, 1991).

[14] L. Kohler, *Hebrew Man* (London: SCM Press, 1953/1973).

[15] On the wider debate of the historicity of the Old Testament, see K.W. Whitelam, *The Invention of Ancient Israel* (London: Routledge, 1996), which offers a challenge to traditional views. To counter this, see W.G. Dever, *What did the Biblical Writers Know and When did They Know it?* (Grand Rapids: Eerdmans, 2001), and, more recently, K.A. Kitchen, *On the Reliability of the Old Testament* (Grand Rapids: Eerdmans, 2003).

[16] See Gottwald, *Tribes*, 245ff.

[17] See {http://freddyandeddy.comessaysandarticles/coupleslivinga-parttogether.htm}.

[18] M. Bietak, 'Israelites found in Egypt: four-room house identified in Medinet Habu', *Biblical Archaeology Review* 29 (2003), 5.41–49, 41ff.

[19] S. Buminovitz and A. Faust, 'Ideology in stone: understanding the four room house', *Biblical Archaeology Review* 28 (2002), 4.32–41, 34–35.

[20] Y. Shiloh, 'Four-room house', *Israeli Expeditions Journal* 20 (1970), 180.

[21] Buminovitz and Faust, 'Ideology in stone', 39.

[22] M. Ottoson, 'The Iron Age of Northern Jordan' in A. Lemaire (ed.), *History and Traditions of Early Israel: Studies presented to Eduard Nielsen*, May 8th 1993 (Leiden: E.J. Brill, 1993), 90–103.

[23] I. Finkelstein, *The Archaeology of the Israelite Settlement* (Jerusalem: Israel Exploration Society, 1988), 254ff.

[24] N.K. Gottwald, 'Sociological method in the study of ancient Israel' in N.K. Gottwald, *et al.* (ed.), *The Bible and Liberation: Political and social hermeneutics* (Maryknoll, NY: Orbis Books, 1993), 142.

[25] Wheeler Robinson, *Religious Ideas*, 128.

[26] W. Eichrodt, *Theology of the Old Testament*, Volume 1 (London: SCM Press, 1961/1975), 39.

[27] Taken from P. Hanson, *The People Called: Growth of community in the Bible* (San Francisco: Harper & Rowe, 1986), 30ff., but adapted by me.

[28] Hanson, *People Called*, 44ff.

[29] L.G. Perdue, 'The household, Old Testament theology and contemporary hermeneutics' in L.G. Perdue (ed.), *Families in Ancient Israel* (Louisville: Westminster John Knox Press, 1997), 223–258, 225ff.

[30] See, for instance, T.H. Robinson, *Palestine in General History: The Schweich Lectures of 1926* (Oxford: Oxford University Press, 1929), 41, 44, quoted in H. Wheeler Robinson, *Corporate Personality in Ancient Israel* (Edinburgh: T&T Clark, 1981), 43.

[31] W. Eichrodt, *Theology of the Old Testament*, Volume 2 (London: SCM Press, 1967/1972), 241.

[32] Eichrodt, *Theology of the Old Testament*, 177.

[33] Eichrodt, *Theology of the Old Testament*, 354.

[34] Johnson, *The One and the Many*, 11.

[35] See Perdue, 'The household', 255, footnote 14.

[36] Johnson, *The One and the Many*, 20.

[37] Kraus, *Authentic Witness*, 122.

[38] Eichrodt, *Theology of the Old Testament*, 233.

[39] Johnson, *The One and the Many*, passim.

[40] This is from M. Elliott and C. Dickey, 'Body politics', *Newsweek* (12 September 1994), 24–25, quoted in C. Meyers, 'The family in Early Israel' in L.G. Perdue (ed.), *Families in Ancient Israel* (Louisville: Westminster John Knox Press, 1997), 1–47, 22.

[41] Johnson, *The One and the Many*, 8.

[42] Eichrodt, *Theology of the Old Testament*, 265.

[43] Eichrodt, *Theology of the Old Testament*, 266–267.

[44] Brierley, *Tide*, 84.

[45] Holmes, '*Spirituality*'.

[46] Johnson, *The One and the Many*, 32.

[47] Fretheim, *God and World*, 265.

[48] Lambourne, *Community*, 31.

[49] Lambourne, *Community*, 58.

[50] S.J. Grenz, *The Social God and the Relational Self: A Trinitarian theology of the imago Dei* (London: Westminster John Knox Press, 2001), 20.

[51] M. Muller, *The First Bible of the Church: A plea for the Septuagint* (Sheffield: Sheffield Academic Press, 1996).

7.

Christ, Paul and Community

The idea that Christ was born into a backwater of Palestine has now given way to new understanding, based mainly on social archaeology. Christ was probably multilingual. Only five kilometres (three miles) from Jesus' Nazareth home was Sepphoris, 'the ornament of all Galilee', a new city being built by Herod.[1] Perhaps Jesus walked there daily since at the time he was a builder.[2] Christ was part of a literate culture,[3] and lived on the doorstep of one of the most cosmopolitan cities in the Middle East. But it seems He never really liked city life, avoiding as much as He could the more urban areas. In His later ministry He returned again and again to Bethany, a quiet village east of Jerusalem. He may have been drawn to Jerusalem by destiny, but He focused much of His ministry around the shores of Lake Galilee.[4] Here He gathered His disciples and did many of His miracles.

The process of recontextualizing Christ's personal life, based on new archaeological and sociological evidence, is now under way in academic circles. But what has always been known is that Christ valued Yahwistic tradition and the record of the Old Testament. In Christ the idea of theocentricity lived again, for He intended to birth a new type of family called Kingdom, emphasizing new covenant relationships focused around Himself. But He also saw many obstacles, symbolized in the Enemy, that were set against the success of this Kingdom (Mk. 4:26ff.; 10:14,24ff.; 12:32ff., etc.). So He needed to equip His followers with a unique new outlook, echoing a *Rapha* Yahwistic perspective, which would give them the spiritual and intellectual capital they needed to hold steady in the numerous battles that lay ahead. As in Exodus 15, Jesus' disciples were told to 'listen to him' (Lk. 9:35). Their wholeness, like that of the Early Hebrew community, was to be found in relationship with Him and one another. For example, His special presence was manifest when two or three of them were together (Mt. 18:20). Christ lived the recovery of theocentric community, with Himself, like Yahweh, at the centre.

Christ came with teaching of a personal Satan (Mt. 4:1–11), and demonstrating spiritual reality (Lk. 10:9; Jn. 14), giving permission to call God 'Daddy' (Mt. 6:9), and challenging His followers to treat this world with a light touch (Lk. 12:31). He showed an ability to know what people thought (Mk. 2:8), while birthing a new wave of reality regarding the spiritual world and Kingdom community. Christ introduced a spiritual Kingdom that existed within everyone who wanted it (Lk. 17:21), while in another sense this Kingdom would not exist until His rule was finally established on earth (Jn. 18:36; Rev. 12:10, etc.). In Christ, community returned to a focus on Yahweh and kinship relationship, though not centred on the *mishpachah* or the Temple, but on Christ Himself as Son of the Father. He brought a new immanence to relationship with God, in both expressing and fulfilling the idea of 'God in our midst', giving it embodiment in calling together a living community instead of the Temple of stones.

Christ taught that the Church would announce this Kingdom, but was not the Kingdom itself.[5] The Kingdom of peace (*shalom*) in the Old Testament becomes the Kingdom of God in the New, bringing with it health and provision from God. For in Hebrew thought sickness of body or weakness of circumstances bring the disintegrating power of death, while health and adequate provision allow one to walk with God in fullness of life.[6] Christ, by offering this Kingdom, was not proposing 'wealth' or 'prospering', and neither am I. Middlemiss helpfully reminds us of the dreadful way God treated Jeremiah[7] and others of His followers. Christ did, however, promise an 'abundance of life' (Mt. 13:11ff.; 25:29ff., etc.) and faithful provision (Mt. 6:25ff.) with joy (Jn. 15:11), which He expected as the norm. Jesus was also concerned about physical health and provision in this world.

This new Kingdom society would be known by both the vanishing of disease and the miraculous appearing of health and healing in Israel. The testing was past. Through Christ everyone could now see the Lord revealed as Israel's physician (Is. 33:24).[8]

In Christ we see the fulfilment of the *Rapha* promise, 'I am Yahweh, your physician' (Ex. 15:26). Christ even said that when He had gone, His followers we would do greater miracles than He had done (Jn. 14:12). Life in this Kingdom included a healthful emphasis and promise rooted in hearing and living the words of Christ. What we are noting is a continual, seamless flow from Hebrew Judaic ideas to Christ.[9]

Christ, Kingdom and Relationships

Christ laid the foundation for *Kingdom community*, both teaching about it and demonstrating how to live it. With His atonement there is both forgiveness and the guarantee of the *Rapha* journey with Christ. Through Christ this Kingdom brings reconciliation, adoption and connection, and with connection there is the community of faith.[10] The eternal Son becomes, through theocentric community and its everlasting covenant, the incarnate Christ (Eph. 2:4–7; Col. 2:9–10; Heb. 2:11–18). Commented Volf:

> Christ . . . who is present in the local church through His Spirit and in this way makes it into the church in a proleptic experience of the eschatological gathering of the entire people of God, connects every local church with all other churches of God, indeed with the entire communion of those who through the same Spirit are 'in Christ'.[11]

Christ and His disciples clearly saw themselves continuing the *Rapha* tradition of both community and its spiritual heritage.[12] By His coming He was restoring something largely lost. Among other things, He re-established the concept of community Assembly (Heb. 12:22–24), where community itself was the leader and each person contributed their own unique gifting toward it. The essence of Christ's teaching was the Kingdom of God, the expression of Christianity in this world. This was a spiritual Kingdom which all of us could enter and contribute to (Mt. 6:33), though with a struggle (Mt. 7:13–14; Lk. 16:16). Some, like Barth, saw Christ bringing in the Kingdom (though it is noted that in his later life Barth recognized that Christ *was* the

Kingdom). Others have argued more specifically that Christ stands at the beginning of a new fellowship of human beings, as its foundation and fountainhead.[13] But whatever perspective we take on this Kingdom, the core theocentric emphasis of Hebrew community remained, now not with Yahweh but Christ as our kin (Jn. 14.8–10; 20:28; 1 Cor. 8:6; Eph. 4:4–6).

The essence of this shift is defined in Christ's teaching us His prayer to His Father, and inviting us to make it ours. (Mt. 7:9–13) It is a prayer announcing the coming of the Kingdom of God, while also helping us to see that both realities, material and spiritual, are brought together in Christ. It also anticipates the ultimate fulfilment of this Kingdom in the return of Christ. Although this Kingdom is spiritual, it is also incarnate among us now, worked out in grace through believers . This Kingdom is also prophetic, reaching out into future history. It is the ultimate destiny for all of us who wish it, demonstrating in this world the living reality of divine community within human relationality. The *perichoretic* intermingling of social Trinity is extended to faith community.

Christ Birthing a Theocentric Community

While Christ was teaching the nature of this spiritual Kingdom, He also created a community of men and women who would be *ekklesia* here and now. For about three years He travelled, taught and rebuked these disciples, forming a core community based on radical Kingdom principles. He demanded personal integrity, the willingness to speak truth at all times, and stressed the importance of one's personal reputation in the presence of others. Such qualities were the fruit of solidarity with God in Christ, who focused this unity around His people, together in intimate communion. Christ was forging a divine-human interdependency, where each person had an active, unique contribution to make and was less of themselves without community. Today *koinonia* embraces the Hebrew concept of theocentric community, God with us, but also adds Christ's own brand of spiritual community, which He calls Kingdom. Through the coming of Christ, kinship *theocentricity* again became a reality. The *koinonia* thus created was ultimately capable of reshaping human history.

To help build this 'Kingdom community', Christ's ministry seems to have created several interrelated groups of followers: those who, during His life mostly stayed in their villages (Mk. 5:19–20), and a core group of twelve disciples that could become seventy (Lk. 10:1), or even more (1 Cor. 15:6). Christ also instituted a renewed 'family' in covenant with His Father .

Although Christ drew His followers from a broad social spectrum, on the whole they were from the poorer classes. He successfully moulded these into a community that stayed together, in obedience to Him, focused on Him (though not always, e.g. Mt. 26:56; Jn. 6:60–66). Christ's strategy was to consolidate all aspects of their worlds into one, seeking a unity reminiscent of the Hebrew settlements. But to do this He required every one of them to change and mature through His words spoken to them about them. The *Rapha* promise became a lived reality, theocentricity taking on human reality in Christ.

We see some fascinating insights into this journey process. Take, for instance, Peter the apostle, who as we see from the New Testament record, clearly had a rugged and difficult journey toward greater honesty and maturity in this life. He learned the hard way that who he thought he was, was not who he actually was. Christ had to expose to Peter his sin and baggage and show him the levels of arrogant self-deceit that he carried. Christ also tested his character by revealing to him the manner of his, Peter's, death (Jn. 21:18ff.). It is hard to conceive how a man could then continue through life, knowing, as Christ Himself had known, the traumatic way he would one day die. A kingdom can be built on such qualities. The *Rapha* principle lived in this relationship of Christ and Peter. Love and trust were built up, so that Peter could eventually become a giver, not just a taker.

This new type of Kingdom community, by the Holy Spirit's help and the maturing of the disciples, birthed the first church in Jerusalem. That first church led, in turn, to a proliferation of other faith communities. Christ's core Kingdom community became the basis of all successive communities in the Church. Among other things, it demonstrated many of the qualities of the *mishpachah*, for instance, its several-generations-extended-family-home character, which was Yahweh/Christ-centred.

From an Old Testament perspective, Christ's death and resurrection brought about a renewing of the triadic foundation of worship, righteousness and compassion (see p. 113ff) as His word was heard and obeyed (Mt. 28:20; Lk. 8:21). Christ's teaching focused on all three (Mt. 14:14). But from Pentecost onwards the Kingdom and its *koinonia* were driven by another divine person, the Holy Spirit (Mk. 13:11). This added dimension quickened the reality of community by promising all of us God's supernatural life to increase our capacity to live relational community in a consistent way (Jn. 14:26ff.). Pentecost (Acts 2:1ff.) meant that relationships in Christ now had the quickening immanent presence of the Spirit of God (Ps. 51:11–12; 143:10). All relationships in this divine-human community now had a supernatural and *perichoretic* dimension. Divine Trinity in human community was theocentric once again. The Kingdom through the Church became the dwelling place of God. Christ thus left the beginnings of a community model (Mt. 18:20), but it was the task of the disciples, one of them in particular – Paul – to introduce and teach theocentric community to the Greek-Roman world.

First-Century Turmoil

During the inter-testamental period the impact of Hellenization on Palestine cannot be over-emphasized. This was a complex issue and various groups within Judaism responded differently, some with accommodation, others with hostile derision. But the Temple desecration by Antiochus IV Epiphanes in 167 BCE and the subsequent Maccabean revolt saw Judaism finally fragment. The Pharisees' messianic hopes put them in opposition to Rome, the Sadducees embraced Rome, while groups like the Essene Qumran community set themselves completely apart from the political, social and religious life of their contemporaries. It was a period of profound social and spiritual crisis. But each group, in one way or another, contributed to Rabbinical Judaism, and hence to Christianity.

At the time of the birth of the Church, Pharisaism was still evolving. After the fall of Jerusalem in 70 CE, within Pharisaism the Jews regarded themselves as a community centred on the

Torah alone instead of on both the Torah and the Temple with its sacrificial liturgy. This prepared the way for a radical shake up in Judaism. The Pharisees now focused exclusively on obeying and studying their Scriptures, completing the process that had begun during the Exile, whereby Judaism became a religion of words rather than a relationship with Yahweh. The final shaping of Judaism following the fall of Jerusalem led to the establishing of the Academy of Jabneh as the centre of Jewish thought and research. This established Judaism with its community of the synagogue – the Judaism we know today – which in turn impacted the Early Church in a range of ways.

But the new community of Christ was not only birthed in the womb of an evolving Judaism, it was also part of the Greek-Roman world. A world which, in Paul's time, was itself undergoing huge upheaval and social change, with increasing polarity between the rich and poor, the political elite and the masses. There was disenchantment with the *polis* or state, and people were increasingly finding their desires fulfilled in voluntary associations, based on *koinonia*, a voluntary sharing or partnership that offered them communal relations denied elsewhere. This was a period within the Greek-Roman world that lacked cohesive community, with the breakdown of culture and commonality. Into this social vacuum stepped two main claimants: a range of philosophies such as the Stoics and Cynics, alongside various 'mystery' or secretive religions or cults. The small Christian communities established by Paul, like the community of disciples established by Christ, must be seen as part of this wider movement of people seeking association with other individuals within society. Christians would have been looked upon as part of a 'cult', in the club or association sense of the word.

Zizioulas noted that Greek thought had no ontology of personhood, that is, it had no theory regarding the person, which meant that it had no framework for relationship. This was in contrast to Roman ideas, which focused on organizational and social concerns, thereby supporting the importance of personal relationships with others. This is illustrated in the Roman ability to form partnerships and associations, enter contracts, set up *collegia* to organize life in the state, and recognize the freedom that can be exercised by the group. This was a tolerant climate for the

Hebrew Assembly, with its community leadership, and its rebirth as Christian Assembly. To any reader of the period, it is self-evident that the wider social climate at the time of the Early Church was conducive to the spread of new ideas. Of these, Christianity was to prove the most radical and enduring.[14] As we are noting, the Early Church began to reclaim Early Hebrew community concepts by acknowledging the centrality of Christ and His *perichoretic* Kingdom community.

Paul and his Churches

Meeks set the tone for the study of Pauline churches by removing both the possibility that we can see just one model of New Testament congregation, and the idea that their success was based on cultish separation. He commented, 'They remained in the city, and their members continued to go about their ordinary lives in the streets and neighbourhoods, the shops and agora. Paul and the other leaders did not merely permit this continued interaction as something inevitable; in several instances they positively encouraged it (e.g. 1 Cor. 5:9–13).'[15]

So although I am focusing on Paul and his communities, I do not wish to deny that much has been written on other communities.[16] The 'New Testament Church' was not a monolith and nothing was set in stone about what congregation should be. Instead, the first Christians left behind a range of models of church.[17] I am not suggesting, therefore, that other communities did not matter, or that Paul's churches were more important. Rather, I would like to suggest that when we look at the types of faith community that quickly established themselves in the Greek-Roman world, we see a 'celebration of diversity'. For the sake of this book, however, and its community theme, I have chosen to focus on one person's efforts, those of Paul.

My main reason for choosing Paul is that he brought to the Church distinct models of community, and we have in his letters and the book of Acts the record of some of his struggles with the churches he established. By the time he began his first missionary journey, his thinking was highly developed, and represented a coalescing of Hebrew thought, Christ's own teaching and the wisdom of common sense in responding to practical problems.

In talking about Paul today in community terms, I have drawn from the helpful writings of Robert Banks,[18] who has done much of the preparatory research. He suggests that the key to understanding Paul's fundamental idea of church community is to see it as Christ-centred, divinely birthed and supernaturally sustained. This seems to me to epitomize Cappadocian theocentricity in *perichoretic* reality. As a result of Paul's teaching, theocentric communities were built that focused on *charism* (the exercising of spiritual gifts) within flat organizations (e.g. no professional, salaried, full-timers) by a living *koinonia* that honoured both men and women.[19] Alistair Campbell reinforces this, 'Nowhere in his letters (with the probable exception of Phil. 1:1) does Paul address one single class or group of people as though they were responsible for the organisation, worship or spiritual well being of others.'[20]

Paul believed that reconciliation (2 Cor. 5:17ff.) was only possible between one person and another when they were first reconciled to God (Rom. 15:7). Christ Himself promoted the building blocks of healthful one-to-one relationships, thus beginning potentially to build communities. Paul also emphasized the need to build up the Body of Christ by deepening relationship with Christ (Col. 1:15ff.). Such a relationship takes us back to the *Rapha* principle, where God speaks to us about us so that we can positively change. We all need to change to be able to contribute to community.

As a guiding principle, Paul, the grounded realist, sought to adapt his thinking to the social culture around him. His own intellectual journey was the fruitful interaction between his Hebrew/Judaic, Hellenistic and Roman surroundings. His background perfectly fitted him to achieve his task. But he seems to have only accommodated or borrowed from the Greek-Roman culture where it neither impinged on the freedom of the gospel nor undermined the person and work of Christ Himself in both community and individual. Paul saw the faith community as an alternative to Roman and Greek claims on people's lives. As Meeks wrote: 'Being baptized into Jesus Christ signalled for Pauline converts an extraordinary thoroughgoing re-socialization in which the sect was intended to become virtually the primary group for its members, supplanting all other loyalties.'[21]

Such Christ-centred theocentric communities, as they matured under Paul's and others' guidance, left people with a simple choice. They could either totally commit themselves to Christ and His community, accepting such change as fundamental to their lives, or not commit at all. Paul saw the need for people to change to be both like Christ and adapt to *ekklesia* as Kingdom community. This process of joining a faith community was the way through which Paul expected people to mature. As in the *mishpachah*, belonging to one of these early congregations would have promoted deep and lasting relations that had the social processes to carry a person through good and bad times. It is especially in adversity and pain that we find the maturity we all need to be able to live in authentic faith community.

As people joined any of the early communities of Paul, they would quickly have had to make deep choices. Christ demanded absolute allegiance, but then so did the pantheon of pagan Roman and Greek gods. But choosing Christ could mean persecution and deprivation, something few of us know about today. There was no easy way of living in both worlds. Christ required that His followers learn and change, and this learning journey demanded an entirely new world view. Such change would also have given the first Christians a 'story' of how they coped with all of the change involved in 'knowing' Christ. Their 'narrative culture' would have been focused around the personal positive change they experienced in their lives, attributing this to Christ and their local faith community. The choices made by the individual would have created distinctives in their lives, delineating what it meant for them to follow Christ. This would have meant living in marked contrast to the way they had previously lived. Such profound distinction was essential, given the Hellenistic culture into which the Early Church was birthed.

Christ, the Axis and Head of Theocentric Community

The conceptual bedrock of Paul's community, following the Early Hebrew model, was relationship with God through Christ, embracing social Trinity and faith community. The obstacles to this being achieved, according to Paul, were found in a range of areas, for instance, compulsion to sin (Rom. 6:17,20; 7:14,25), being hampered in finding God (as Jews, see Rom. 10:1–3, or for anyone else, see Rom. 10:14) and being in bondage to realities outside ourselves (2 Cor. 4:4; Eph. 2:2). Christ came to give us freedom from all of these (e.g. the *Rapha* principle), but for Paul this freedom could only be possessed in relationship with Christ and *one another*. Paul saw salvation not only in personal terms (Rom. 11:17ff.), but also as focused on encounter with Christ within community. Salvation was possessed now, as well as being a future hope. It required a maturing of personal integrity and a growing positive reputation with others (1 Cor. 11:27–32).

Such a view of salvation makes Paul's expression of Christ a corporate relational reality *now*.[22] This new liberty in God, in relationality, can also lead to new freedom toward others, which must at all times be birthed in love (1 Cor. 9:19; 1 Thes. 2:8). This theme of love, and its binding interdependence, is central to Christ's teaching and to Pauline and Johannine thought. It has also been a recurring theme throughout the history of the Church, for example, among the Lundensians,[23] a community in which, as in the social Trinity and the Hebrew *mishpachah*, each individual member had an active and unique contribution to make.

In Pauline thought we see the earlier Yahwistic example of a deliverer-God inviting personal transformation from both the individual (Col. 3:12–15a) and the community (Eph. 4:31–32), eliciting from them praise, righteousness and compassion (Phil. 2:1–11). Paul's deliberate policy was to seek to bring people into intimacy with God in Christ, which in turn would lead to deeper personal relationships with one another (Rom. 15:7). Accepting Christ should compel us to accept all those already in Christ. For the gospel (Phil. 4:2–3) and the Spirit (2 Cor. 13:14; Eph. 4:3; Phil. 2:1) are both shared. Therefore, to embrace the gospel is to enter community. Let me share some of the observations of folk in CCD on the theme of knowing Christ and others.

Knowing Christ and others

* It has shown me that my relationship with Christ, myself and others is what being a Christian is all about

• I would like to think of myself as being a Christian. I have a relationship with God but I would still like to know and love Him more. I never thought of myself being a Christian until coming to CC. I would say now, I have a slightly better look on life and God since joining CC

• To me, a Christian is someone who believes God can heal you if you let Him – a Christian wants to love God and others, no matter what He shows you

• I should describe myself as aspiring to be described by others as Christian

• Being / becoming a Christian is not about me, but about Christ in me for others

• I always knew that I had decided to follow Christ, but now see the hope of sins forgiven and being free, as the Bible had always said I could be, yet I knew I'd never experienced

• Now I think being a Christian is more about an emotionally led relationship with God based on Him talking with me about myself

• Christianity is not bullshit any more. It's real and I can really have a relationship with Christ instead of imagining one

• It has meant that things that I have known in my head have started to become more real in my spirit

• The emphasis of the journey is about seeing Christ's perspective. This is far more in keeping with being a Christian than I previously thought

The Assembly, or gathering of people, with whom one makes the journey of learning to know Christ and others, is called an *ekklesia*.[24] But unlike any other meeting of people in the Hellenic sense, the Church is described as belonging to the One who has brought it into existence, Christ Himself. He dwells within it, sustaining and giving life through the Holy Spirit. This makes Christian *ekklesia* divine and supernatural (Rom. 16:16; 1 Cor. 1:1; 2 Cor. 1:1, etc.). It is a theocentric kinship community, a community of countless equals under Christ. Its owner, Christ Himself, remains its Head. This body exists on earth, meeting intermittently, while permanently in session as a heavenly community (Col. 1:2; 3:3–4, etc.).[25] After Christ's ascension, His mission[26] and its commission continued corporately as a household, family and community[27] in the Early Church.

I do not share the vision of those Christians who seek to recreate in the twenty-first century the way of life and achievements of the Early Church. This is partly because we actually know very little about how the first Christians achieved their success. Also, given the cultural uniqueness that exists today here in Europe and North America, if they were translated to our contemporary world, I doubt they would fare much better than we have done. Even the Early Church struggled when they had to adjust to a fundamental change of climate. By the time of Constantine the Church began to abandon many of its early values and demands. The changes that took place in the Church after the first two or three centuries included the loss of the significance of the home as a centre of congregational life (as the institution of the Church began increasingly to centralize and construct church buildings), and weakening demands upon people to change personally (as persecution lessened and Christianity became the official state religion, see below). We also see the creating of more structured hierarchies of leadership.

Although I doubt that the Early Church would prosper in our postmodern age, I believe it has a number of things to teach us about being relevant to contemporary culture. We have already noted in some detail the evolving idea of social Trinity. But there is much else that we can learn from their early success, much that is now largely missing in our contemporary churches. Let us focus first on the Early Church's application of the *Rapha* principle and its place in theocentric community.

The Importance of Personal Positive Change in the Early Church

In the Early Church there was an expectation that everyone would need to experience personal positive change if they were to be active members of a faith community. Paul, taking up the theme of Christ the disciple-maker, speaks of maturity in terms of union with Christ (Col. 1:28; Rom. 8:29) and moral stature (Eph. 4:13, *Williams New Testament*), neither of which is assumed to pre-exist in anyone who turns to follow Christ. It would take substantial change to know either union with Christ or moral stature. Comments McGrath, 'The New Testament suggests that salvation is inaugurated, but not completed, in this life, but it is clear that a decisive transition is envisaged.'[28] This therefore begs the question: Are we to assume that Christ-likeness, making disciples, union with Christ and moral stature when practised, should be the duty of every person who wishes to join a faith community? I believe they should, and I would like to suggest that this is anticipated in the 'healing' envisaged in the *Rapha* concept of Exodus 15:26.

Paul's writings in particular illustrate the extent of the change expected and required. At no time in the New Testament does this change appear to be optional or only for those in desperate sickness or need. Instead, the impression I have is that the first three centuries saw, at both a personal and group level, a pattern of discipleship change that was foundational. An expectation and requirement of personal positive change was basic to belonging to Christ and one another in *ekklesia*.

The Early Church developed a whole range of programmes intended to 'perfect' new converts, a process that involved considerable personal change. For an outsider's perspective, see MacMullen, for an insider's, see Field.[29] Both books illustrate the stringent and deep changes expected of new converts, which Field suggested meant a minimum of three years of 'training and exorcisms' before a catechumen (a Christian convert under instruction) was baptized into the Christian community.[30] The Early Church even had this special word – catechumen – to distinguish such a person. The radical nature of the change from a pagan to a Christian culture cannot be over-emphasized. This shift would have impacted every area of the person's life, no part remaining untouched. Such a dynamic culture, and the deep change it offered, was clearly both attractive and successful, as is seen by the numeric growth and the boldness of Christians in martyrdom. The change would be dramatic for either the Jew or

Gentile who chose to become Christian.[31] T.M. Finn writes: 'Catechesis was only half the battle, and "battle" is the correct word: The purpose of the catechumenate was literally to "reform" the candidate . . . Thus, as the catechumens' convictions changed from old values to new, their conduct had also to change from old ways to new.'[32]

Creating a climate of positive change in the way that we see it existing in the Early Church is a challenge that we have tried to take up in CCD.

Problems of positively changing

♦ Community is a scary thing. I personally cannot do it that well. There's only a handful of people I see who are doing it well. Community is a good thing in CC for many people, and it has helped others a lot . . . I cannot handle anyone being nice to me

♦ And even changing the job that I do. I am working with people that I worked with 20 years ago, they still look at me as the same person I was 20 years ago, they don't give the new person the chance

♦ It is a community of people that want to give something back into the community, to be available to the community

♦ When I joined the church (not CCD) they would say the search has pretty much come to an end. But for me that was when my Christian life went down the pan because there was nothing to do any more, nothing to find, because you had everything in Christ and the official teaching was you have everything in Christ so you don't need to search for Him, all you have to do is ask and God appears

♦ I do find it amazing that every week you will meet some-one and you will meet them a week later and they are differ-ent – it is bizarre

♦ The other difference is that because you see people chang-ing around you all the time and it is such an obvious change in so many people, you can't stay still yourself

♦ I have always wanted to be very much on my own, never worked in a team in real life, not real life. Always been on my own and always purposely avoid being in a team

♦ It is community, big time. It is, you will let us come close

Discipleship for the catechumen was inevitably 'therapeutic', in the sense of bringing about positive personal change by separating new believers from their pagan and no doubt sometimes toxic pasts. But such disciplines, and their importance for promoting personal positive change, clearly did not survive the heavy waters of Constantine's reign when Christianity became the official religion of the Roman Empire. For one thing, discipleship was less important in an accepting culture than in one where distinctives were essential in order to know a friend from an enemy. Also, the lessening threat of persecution and martyrdom meant that a person did not have to pay the price that could once have been required to join a congregation. When Christianity became the state religion, and the Church was no longer attacked as seditious, it also became more fashionable and advantageous to be a member. This seems to be a problem shared with the twentieth century, when many were born into or joined the Church with little requirement of radical change.

Here in CCD, partly because we work with so many people who know they need help, we have come to value a culture in which change is expected. One of the most valued features of life in the community is the presumption of personal positive change. This is the expectation for everyone in our community. If you do not like someone today, you will like them next week because both you and they will be changing. If you struggle with each other's baggage, or do not have the capacity to love, expect this to be resolved by continual, mutual change. Thus a social culture where people are changing is, in a counterintuitive way, a place of real safety. For where attitudes and values become dogmatically entrenched, relationships harden and decay. In any group of people such a climate does little to promote deep trust and personal positive change. In contrast, we have encouraged a valuing of change that allows people to remain fluid in relationships and accepting in a helpful sense toward the failures and shortfalls of the learning journey. This fluidity within relationships leads to a cohesiveness that strengthens the internal allegiance of one to another.

The social culture of any faith community has to compete with numerous external claims. Its values have therefore to be internally very strong if it is to survive. They must also be distinct enough for members to be able to make a conscious choice to join and continue their commitment. This was clearly true for the Early Church. For those in our community it is important that they feel safe, particularly if they are to continue to change. So it is key that the distinctives and values of the community should be such that people's reactions can be trusted. As people begin to deal with deep issues in their lives, they will be able to do so within the safety of the community. Let me illustrate this from members' comments.

CCD as a safe place

♦ It is a safe place to be

♦ I see it like a network of people. It is as if in spiritual terms we have all got as many hands as there are other people within the community. We can hold hands with all of them and that is what gives the strength to any one member of the community stretching to someone outside it, because they carry in their single offered hand the strength of all the other connections within the community

♦ For me it is the whole thing with community, extended family

♦ Community, scratch community put relationship. That is probably the one thing that makes me squirm the most. Being in community means being available and vulnerable for everybody else. And I haven't cracked that one either. And it is a struggle. With me very much on the outskirts of the church life and choosing to be there, rightly or wrongly

♦ I always thought community was when a group of people lived in a great big building together. We did that before in

Wales. Now I realize community is a group of people and you don't have to live in one building, you can have lots of different houses around but you have got some common values or a common direction you are all going in. And you are still allowed to be an individual in that

• We may not have it perfect here but it is a million times better than where I have come from

• Christ Church sells itself

• It is not going to be 100 per cent safe because we are people

Leadership in Paul's Community Churches

A Christian faith community or local congregation is a voluntary association, existing by divine authority, expressed in its earliest form in household units.[33] These 'house churches' were a visible manifestation of what was to become a universal, eternal, spiritual commonwealth built on the foundation of the work of Christ and the Holy Spirit through social relations. The essence of church as we know it is divine and human relations co-mingling.

Earlier in this book I confessed to the prejudice that I had had against the importance of community for men, shamefully admitting that I had seen community more as a female need. In recent years a lot has been written about the role of women in church life, and the subject is now in vogue. Paul does not seem to have seen this gender distinctive, since it appears that all who belonged to the community, male and female, shared responsibility for the general conduct of the church's proceedings. Paul gave to everyone the responsibility to hear and discern God's mind and perspective (Rom. 15:14; 1 Cor. 14:31; Eph. 4:15, Col. 3:16), while tempering it with the Greek unease of women taking a lead in front of men.

This was in contrast to Roman hierarchies and organizational structures. With the birth of the Early Church we see a return to the Hebrew idea of the one and the many. All members were personally responsible for their actions and aware of the shared commitment of belonging. By giving each person individual responsibility, Paul seems to have been seeking to avoid the heavily regimented religious structures and hierarchies of the Greek-Roman world. Instead, he gave each person the duty to build community, and seems to have been suggesting a more flat organization. Such a strategy remains a challenge even today, as folk from CCD will tell you.

Taking responsibility

> ♦ From my perspective . . . if someone came to me asking me about Christ Church, it would actually be to turn the question back onto them and ask them why, 'what do you want from it'. And pick from them their reasons of wanting to, rather than giving them reasons, so instead of me putting a path in front for them to walk, actually to get them to put their own path in front of them for them to walk. It is easy to say but that is what was done for me, actually 'what do you want'

> ♦ I certainly endorse the empathy and care etc., but I would put a reservation that the commitment is conditional. In other churches it's not conditional, it is unconditional, we will help you whatever, we will help you and the responsibility becomes the churches. But here the commitment is in equal measure

> ♦ It is your own personal responsibility to change, and to look at your situation and yourself, and it is your own responsibility to grow and take up responsibility in the church . . . I think that was probably the hardest for me

> ♦ So it is your responsibility to be part of the community

In Paul's communities, as in Early Hebrew communities, leadership seems to have been corporate. Each home would have had its 'elder' and each cluster would have had a council made up of its members. This is in marked contrast to our human instinct to build hierarchies and authority structures. Paul seems to have grounded equality at the heart of his churches by suggesting that

Christ was available to all. But for Paul equality seems always to have been subservient to the idea of unity. In this Paul was following Hebrew values. We can be guilty of reading into the New Testament writings values that we hold today. So our contemporary emphasis on the individual fits comfortably with Paul's emphasis on individual responsibility. What we sometimes fail to see is that Paul's emphasis was intended to contrast with the Greek-Roman practices of creating hierarchies and structures. I am suggesting that in Paul's emphasis on individual responsibility, he was returning to the Hebrew balance of the one against the many, not endorsing Enlightenment ideas. His churches were far more egalitarian than our modern prejudices are often willing to admit.

In CCD we have sought to take up the idea of a flat organization. By this I mean an organizational structure that has very few 'layers', as in a business where you have to go through very few people to get to the managing director. Easy accessibility to the leadership is important. Paul never used the word 'priest', but addressed most of his letters to towns and cities, to the whole church in an area. He spoke little of organizational structures and hierarchies. He seems also to have held an assumption that spiritual and natural gifting would spontaneously surface in these modest house church communities. Similarly, he seems to have assumed that leadership would emerge from among the members, especially among those naturally gifted, who would be sought out by those in need. As any church leader will tell you, the person who provides pastoral support to church members is the one who is effectively helping them find faith and wholeness. Here in CCD we elect most of our Leadership Team (LT) of ten men and ten women, and choose a chairperson from among this group. All are lay people and work on a voluntary basis.

At least half of the LT seems to change every year. We also have a 'wild card' principle whereby we choose one or two of the team from people who did not get enough votes to be included but who we feel would benefit from exposure to leadership. These 'wild card' members are decided by representatives of the new LT. They are often talented newcomers to the community or those who, because they are serving in less high-profile roles, do not normally attract the 'votes'. The office is run on a job share by several very talented men and women, supported by a host of volunteers. Such arrangements militate against individuals having power over others, or developing a power base within the congregation. There is no doubt that such structures are not always the most efficient way of getting a job done, but by prioritizing relationship over goals, and putting people ahead of tasks, we have endeavoured to mirror social Trinity.[34]

Sociologically, the persistence of Hebrew ideas over Hellenistic ideas is now beginning to be recognized and accepted. In the past the orthodox view was that Hebrew influences were fast lost in the Early Church as the Gentile expansion of the Church quickly moved Christianity away from Jerusalem and Jewish cultural centres, and more and more Hellenic ideas were absorbed. But today this view is being challenged by a number of scholars. Skarsaune, for example, argues in his recent book for 'the persistence of the Jewish heritage'.[35] Early faith communities seem to have been far more mixed than we had thought, with Greek, Roman, Jew and many others all making up the membership of local house churches. Skarsaune proposes that a range of foundational beliefs and practices adopted in the Early Church were all deeply influenced by Hebrew thought. For instance, Christology, the formation of liturgy, types of worship, the Christian calendar, Passover and the Eucharist all evolved under Hebrew influences. He reminds us that Paul went to the synagogues in each city, the implication being that both Jews and Gentiles made up each local Pauline faith community.

Home and Family in Theocentric Community

The more we research such matters, the more we realize that we know surprisingly little on the subject of how the Early Church was structured. It is dangerous to speculate. But what we do seem to know is that practically and theologically it was built, like the Old Testament *mishpachah*, around Hebrew ideas and the contemporary Greek-Roman family. Family was community. Paul, however, was not using the term 'family' as we use it today to describe a man, wife and two and a half children. Instead, he imposed his own meaning into the term, using the terminology of family creatively as body, household, steward, slave, brethren, neighbour, my brother, and my child. It was around the metaphor of the family, with Christ as the Head, that Paul built his faith communities.

It is interesting that the obvious import of Paul's use of these familial terms, with the meaning he gave them, is largely overlooked today. These local communities saw one another primarily as members of a common extended family (Gal. 6:10). The radical nature of this family concept is not fully comprehended until one realizes that nowhere in the Old Testament is Israel called 'God's family', though it is sometimes referred to as a 'household' (Je. 38:26; Am. 5:25). Paul seems to have been the first to apply the analogy of family to an extended, adoptive and impartial social grouping called church (*ekklesia*), existing by fellowship (*koinonia*). It was an obvious metaphor, given that the Church lived, breathed and grew in people's homes.

One of the values of the Early Church was the emphasis on the Christian life being centred around the home. The first Christians had few congregational buildings, and instead used the home to build faith communities. This is something Roger Gehring has ably documented: 'The basic structure of the family has proven itself as the incubator and nucleus of the mission church.'[36] Likewise, when we planted CCD, we decided that we would not put money into buildings, but into people. This was not a difficult decision since we had little money! As the congregation has grown, we have seen the Lord provide us with a range of very suitable accommodation for our growth, mostly rented or leased, at very modest cost, as we have needed it. This has allowed us to focus on our people programmes and the homes they offer. Interestingly, some of this accommodation has proved particularly appropriate, such as a refurbished 150-year-old seamen's chapel built in 1878 by Pastor Stanley Treanor that we now use for workshops and a range of other meetings. We also use the local theatre for Christmas celebrations, and the rowing club for parents and toddlers, as well as a range of homes for discipleship groups, support groups, homework weekends and business meetings.

Without a 'sanctuary' to build or finance we have stayed a faith community rooted in homes. In a town less than two miles long and only a mile wide, we have little trouble visiting each other. A church building complex that is open much of the time can have the tendency to centralize the congregation's activities and even isolate them from the community and the home. But we do have a small office, and often open homes where people can drop in. A lot of this 'house to house' visiting goes on in a spontaneous way. Similarly, I cannot walk through the shopping precinct without meeting friends, and will stop for a coffee when I have time. This all begins to feel like community, but if we had a church building one would go there to talk, not into the local library, café on the pier, or one of several very inviting 'greasy spoon' cafés.

We encourage this focus around the home, and some in the community see it as part of their calling. One elderly lady saw her ministry in part as baking, every week, several fruitcakes, chocolate banana cakes and iced strawberry sponge cakes for the office and for Waterfront. Our own home, Waterfront, is open all hours and people come in at all times for tea, coffee, cake and a chat. I decided when we planted the community that it would only work if I and others were available as far as possible on a 24/7 basis. So someone is nearly always at home to welcome people. Mary, my wife, has a key role to play in helping this happen. This is not, however, as onerous as it might sound. We have the whole top floor for personal space to retreat to. CCD has grown and prospered on this principle of openness of homes, and the availability of people to talk to. Let the community themselves comment.

Being available 24/7 for each other

> • It is having the people that are prepared to be there 24 hours a day for you

> • I see it as being a safe place and knowing that you could pick up that church list and ring up anyone and drop in on anyone and know you are not going to be told to bugger off. You trust people and feel at ease with people, feel safe with people. Feel you have something to offer, something to give that will help others. And want to give it freely without being asked

• Unless you have a sense that people are genuinely concerned about your welfare and you are genuinely concerned about theirs, you haven't really got the beginnings of a community. That is why it is so unique

• I have been thinking of it being a place where you can give. But it is also a place where you can receive. My baggage is that I don't like people helping me

• The thing about this (community) is that it doesn't suck life out of you, and you don't have to be a certain way to become part of the community. It actually gives life

• It is benefiting the majority, not a minority

• A culture of honouring each other

As part of being family together, we have largely dropped the more traditional idea of first requiring allegiance to Christ, then teaching people what they need to learn to be an effective part of the Body of Christ. Instead, maybe because of the type of people we work with, we first begin to build relationships of healing trust with them. We even remind them that if they so wish, they can begin their journey, especially during the early stages, without the apparent direct help of God. Very few of the unchurched who have joined the community or *Rapha* have ever been asked to commit to Christ as a first step. Neither have we subsequently pushed this on them. A number have said that if we had required that, they would have left. Likewise, Christians in the community say that if we were to adopt a more conventional approach, they would struggle to bring their needy unchurched friends into the community. So as a community we remain solidly committed to 'evangelism', but in a more natural, low-key way that many postmodern people find more acceptable. Let me illustrate.

Being a non-Christian in CCD

• It is all down to earth and mostly on 'their' level (without airs and graces or religiousness) • Yes, because people will be real and relate to them at their level and not see them as fodder for 'Jesus' ✦ I believe the teaching would resonate with Christian and non-Christian alike. It starts where people are at ✦ What we are into is real, and has something to offer ✦ Truth is taught and there's no them and us ✦ My own example I hope would be enough to motivate them ✦ People meeting God on His, not their own terms ✦ It's welcoming, easy, fast-paced, untraditional, up-beat as well as tender-hearted and real ✦ They can be themselves and I don't have to be responsible for them

✦ So the willingness to explain to people how they work, the whole teaching on the human spirit is so, I don't know, the response from the non-churched is that it makes perfect sense, they are hungry to hear it, want to hear it, now it gives me something to think about, something to work on

✦ Within Christ Church there is no us and them . . . we are all made in God's image which is the community of God, and we don't need to be saved to be in that community, we were created to be in that community

✦ It used to be such a big thing, are you a Christian or not and that depended on how you could, like, talk with someone. For me personally it is such a relief that I don't even have to think about whether she is a Christian or not

To some Christians such thinking might be shocking. To help balance the low-key approach, I have written a weekend workshop called 'Meeting Jesus', but to get to this place, people need to go through several stages. The first step with those with no Christian background has got to be building trust. This begins with one person, maybe a mentor, but in time is extended to a circle of others. It is usually some time later, often months, or a year or two, before they declare that they want to begin to trust God in this same way. Some never do, and leave after a time, taking the wholeness they have gained. In much the same way, Christ gave people their healing unconditionally, without requiring that they follow Him first. This process can appear to reverse traditional methods of 'evangelism', but I suggest that it may be just as Biblical. Christ saw positive healing in people before He gave them the Great Commission. Such an approach is more acceptable to contemporary unchurched people. One of our observations is that postmodern people do not like to be pushed into things. In fact, they seem to loathe defining themselves by religious dogma that does not reflect their authentic experience of life. Many are now looking beyond religion for their spirituality. They prefer to do things slowly over time, thinking them through, seeing for themselves whether they make sense, or are relevant to their lives.

The Priesthood of All Believers

In practice, Paul stands behind Christ in using the language of both family and love to describe the community of believers (Mk. 3:34–35; 12:30–31). Paul saw Christ as truly and wholly present in any group of believers (1 Cor. 12:13). Theologically this is key as it endorses the possibility that anyone may have a full relationship with Christ and everyone else. Although Paul used the terms 'elder' and 'deacon', echoing Hebrew thought in acknowledging the 'elders' of each *mishpachah*, he nowhere used the common Greek word *hierus* (or priest). Christ returned to the ideal of Yahweh being the head, with everything under Him. In this sense, Christ was the ultimate priest (Heb. 4:14) because He made the last great sacrifice of Himself once and for all. Therefore, no one else could be a priest, and the ceremonial sacrifices were redundant (Rom. 5:6ff.; Heb. 7:11–28; 9:25–28).

What I am suggesting is that our modern practice of one priest leading a congregation is in danger of usurping what Hebrew thought and Paul are actually saying to us. It is the 'priesthood of all believers', as Peter suggested (1 Pet. 2:9), that should form the foundation of local congregational life and leadership, not just one man or woman. We are in a post-individual age where teams and groups raise less suspicion than a single leader. Paul understood better than most what Christ intended, which is that all believers together need to acknowledge Christ, and Him alone, as the living Head. Paul was building on the Early Hebrew theocentric community concept, the ground of which had been prepared by Christ Himself. Even in the Hebrew period we see both priests and

Levites, but, as Paul suggested, such offices should not be at the expense of either personal responsibility or relational mutuality. Paul did not expand on any of these obvious truths and ideas, no doubt because everyone was already living them. Such values as equality and mutuality were accepted, so did not need to be talked about, as were the importance of extended family and congregational life lived within Trinity. Paul largely addressed matters in his letters that were not working well.

The Church, therefore, is not just the Body of Christ but 'in Christ . . . one body' (Rom. 12:5a). Christ is the source of its unity and the means by which it exists. Everything in creation owes its life to Christ (Col. 1:15ff.). He alone is the image of the invisible God, and the Church as Kingdom community is to grow up in every way into Him (Eph. 1:12,15–17). According to Paul, all who are genuine members of this community have the Spirit of Christ (e.g. 1 Cor. 12:13; 2 Cor. 3:18; Gal. 5:22ff.; Eph. 2:18, etc). This means that all members are spiritual in a Christ-centred sense. All members have the capacity, not only for relationship with God, like God Himself, but also for hearing Him for themselves (Jn. 14:26), the *Rapha* principle. Both intimacy with Christ, and holiness through Him, are for everyone. In this sense, Christ, by making Himself fully available to everyone at a personal level, is building on the theocentric *Rapha* principle. The authority for our claim to be able to become more fully human is that Christ, as fully human, can now teach us how to claim our full potential, both human and supernatural.

In Summary

We began this chapter by noting the teachings and practices of Christ regarding the building of community, and His forging the band of disciples into a community that would change the world. Christ is the Head of this *ekklesia*. We then went on to note Paul building his congregations around the home and extended family, along similar lines to the *mishpachah* of the Hebrew period. We have seen that Paul used the analogy, first adopted by Christ, of the 'family of God'.

It is very evident that the expectation of change was of key importance in the lives of all those who came into contact with, or who joined one of the early house churches. The Early Church, as a community-building movement, relied very much on the significance of the individual in relationship, rather than the Greek-Roman administrative structures of the day. Paul placed great emphasis on the individual's relationship with Christ and others. This whole network had to be forged in love. The 'priesthood of all believers' was the way of implementing this corporate responsibility. We now need to move on to the next step in our journey. This is the idea that we all need to be on a journey to change to be more Christ-like, and that this change can be both positive and health-giving.

Notes

[1] Skarsaune, *Shadow*, 70, note 78.
[2] M. Chancey and E.M. Myers, 'How Jewish was Sepphoris in Jesus' time?' *Biblical Archaeology Review* 26 (2000), 4.18–33.
[3] A. Millard, 'Literacy in the times of Jesus', *Biblical Archaeology Review* 29 (2003), 4.37–45.
[4] J.E. Stambaugh and D.L. Balch, *The Social World of the First Christians* (London: SPCK, 1986), 103.
[5] D. Harrington, *God's People in Christ: New Testament perspectives on the church and Judaism* (Philadelphia: Fortress Press, 1980), 27.
[6] A.R. Johnson, *The Vitality of the Individual in the Thought of Ancient Israel* (Cardiff: University of Wales Press, 1964), 108–109.
[7] Middlemiss, *Charismatic Experience*, 165ff.
[8] Lohfink, *Pentateuch*, 95.
[9] H.C. Kee, *Who are the People of God? Early Christian models of community* (Yale: Yale University Press, 1995).
[10] L. Crabb, *Connecting: Healing for ourselves and our relationships, a radical new vision* (Nashville: Word Publishing, 1997), 46.
[11] P.E. Volf, *After Our Likeness: The Church as the image of the Trinity* (Grand Rapids: Eerdmans, 1998), 145.
[12] E.g. H. Miller, *Christian Community: Biblical or optional* (Ann Arbor, MI: Servant Books, 1979) and Hanson, People Called, 382ff.
[13] Grenz, *Theology*, 352.
[14] Modern study probably began with W.A. Meeks, *The First Urban Christians: The social world of the Apostle Paul* (Newhaven: Yale

University Press, 1983), followed by the social history of R.S. Ascough, *What Are They Saying about the Formation of Pauline Churches?* (New York: Paulist Press, 1998), and its sociological analysis by C. Osiek, *What Are They Saying about the Social Settings of the New Testament?* (New York: Paulist Press, 1992). See also Kee, *People of God*, 13ff., R. Stark, *The Rise of Christianity* (New Jersey: Princeton University Press, 1996), C. Osiek and D.L. Balch, *Families in the New Testament World* (Louisville: Westminster John Knox Press, 1997) and E.W. Stegemann and W. Stegemann, *The Jesus Movement: A social history of the first Christians* (Minneapolis: Fortress Press, 1999).

[15]   Meeks, *Urban Christians*, 105.

[16]   See, for instance, J.G. Gager, *Kingdom and Community: The social world of early Christianity* (New Jersey: Prentice-Hall, 1975).

[17]   R.E. Brown, *The Churches the Apostles Left Behind* (New Jersey: Paulist Press, 1984).

[18]   Banks, *Community*.

[19]   Banks, *Community*, 150.

[20]   R.A. Campbell, *Elders* (Edinburgh: T&T Clark, 1994), 99.

[21]   Meeks, *Urban Christians*, 78, 104ff.

[22]   Banks, *Community*, 25.

[23]   See A. Nygren, *Agape & Eros* (London: SPCK, 1932/1982) or N.F.S. Ferre, *Swedish Contributions to Modern Theology: With special reference to Lundensian thought* (London: Harper & Bros., 1939).

[24]   See Volf, *After Our Likeness*, 137ff.

[25]   Banks, *Community*, 41ff, and Oden, *Systematic Theology*, 283.

[26]   A.J. Kostenberger, *The Missions of Jesus and the Disciples According to the Fourth Gospel: With implications for the fourth Gospel's purpose and the mission of the contemporary church* (Grand Rapids: Eerdmans, 1998).

[27]   Oden, *Systematic Theology*, 280.

[28]   A.E. McGrath, 'Sin and salvation' in D.J. Atkinson and D.H. Field (eds.), *New Dictionary of Christian Ethics & Pastoral Theology* (Leicester: IVP, 1995), 78–87, 28.

[29]   R. MacMullen, *Christianizing the Roman Empire* (ad 100–400) (New Haven: Yale University Press,1984); A. Field, *From Darkness to Light: How one became a Christian in the Early Church* (Ben Lomond, CA: Conciliar Press, 1978/1997).

[30]   Field, *Darkness to Light*, 19ff.

[31]   See Skarsaune, *Shadow*, 354, 229.

32 See T.M. Finn, *Early Christian Baptism and the Catechumenate: West and East Syria* (Minneapolis: Liturgical Press, 1992), 5–6, quoted in Skarsaune, Shadow, 229.

33 See H.L. Ellison, *The Household Church* (Exeter: Paternoster Press, 1963), P. Stuhlmacher, *Der Brief an Philemon* (Zurich: Benzinger Neukirchen & Vluyn, 1981) and Lohfink, *Jesus and Community*, 98.

34 As I write, we are reviewing our Leadership Team structures. We have struggled to get a balance between the immediate practicalities and mature exercising of spiritual gifting. This challenge has increased as the community has exceeded 150 adults.

35 Skarsaune, *Shadow*, 279ff.

36 R.W. Gehring, *House Church and Mission: The importance of household structures in Early Christianity* (Peabody, MS: Hendrickson, 2004), 300.

8.

A Journey Model toward Christ-Likeness that Builds Community

The idea that as Christians we need to change to become more like Christ has always been part of the culture of the Church. But what I am suggesting in this book is that this process is not some mysterious force or drama that happens to us as we attend church, talk religiously or even read the Bible. Instead, it is a journey that each individual must purposely and personally take responsibility for, and positively seek to promote in their own lives. They must treasure their own becoming rather than their being. This is a journey of learning to relate to and obey God, through the Holy Spirit, Scripture and those we are committed to. Christ-likeness is not some force that comes on us just because we passively believe in Christ, or regularly attend a local church. It is a journey we intentionally decide to make, and is, I believe, an essential prerequisite to our being able to contribute positively to building faith community. What this book is suggesting is that without this positive change it is unrealistic for most of us to have the ability to contribute positively to the type of faith community God created us to be part of. He wishes to promote this positive personal change.

Linked to this idea of all of us needing to pursue a journey is Exodus 15, and the suggestion that the Lord wishes to help us on this journey. Christ, both in Himself and by His example with His disciples, teaches us how to be free from the damage of the disease called sin. When we bring these ideas together, and look to the experience of the Early Church as a guide, we see that ongoing personal positive change is at the heart of authentic

Christianity wherever it is successfully found. But what I am out-lining here, a journey toward Christ-likeness in the twenty-first century, is a form of Christianity that combines both traditional Biblical and contemporary ideas and practices.

What is not realized by some when they first hear of the teach-ing of CCD and *Rapha* is that we are drawing on long-held Biblical traditions on discipleship, sanctification and transforma-tion, but are employing contemporary language, found more commonly in folk psychology and therapy, to describe in practi-cal terms how to live these ideas. For example, we teach and apply the idea that we can all know as much personal positive Christ-likeness in our lives as we desire. This is the Biblical tradi-tion of discipleship, but expressed in our work with a dimension more readily intelligible to an unchurched visitor to our work-shops. None of us need be limited by the skill or spirituality of our priest, congregational leadership or therapist. We do not have to be thrown because someone on whom we might be rely-ing is having a bad day. Instead, this is a journey that we can all actively take for ourselves in a way suited to us and the Lord. The change we are describing and that we teach is based on the expe-rience of Biblical characters. It also draws on the teachings of Scripture, especially the *Rapha* promise in Exodus 15:26. God is more eager to talk to us about this need to positively change than we are to listen.

People at CCD who respond to this invitation to change and seek out others, or come to me for help, generally fall into two groups. One group could be described as the frustrated-but-never-knowing-when-to-quit Christian. These are the people who are too stubborn to give up Christianity, and give testimony to how wonderful it is, but admit within themselves that it is not working for them. God is a million miles away and they are weary of pretending. Such people need to begin a journey, with the Lord's help, of personal positive change. The other group are those, both Christian and unchurched, who know they are in need or are unwell. Their need may be physical, emotional or both. It may be one specific area of their lives, or extend into many areas. Some, by the time they reach us, are close to giving up, or have already given up, and are in deep personal despair. They are also often very isolated, with few friends, and have been unable to break the cycles of trauma and pain in their personal lives. Others have apparently been coping well for many years, hiding the damage even from close family and friends. These people also need a journey of positive personal change.

To these two main types one can add a range of other people, for instance, those who have tried and failed either to change personally or to meet the Lord. There are also those who in the past have blamed others for their condition, perhaps paying professionals to solve the problem, while refusing to take personal responsibility. Regardless of where they have come from, for most, their position will distil into one simple question: Am I 'hungry' or desperate to change?

Those of us who carry a desperation to change, will, like the catechumen, find that new values and a changed lifestyle will inevitably accompany the journey of discipleship. Perhaps this is why Christ delighted in surrounding Himself with the sick, rather than those who believed themselves to be healthy. As noted already, it is through such 'desperate' people that our own community has grown. Mentors and leaders alike need to hear people admit that they cannot live this way any longer. Let me illustrate from comments by members of CCD.

Being desperate

♦ It's a choice, because it isn't comfortable or easy, but it heals you – because each relationship or situation you encounter in community shows you more of yourself – good and bad!

♦ The only people I would tell or whom I would consider telling [about CCD] would be those who were not only in desperate need but knew it also. Coz it is a place of healing. With immense cost. It is a deep place not to be trifled with. And being desperate is a qualification for knowing about us

♦ Sometimes people are not willing to admit to themselves just how desperate they are, and it is therefore a place where you can explore whether you are desperate or not. You will soon find out. And the door of Christ Church is open for people to come and then leave because they are not at that place yet. And to say to someone, maybe Christ Church isn't the place for you at the moment, but it might be in time, and if it is, then the door will be open to you. But there are possibly other churches in the town which for the time being may suit you better

• It is therapeutic community, it's a clinic. And a person who comes to a clinic has lost his life or will to live. It is OK to be amongst those people in our church because it is a place of beginnings and ends – the end of the past and beginning of a new

• People dressing up in their suits on a Sunday, the goody two shoes. These people who socially had comfortable lifestyles, and didn't know what it was like to be hungry, traumatised, rejected, not to have family around, didn't know all these issues, so how could these people possibly help anybody on the street?

• When I arrived here I knew that a life-long search for something was over. I was so profoundly aware of it. That when I came to this church I didn't know what that search was, but I was aware that whatever it was I was looking for had come to an end. It was here. There was great comfort in that

• There is a reason you are like you are. If there is a reason there is an answer

• I learned to live in my defences. So my whole life was based on defending myself. It is only once you start to disassemble that that you have a chance

Congregational Life as a Healing Community

Although the Christian Church has a remarkable track record of helping those who are sick and desperate, today such people would not instinctively turn to the Church. Many of its former responsibilities are now carried by the state. But these state-run health care services are under enormous strain. For instance, here in the UK one in four adults will at some time during their adult life experience prolonged mental or emotional illness. This sub-group now represents the single largest demand on the health care services. Some in the wider Church are responding to this need. We can all point to these exceptions. There are independent caring groups such as L'Arche and some that are seeking, for example, to help those with learning disorders. But such exceptions make the point that most congregations do not get involved in this area except where they need to, for example, with existing congregational members. This could be because emotional and mental illness is something that we all assume the state takes care of, so we feel that we do not need to be involved. Or is it, maybe, because we see this as a specialist area that counsellors and psychiatrists are responsible for?

Whatever the reasons, it is now true that overall the Church has substantially retreated from these areas. Even where it has entered the fray, it tends to follow a classic psychoanalytic or therapeutic model based on one-to-one counselling. Congregations tend to adopt this one-to-one model, with Biblical modifications, as part of pastoral ministry. For me all of this is very sad, given that we are the Church and a communion with a social Trinity, and we have received the command to heal (Lk. 9:1ff., 1 Pet. 2:24). So for a number of years I have been looking for a model of congregational life that will be both fun, healthful and faith building, a model that has the capacity to hold on to historic Biblical beliefs and traditions while also being able to serve the person who needs help. The Church's response to date has been to borrow much that is, on the whole, already being competently delivered by therapeutic counselling models in the health care and private sectors. Intentional theocentric community is the alternative I have been looking for.

The principles of both person-in-relation and *perichoretic* co-mingling provide the Church with a radically different model, one that is able to stand in dynamic contrast to the dominant one-to-one therapeutic practices of today's state-run services. Building on the community models of Christ and Paul, this book is calling for an *intentional* faith community movement able to provide an environment that has at its core personal positive change as a relational process. I have already suggested that this type of change is necessary in order for us to be able to contribute to theocentric community.

But I am also proposing that without involvement with the Other (in Macmurray's sense of the word, see page 65ff), without the mutuality of giving and receiving in relationships of love, personal positive change remains a private and confining matter. Such an approach fundamentally restricts its benefit. Being-in-relation and personal positive change are both interdependent ways of living that ultimately find fulfilment in the divine-human relationality of the Body of Christ. Intentional therapeutic faith community invites into the twenty-first century Church the philosophy and lifestyle of the *mishpachah*.

In CCD we have now been seeking to live this journey of intentional therapeutic faith community for a number of years. To be involved in each other's lives, to belong together rather than simply to attend meetings, is a proactive choice. We have not got everything right, but we are trying. One way in which we are slightly different from many congregations is that, as I have already indicated, we have structured church life to allow a number of mentors to help and support those who are on this journey with them. Within the congregation we encourage people to begin this journey of change relationally with others who are 'experts-by-experience'. Anyone can be a mentor – they just need to be one step ahead of the person they are mentoring. This allows the whole process to move forward that much faster and with greater ease. It also avoids the 'bottleneck' of having one or even a handful of leaders on whom the whole congregation relies for guidance and growth. The solitary saint may have made progress in the past, but we can be greatly helped by doing the journey relationally with those who have already successfully overcome areas of baggage and need in their lives. When you then also call on social Trinity within faith congregational community, the whole process of becoming more like Christ is much less tortuous. In mirroring God's nature of sociality, we must as Christians create more space to support and facilitate this journey.

Therefore in CCD we have emphasized the healing power of relationships with Christ and one another, developing the culture of experts-by-experience. So when people join our community or come to a *Rapha* workshop with emotional disorders, or a range of other problems, we can usually find within our network several like them to help them when they want help. We now have, in the people in our community, a deep therapeutic healing journey IQ that is available to anyone who joins us and genuinely wants help. This has allowed us to turn congregational life into therapeutic faith community.

The concept of social Trinity is at the heart of this. The idea is that the three persons of the Trinity, through the *Rapha* principle, can talk to us about what they see are the reasons (e.g. baggage and sin) that stand in the way of our becoming more whole. The combination of the Lord talking to us about ourselves, together with a simple range of Biblical, health-giving principles, helps us support all those in need. One such principle is our need to acknowledge that each of us is not all we could be, which helps open the way for us to positively change. Another is the idea that we need to admit that we need help from both the Lord *and* others. Here our mentor programme can step in and help speed up a person's journey. All of these together bring the significant benefits of relationality with its social process and social rules, and when people see this, they begin to believe that they really can change.

For most of us in CCD and *Rapha*, this means, if we want it, daily positive input from others, which is more consistent and supportive than a chat with the pastor or a 50-minute session with a therapist once a week. In a therapeutic community like CCD it is the power of relational healing through the exchange of experience *between* sessions that offers deeper wholeness. *Perichoresis* means that each person simultaneously gives and receives as part of the Other in daily relationality. So the whole idea of a journey into maturity in Christ takes on a more relational dimension.

Maturity and Community *Together* as Wholeness in Christ

As we look beyond Paul to the rapidly expanding Early Church, we see the importance of the family, and the Lord's strategy to extend these Christian ideas of family into the wider faith community. It is thought that for the first 300 years communities remained relatively small and tightly knit.[1] Large crowds drew too much attention to themselves. These small groups clearly had a high degree of autonomy, while retaining moral and social cohesion. From the records we have of this period, we know that many members and even whole communities were suffering persecution. To survive, they each needed strong internal social processes that helped support the individual, giving a reason to hold steady. Such a culture would generate its own integrity that held the theocentric *Rapha* value system in place. This culture of positive change gave people a good reason to follow Christ. Change and belonging were what they were looking for.

In my ministry I associate this positive change with growing up, becoming personally more mature. Earlier in this book I suggested that in the Early Church this change had a therapeutic dimension in that people were able to let go of toxic aspects of their past. This new-found wholeness allows the person to begin to experience deeper relationships. But in CCD we also relate this wholeness journey and its positive change to becoming more like Christ.

In part, becoming mature in Christ is about having a greater capacity to live more fully, to live life well. In my previous books I have related this change to our having an increasing capacity to let go of our pasts with all their toxic pain and failure.[2] But I also relate this positive journey and its outcomes to our capacity not only to become more Christ-like, but also more human.[3] I liken this to our need to be more sensitive, more loving, more mature, more balanced and less toxic. This need also includes our being able to live at ease in spiritual reality, anointing and gifting, being able to discern in a mature way what is good and what is dark in ourselves, others and the spiritual world (Heb. 5:13–14). In a world where increasing numbers are seeking to be more spiritual, I share C.S. Lewis's sentiment[4] that in some ways we need to be more human.

This process of becoming more human is a process of growing in maturity and holiness, earthed in the reality of our own humanity and its damage. I am seeking to describe a type of Christ-likeness that helps us understand and love contemporary people while also giving us the capacity to relate to them. We talk in CCD and *Rapha* in terms of a discipleship model of personal positive change toward more maturity and Christ-likeness. But this maturity does not just happen routinely. I am suggesting that it takes place most successfully in intentional faith community, with others who are also seeking the same ends in their lives, drawing on the voice of God, Scripture and the support of all those who are committed to the same journey. This we describe as working together in common purpose. Here in CCD, as we have noted a couple of times earlier in the book, we call this approach to faith community a therapeutic culture or therapeutic faith community. Let members of the community comment on how they see this approach to Christ-likeness and spiritual maturity.

Maturity

♦ Putting others first ♦ Letting go of your damage as soon as you see it ♦ Knowing Christ ♦ Knowing yourself ♦ Walking in the real you ♦ Honouring yourself ♦ Loving yourself ♦ Loving other people, honouring them ♦ Being at peace ♦ Knowing anointing, gifting ♦ Doing your homework in your quiet times, cover the baggage the rest of the day ♦ Bigger capacity ♦ Humility ♦ Not being critical ♦ Standing in love ♦ Knowing you are not going to get there ♦ We are allowed to disagree ♦ Also the closer you get to God the more you become you ♦ You move into maturity together ♦ Everyone in their own uniqueness ♦ Consistently being the person that God created you to be ♦ We humble ourselves to each other. We make ourselves humble to each other, transparent. That to me sums up maturity in every way ♦ I am beginning to do things now that I never thought, never thought I would get a degree, to do things that were never possible before

♦ Maturity in Christ, I suppose the overall aim, the overall perspective, the area to be, is to be able to give Christ to anybody in any situation without having to pick out your own drive, your own agenda, and your own garbage, baggage, sin, disorder, whichever word you want to use. That you can honour that person in Christ. And I haven't got a clue how to do it and I know I haven't got there personally

♦ Something else that has sprung into my head about what is different in Christ Church is that we are constantly being encouraged to go beyond what we think we can do (giggles in agreement) . . . the things she thought she couldn't do I always thought she could and vice versa. So I used to think if she thinks I can do it then maybe I can. It has happened a lot with relationships. It has helped me to do things that I wouldn't have thought I could do. So that is quite a big thing

It has been the experience of CCD and those pursuing the *Rapha* discipleship journey that living community relationships is one of the key means of achieving personal wholeness. To be more fully human one must live as a 'person in relation'. However, as we have also learned over the last few years, such a community or commitment to relationships requires each of us to take a painful path of personal change. This cannot be done quickly. It takes time to learn to live in deepening relationships and few of us, either female or male, do it naturally. Maturity only rewards us when we are persistent over several years. But a healing salugenic community environment is, I believe, part of the background to Christ's and Paul's discipleship models. In an instant age of quick returns this is a very hard message.

In Paul's writings we see the concept that faith community should be the context that promotes the change necessary for Christ-like wholeness. But such thinking also brings with it numerous other implications. Throughout Scripture the modelling of becoming more fully human is neither exclusively personal nor entirely private in the way that it is often thought of today. For Paul, growth and maturity are spoken of in terms of ever-increasing integration into Christ, as well as a living love in and through one another (Eph. 4:15): 'Since for Paul Christ's resurrection and the abiding presence of Christ's Spirit within the community of faith formed the centre of God's new initiative, he defined the Church as the body of Christ, called by grace to carry on the mission of reconciliation it had already experienced.'[5]

It is important to note that most of the time when Paul spoke of maturity, he addressed the issue corporately (1 Cor. 1:10; 14:20; 2 Cor. 1:13–14; Eph. 4:11–16; 5:25–27; Col. 1:21–22; 4:12, etc.). As we have seen, this is in marked contrast to Western Christian thought, which much of the time understands maturity in Christ in personal private terms. Maturity for Paul was defined as an ever-closer approximation to the 'likeness' of Christ, an increasing reflection in our lives of His values and attitudes, as well as our mutual participation in His activities (Col. 1:15–19). In this sense, it is Christ speaking to us both personally and corporately that promotes authentic personal maturity and the community that goes with it. Wholeness, from a Pauline perspective, is holistic in the sense of involving the whole community and embracing every one of us. Wholeness is experienced when faith is lived out in corporate natural/supernatural relationship, the two co-inhering within one another. The whole body of Christ, with all its diversity and differing gifts, will contribute, if we allow it to, to our own maturing.

Paul saw this process of 'maturing' as a learned journey on which the first Christians progressed as they received the knowledge of Christ (Eph. 4:20; Col. 1:7, etc.), which was taught by both Paul's words and by his life (Acts 19:11ff.). This knowledge was specific and its sole purpose was to promote relationship with Christ. Paul was not prepared to tolerate any other talk except that which promoted personal and corporate deepening of this relationship. He specifically stated that growth took place only as the members of the community were 'increased with', 'enriched by', 'renewed through' and 'filled with' Christ-centred knowledge (Phil. 1:9; Col. 1:9–10; 3:10). It is interesting to see the parallel with the *Rapha* idea of Yahweh talking to the individual. What Paul is suggesting is that we can all learn, and as we learn we change. Learning is not merely cerebral, but life transforming. Ever since the early Middle Ages, when universities began to be established outside monasteries, learning has been separated from a requirement of personal positive change. I believe that as a Church we need to recover and live this connection.

Growth for Paul was thus not only a rational and ordered process, but also a learning journey of personal change. To describe it, he used numerous Greek terms: *nous* (mind), *noema* (thought), *gnosis* (knowledge), *sophia* (wisdom), *sunesis* (understanding), *aletheia* (truth), *phronein* (to think), *logizein* (to consider), *anakrinein* (to discern), *peithein* (to persuade), *dokimazein* (to test), etc. Each person internalizes the truth of Christ by their commitment to it (Rom. 10:9–10). In describing this learning journey, Paul was expecting such truth to come from God Himself as

He talks to us in a range of ways, together with the painful and life-changing processes that we experience within faith community. This was expected to produce over time a growing, deepening knowing of Christ. The vehicle through which such faith and knowledge of the person of Christ grew was understanding given by the Holy Spirit. Banks noted that Paul nowhere limited this knowledge of maturity to an elite.[6] In fact, as we are noting, one major distinctive of these New Testament divine Assemblies was the strong internal culture of personal change required of all new disciples as they earned acceptance into the Kingdom/family.

Introducing the Gender Continuum

Paul was also part of a culture that recognized gender distinctives. Greek-Roman culture subordinated women, while within Hebrew culture one sees much more equality. Paul, by emphasizing that salvation was for all, brought a redressing of this imbalance against women.[7] We have sought to mirror this equality in CCD by using the idea that both male and female together reflect more fully the nature of social Trinity. This is seen in our leadership team and the division of responsibilities both within *Rapha* and CCD.

A number of years ago I developed a simple tool that I call 'the gender continuum'. Across a sheet of paper I draw a horizontal line. This represents both male and female. Then I bisect this line vertically at the centre, with one side becoming female, and the other side male.

WOMAN			MAN
very female	female male	male with female	very male

Everyone is somewhere on the horizontal line. All men will be on the male side , although some may be closer to 'female' in their skills and preferences. Likewise, all women will be on the female side, although some may be closer to 'male' in their skills and preferences.

This idea has proven very significant in many people's lives, for a range of reasons. To begin with, the gender continuum makes a clear distinction between male and female. But it also suggests that each of us is unique. We are all somewhere on the line, though some of us may see ourselves at more than one place, reflecting different abilities and interests in our natures. For some men and women, a lot is explained by the concept that they might have aspects of their character that are more typical of the opposite sex. It gives them permission to begin to accept sides of their nature that they may have been embarrassed by or uncomfortable with, or felt were discriminated against in society. For others, it means that they no longer need to think that they may be the wrong sex. For instance, a woman with a brain at the male end of the line, who shows more of the abilities of a man, is able to make peace with this and begin to enjoy her natural gifts, rather than feeling guilty that she is not 'more female'. Likewise, knowing that they are at the female end allows men to accept themselves, and begin to explore who they really are in a more honest way, without feeling ashamed.

The gender continuum is a particularly beneficial concept for those believing that they are trapped by unhelpful gender stereotyping. Women in particular are able to accept that they mirror God as much as men do. From God's perspective they are not second-class Christians. The concept also suggests that we all have the ability to 'grow' along the horizontal line. As our personalities are enlarged in this way, and we feel able to express a better balance of male and female qualities, we become more mature. Susan and I have devised a questionnaire that we use in one of our workshops to help individuals find out where they are on the line at a particular moment in their journey. We suggest to those attending these workshops that Christ represents the whole line, an ideal example for both male and female.

Here are some comments from men and women in CCD regarding this gender perspective.

Comments on gender issues

> ◆ I can see that an enormous amount of healing is coming from encouraging men to be men and women to be women ◆ It has been helpful to work on a gender exclusive

basis originally, as this gave me the ability to work with my difficulties with each sex systematically • In some respects we are the same, in others we are very different • Men and women are fundamentally different, equals but different • A place where women are allowed to be women. Men are allowed to be men and we can learn to let each other be who we were created to be • Together they reflect the whole of God's nature • We are all responsible for our own sin, be it male or female, we are both equally guilty of our sin • I have learned much more about men and women, how and why we do certain things • It has helped me to understand why my marriage was as bad as it was • Shows and explains why couples divorce and can't get on • Our expectations of our own gender and of the other need to be re-evaluated • Gives women a real insight and chance to change their behaviour of the damage they do to themselves and men • Helped me to accept my womanhood more • That men can be real, that the superficiality, macho lies that we live, can be put right and that men can be having to compete with men! • In the politically correct atmosphere of American Education it is one of the highest commandments that you will not make any comment that is in any way critical of a woman

The gender continuum also helps people to break stereotyping. It gives people permission to be uniquely themselves, no longer needing to clone themselves on their leaders or heroes. Learning to live in our uniqueness is part of our life of worship.

Early Church Incarnational Community

A characteristic for Paul of faith community life was that people did not go to church to 'worship'.[8] Rather, Paul saw one's whole life as worship (Rom. 12:1–2). To use a modern term, the meeting together in Paul's communities would be better described as 'mission', that mission being to express theocentric community in Christ. Paul saw the purpose of meeting corporately as the spiritual strengthening of one another (1 Cor. 14:12,19,26). This was done through sharing gifts in mutual ministry or *charism* (Eph.

5:19; Col. 3:16–17), the exercising of spiritual gifts for the benefit
of all present. Christ Himself is the first gift (Eph. 2:8), and all the
other gifts were exercised through the gift of the Holy Spirit and
should reflect and point to Him. Though the gifts may differ in
their *effect*, the entire thrust of 'giving of gifts to one another'
must ultimately deepen one's individual relationship with
Christ, and subsequently further transform the group.

One further quality was mandatory in all of Paul's communities, and that was the presence of love in relationship. Christ is
love. The social Trinity exists by and through love. So although
knowledge of Christ is important for Christ to be formed in us,
knowledge is not all-important, for love surpasses knowledge (1
Cor. 13:8; Eph. 3:19). Knowledge without love merely feeds pride
(1 Cor. 8:1; 13:2). For Paul, it was love within faith community life
that created the most conducive environment for both a fuller
presence and a deeper understanding of Christ (1 Cor. 12:31ff.;
Col. 2:2). The pastoral duty always to act in love was assumed to
be incumbent on *every* community member, not just a mature
elite.

It is interesting to note that some of the ideas and practices
sound counterintuitive. For instance, in CCD we emphasize the
idea of living as community 24/7, rather than relying heavily on
the Sunday or mid-week meetings. As we have already noted,
this gives us the freedom not to meet at all one Sunday a month.
Numerous pastors and Christian leaders have asked me over the
years how we can do this. They will often exclaim that if they did
such a thing, their congregations would fall apart. But is this not
the point I am making? Taking a break from Sunday church
allows people to do the important job of developing relationships
in Christ, the building of community. The Sunday off also gives
them the chance to do tasks that they need to do some time (travelling to meet family, etc.) without missing church. For a number
in the community, the Sunday off is a nuclear and corporate family day for spending more time together, which in turn promotes
community.

The focus of Paul's meetings was Christ and the fellowship
meal, the Eucharist or Breaking of Bread (1 Cor. 11:17ff.), sometimes called the Holy *Communion*. In CCD the first Sunday of
every month, that is, the Sunday following the Sunday off, we

meet and celebrate the Eucharist. I believe this to be the centre of 'mission' in the church: the celebrating of Christ among us. I see the Eucharist as the fullest expression of love within community[9] celebrating Christ, as Lord, Friend and Master. At the Last Supper the breaking of bread took place in the middle, the wine at the end, of the meal, and in between came the food of warm relationships (1 Cor. 11:23–25). For us, and the Early Church, Communion is a community meal, focused around a family event, usually with guests, friends and strangers.

For Paul, this event was to be shared with Christ and one's friends. At the heart of Pauline community was a meal, celebrated together, when believers remembered the Lord and took stock of their state in Christ (1 Cor. 11:27). So strong was Paul's belief in the power of the communion-community aspect of this meal that he warned participants that if they were not sensitive to the physical needs of others in the community, in taking the meal they might offend Christ and harm themselves (1 Cor. 11:27–29). Healing and wholeness should be seen as part of this sacrament.[10] Here Paul was using what is called a *diachronic* principle,[11] the encouraging of a participatory society involving everyone in mutual allegiance within community in Christ. It is interesting to me to see the extent to which we have individualized and privatized our faith, even though, ever since its inception, Christianity has had at its core a fellowship meal or celebration that requires all Christians be together.

A long debate has continued over the question of what Paul actually used as a model for his churches. I am suggesting that it was the concept of theocentricity, but the truth is that we do not actually know. It seems to have taken different forms in different places. But what we do know is that for Paul communion-community focused around the home and extended families,[12] which was at the heart of his young churches. It is interesting to note here that neither Christ nor Paul insisted that the Breaking of Bread should be practised at a certain time. Instead, it is suggested that it should be as often as people meet (1 Cor. 11:34). Such a celebration should be happening all the time, not just at a special time or occasion. Celebration of Christ, His person and work, should be the centre of all that we do and are. Such a theocentric focus, the ongoing manifest presence of Christ, is what raises meetings of believers above the cricket, bowls or local bonsai clubs.

In both Christ and Paul we see the maturing of the ideas we noted from the Early Hebrew period: theocentricity and its learning relationships, the concept of Assembly and its community leadership. We also find the importance of personal integrity and reputation and the promoting of community interdependence where everyone has an active and unique contribution to make. This suggests that each person must show a willingness to change and mature in order to express more fully 'God in our midst'. God lives both in us and cohesively between us, binding us together.

For Paul community life was the expression of the gospel in corporate, visible, enticing form, the instrument that would persuade the outsider to become an insider. But as a tool, community was as fluid as the *mishpachah*, and as stable as the Assembly. Banks suggested that Paul might well have been the first individual to formulate and implement an idea of religious community that was not subservient to the family or the state.[13] Paul's communities were not based on one specific analogical model. Each community matured differently, having a unique range of characteristics and difficulties. All of them were experimental, non-standardized and genuinely 'incarnational'.[14]

The picture that emerges is of a Church primarily meeting in homes, each household church, because of the size of most homes, probably having not many more than 30 members. Groups of this size were culturally adapted to the social climate prevailing at the time. These communities were focused around Christ, having the desire for His continued, incarnate presence among them. Paul described his communities as 'family'.[15] The goal of life within these communities was to bring everyone to a mature, personal knowing of Christ, but at all times within the context of relationship with one another. Each person, through the *Rapha* promise and its *charism*, heard Christ for themselves and this released *charismata*, spiritual gifting. Each community was conceived in love, focused around the celebrating of 'Communion with Christ', energized through the Holy Spirit by the exercising of spiritual gifting and its fruit. Leadership seems to have emerged on the basis of an individual's anointing and gifting, though everyone had to be honoured, particularly the least esteemed in the community. This life and practice of Christ-centred theocentric community would have extended into a world that was created by God to participate in the life of the social Trinity.[16]

The importance of relationships

♦ It has brought me in touch with a whole community of people who want to do the same thing that I want to do, to start to possess some kind of meaning in my life and find out what is really going on in my life, in myself and in the world around me. It is meaning, I think. I am starting to find out what love is. And starting to see how persistent and deep the lies are which I have lived in for all of my life. And Christ Church has enabled me to start to see this, because there are a group of people who want to try and see the same thing. And the covering which the church provides to make a place safe enough for me to be able to start doing this in relationship with other people has been the most significant thing for me, the safety and consistency

♦ You can find part of yourself that you never knew you had. I wouldn't say their spirit, although I would say that as well. I would tell them that it is a way to find part of you. With a lot of people that is what they are looking for, themselves really. They feel very far away, travelling to find themselves.

♦ The most important thing for me was testimonies. I needed to hear different people's testimonies every day

♦ (speaking of outsiders) Half of these people don't know what it is, they could probably never remember any time in their life where they were in some kind of community, unless it was someone who was in the armed forces and even then their description of the community was something completely bizarre, it is fair to say I have had 6–7 people ask me and they have focused every time back on this ability to come to one person and initially to find some answers

What we are beginning to visualize in this book is a divine community and a redeemed people living within a renewed creation, enjoying the presence of their God.[17] Such community is the life of Christ on earth, having a theocentric *heart* where God speaks to each one personally while actively and manifestly dwelling among them corporately. Yahweh established Israel as a community through his speech – in His covenants, and by personally speaking to individuals about themselves.[18] This is something that Christ through the Holy Spirit replicated, fulfilled and endorsed. Language, with its power to teach and change us, is the marrow of community, the divine co-inherence by which human beings are capable of living together in growing wholeness. Just as Yahweh spoke His covenants that brought about community with a common purpose, so, through the social nature of language, the Church still integrates the learning of the message of the Kingdom with the formation of community.[19]

Echoing Bonhoeffer,[20] the relationship of God to us is the one on which all other relationships must be built. Triadic covenant with Yahweh established a foundation within the community of righteousness, compassion and worship. Like Hanson, I see the concept and practice of righteousness as corporate: 'In considering the Biblical notion of righteousness, we thus must conclude that an asocial private piety is simply unbiblical.'[21] The suggestion is that divine presence rests in community in a uniquely powerful way.[22] God, through such community, has the capability of creating a single unified world.[23]

Notes

[1] Gehring, House Church, *passim*.
[2] See Williams and Holmes, *Letting God Heal* and P.R. Holmes and S.B. Williams (eds.), *Changed Lives: Extraordinary stories of ordinary people* (Milton Keynes: Authentic, 2005).
[3] Holmes, *Becoming More Human*.
[4] Lewis, *Psalms*.
[5] Hanson, *People Called*, 485; see also, D.J. Bosch, *Transforming Mission: Paradigm shifts in theology of mission* (Maryknowle, NY: Orbis Books, 1991).

6 Banks, *Community*, 149.

7 Stark, *The Rise of Christianity*.

8 Banks, *Community*, 91.

9 See T. Maertens, *Assembly for Christ: From Biblical theology to pastoral theology in the twentieth century* (London: Darton, Longman & Todd, 1970) and W. Pannenberg, *Christian Spirituality and Sacramental Community* (London: Darton, Longman & Todd, 1984).

10 M. Israel, *Healing as Sacrament* (London: Darton, Longman & Todd, 1984).

11 Banks, *Community*, 150.

12 Gehring, *House Church*.

13 Banks, *Community*, 189.

14 Ascough, *Pauline Churches*, 98–99.

15 See, for instance, G. Nardin, *The Open Family: The vision of the early church* (London: New City, 1996).

16 Grenz, *Theology*, 112.

17 Grenz, *Theology*, 113.

18 J. Plaskow, 'Transforming the nature of community: Towards a feminist people of Israel' in A. Bach (ed.), *Women in the Hebrew Bible* (New York: Routledge, 1999), 403–418.

19 C.G. Christians, 'The sacredness of life', *Media Development* (1998, Online). Available from http://www.wacc.org.uk/publications/md/md1998-2/christians.html (Accessed 26 March 2003).

20 D. Bonhoeffer, *Life Together* (London: SCM Press, 1949/1970).

21 Hanson, *People Called*, 510.

22 Plaskow, 'Transforming', 407.

23 Kirkpatrick, *Community*, 198–201.

9.

'The reconciliation of all things' (Col. 1:15–23)

In this final chapter I would like to summarize some of the themes of this book, putting into focus what we have learned and where we might go from here. But I would also like to introduce an idea that draws together a number of the themes. This is the idea of reconciliation.

In the previous chapters I outlined some of the ideas we have sought to implement in the life of CCD and the *Rapha* Fellowship. As you will have gathered by now, some have been very successful (e.g. taking the last Sunday of the month off as a break from church) while others have not proved so significant (e.g. putting the worship group behind the congregation). Others, such as the idea of practical relational holiness, are still evolving. All these ideas have one thing in common. They are all intended to promote relationality in mirroring social Trinity.

But much of what we have innovated, and are still exploring in CCD and *Rapha* goes beyond mere relationship promotion. What we are seeking to do as a community is to bring people together, to enjoy deeper trust and transparency in relationships. We value openness, 'truth' and honesty, the banishing of masks and spiritual pretence. We are exploring how to honour the diversity of perspectives and avoid the constraints of hierarchical structures, while also facilitating fluidity and ongoing change. We seek to hear one another without filtering everything through our own hidden agendas and the negative scripts that we so often like to deny in ourselves. These deeper personal relationships, however, good as they are, are not a goal in themselves. They must lead to something more. I believe this 'something more' is reconciliation.

A traditional definition of reconciliation is: 'to restore to friendship, to make acquiescent or submissive, to harmonize, make compatible (with), to settle differences'.[1] When considered within the idea of social Trinity, reconciliation suggests divine harmony, the norm for God Himself. Yahweh, who is 'social Trinity in eternal harmony', models reconciliation. God is Himself already living as authentic community in perfect harmony. Two persons are a relationship, while three a community. God's intrinsic *perichoretic* union of eternal co-mingling therefore represents harmonic, unbroken, divine reconciliation.

When God's reconciliation is extended to human community in Christ, we find that many more levels of potential relationality can be achieved. The three persons of the Godhead draw in a fourth idea or person, the living reconciliation of divine-human indwelling. In seeking to become who we were created to be, we also find, within ourselves, the integration of intrinsic reconciliation. No longer do we need to live under the fragmentation to which we have become accustomed. Reconciliation with one's Creator leads to reconciliation within one's self and also with creation. All these areas of potential harmony enable reconciliation with the Other in intentional theocentric community. What I am suggesting is that one aspect of authentic wholeness and healing has got to be reconciliation. If such fruit is not present, wholeness cannot be claimed.

But taking this idea further, to be out of harmony is not even a possibility within the nature of God. We have no record of the persons of the Trinity ever falling out with one another! Contrast this with people, who often find it inconceivable to be in harmony with anyone, or even with themselves. Instead, the norm for most of us is to have a few friends, but to be out of harmony to varying degrees with almost everyone else. This could be because we cannot get on with them, or because we do not want to. We so often control exposure to relationships in order to keep others at a distance. If we fall into the latter category, it does not bode well for us, especially if we want to contribute to intentional and authentic community.

Authentic community requires personal maturity, and is only possible where people are both mature (e.g. learning to let go of the damage of sin and its baggage) and willing to become givers, rather than remaining just takers. What must happen is that we must develop a greater capacity to both receive and give love, endure gracefully abuse from others, and have a long-suffering attitude to the possibility of people (eventually) changing in positive ways. As we are reconciled to ourselves and to Christ, we also develop the capacity to be reconciled to others. Some believe we can 'give' to community without taking such a journey of positive personal change. But if intentional community is built on the harmony of reconciliation, then any part of us that is fragmented will obstruct the social processes of theocentric relationality.

God's perspective, given to us in Scripture, shows us our darkness and its sin (e.g. conviction of sin), then through Christ, by a journey, reconciles us with ourselves, others and Him. We see this effort on God's part in, for instance, Exodus 15. He wants to talk to us, and asks us to pay careful attention to His voice so that we can be obedient to it and find the transformation that the Mender brings in sewing us together. In pondering on these ideas, I have concluded that reconciliation *is* God's nature, as well as His goal and intention. A God of relationship, a social triune God, would want all of us to experience who He is. Instead of the severing of relationships, He seeks their healing. His nature is to use healing relationality to bring reconciliation.

Scripture illustrates this reconciliation in a range of ways. In our estranged state we are all enemies of God (Rom. 5:8–11). Our only hope of reconciliation to God is through Jesus Christ (2 Cor. 5:14–21). For in being reconciled to Him, we adopt values that require that we also be reconciled in all other areas. We see this in the teachings of Christ – for instance, in the parable of the prodigal son (Lk. 15:17–24). Here Christ suggests that even our profligate, wasted lives are not enough to offend His love toward us. Along similar lines, God is seen as the debt-cancelling King (Mt. 18:23–27). We have a duty to show mercy to others in the way we have received mercy. Jesus even takes this idea of responsibility for reconciliation further in suggesting that we must take the initiative in reconciliation when fellowship breaks down (Mt. 18:15–16,33). Much of Christ's teaching, one way or the other, focuses around our lost lives, and our need for reconciliation with ourselves, God and others.

In the writings of Paul we also see other grand themes of reconciliation. A future cosmic reconciliation (Col. 1:20–22) will
bring together under Christ all aspects of material and spiritual
reality. Both Paul's relationship with Christ and his own learning
journey had taught him that eventually everything and everyone
must answer and submit to Christ. Such a mission of reconciliation is encapsulated in the return of God's Son, Christ, which will
be the final end of all human efforts at reconciliation. Creation
will then be reconciled to God in the way He intended, with the
damage of Adam finally dismantled. We therefore see two recon-
ciliations: one here and now as in Christ we begin to enjoy human
Kingdom community within divine social Trinity. But also a reconciliation that is yet to come, when Christ returns to human
material reality, reordering all human injustice, and completing
the reconciliation of all of us to Him if we so wish.

In a sense I have always seen the Church as mirroring this mission in a modest way by carrying a calling to reconciliation. But
as ideas of social Trinity have grown in me, I have come to see
this as our central mission. We are pre-eminently called to live
reconciliation within ourselves, others, God and creation. I see no
better or more convincing way to witness to Christ in a sceptical
world than to show we have the capacity for love because we are
being reconciled within ourselves and to Him. By such love others will know that we are His disciples (1 Jn. 4:7ff.). In our becoming we move into step with the becoming of social Trinity. As a
consequence, the aroma of Christ will be unmistakeable.

From her own research Susan Williams is developing these
ideas academically, speaking of a 'social place' that we create in
relationship together. This social place allows us to build on one
another's growing experience and journey of positive change.
But this 'place' is not a geographic location, such as a church
building, meeting or evening out, but a 'spiritual', emotional,
relational connecting of ourselves with others. Having been
formed, it continues to exist relationally, even when we are apart.
In one sense, it builds on the traditional idea of therapeutic community whereby any encounter has the potential to be deeply
and mutually beneficial. It is a 'place' of belonging, of trust and
openness with others who are committed to the same values. It
offers ongoing reconciliation as a daily way of life.

The priority of reconciliation puts community into a whole new context. Living as authentic faith community is a mission of ongoing reconciliation, and this message must be at the heart of therapeutic faith community. This one idea alone should radically change our view of community and our duty to live it. I am beginning to see that one of the challenges facing contemporary Christianity is to understand how it is that we, who worship a God of harmony, should ourselves be damaged and sometimes angry people living in a fragmented, broken world of damaging relationships. Our personal lives do not convince others of either our values or our beliefs. We do not live as though we are saved, healed and better off with Christ. So the core of our damaged selves, our human nature, is at odds with Father God and His intentions of reconciliation in and through His Son Christ.

The Human Condition

In contrast to God's divine plan of reconciliation, there is for most of us our sad human condition. Much of the time our heads rule our lives, dismissing our hearts and their emotionality as invalid. As we have noted already, we see life from our cognitive perspectives, passionately convincing ourselves that we are okay. Because we are ruled by our thinking, and not by our feelings, we begin to believe that what we think is all there is. We all have the tendency to believe that we are always right, regardless of how little we know. Our lives centre around proving a point, or defending what we believe, and, as we have noted, this becomes more important than the relationships themselves. We either refuse to admit that we have a dark side to our nature, or do not allow that it is more active than we care to acknowledge. We also deny the possible enriching of our lives through our emotions. Our feelings can equip us with a range of alternative views of reality that will often question our more dogmatic intellectual conclusions.

Put another way, our cognitive drives are so strong, and our EQ (emotional intelligence) so underdeveloped that we refuse or are unable to see the damage we are causing. We will fight, and even die, for our rights, and our being right. We all tend to put rights and their rules before friendships and even before love. Standing up for our rights is our most likely path, even though this may damage relationships. Ending a conversation by making a point is often more important than honouring the person we are talking to. Our human condition, in its damaged state, is hardly ideal material to build authentic (to the outsider, convincing) faith community.

Our striving to protect our rights, or keep control, will in fact cause us much pain, putting us in danger of losing relationships as well as friends. Put in a more brutal way, it means we are poison to community. We get in among the members and begin to divide them for our own ends. Because rights are cognitive, and friendships, much of the time, of the heart, we usually do not stop to ask what our actions might do to adversely change relationships. The brain prevails. Even the hurting friends and broken relationships that we see before our eyes are rarely enough to make us change our minds, or drive us to restore damaged relationships.

But behind most 'I'm right' attitudes is, as we have seen (see Chapter 4), something much more sinister. For the belief that we are right feeds our pride. We not only believe what we believe, but judge all others to be wrong so that we alone are right. We measure every conversation as it is spoken and then decide whether we agree or disagree. It never occurs to us that our conclusions might not be the only valid viewpoint. Pride separates us from the possibility that we might be wrong! Our own views are the right ones, and others should agree with us by adopting them. Other lesser mortals who persist in disagreeing with us are sad and misled. This conviction that we cannot be wrong is an idolatry of the self.

Within a church context, such an attitude is sadly very common, and can be devastating. Because we are careful to suggest that our perspective is the one shared by God, it gives us power to abuse others. Instead of promoting reconciliation, our chosen cognitive blindness tends to promote fragmentation in our own lives, and in the lives of those very people in faith community who our lives are intended to heal.

Equally damaging is the idolatry of our self-hate, which leads dogmatically to the belief that we are wrong, unworthy or unlovable. This form of pride is more deceptive, veiled as it is in a guise of acquiescence and uncertainty. Instead of abdicating our responsibility to listen to others, as in the case of those who believe that they are perfectly right, we avoid taking responsibility for what we intuitively know. We know that we are right in believing we are wrong! Reconciliation is impossible when we are unable to bring ourselves to the relationship.

This book is therefore suggesting that personal rights cannot always be sustained, and being right all the time cannot be sustained at all, if we are to live authentic faith community. Fragmentation and loss of friendship because of principles is not acceptable behaviour. Our self-righteousness or self-hate makes us toxic to building authentic faith community. Being right is worth nothing if we are right but alone. If we are to live Christ-like lives, following social Trinity, then we carry reconciliation as our mission: reconciling people to themselves, to God, to each other. The whole *Rapha* journey is based on the premise that as we grow up, become more mature and move into greater wholeness, we are also more able to be social and public people. Therefore our capacity to live in a reconciled way in all areas of our lives is a measure of our Christ-likeness, healing and wholeness.

Put another way, our emerging self is a public self, our sick, dark self is an isolated, broken and damaged person. Someone who is struggling with relationships will have few of the resources that are needed to build hope and promise with others. The baggage and sicknesses in our lives steal the capacity for relationships. We spend so much time managing our disorders that we have little energy or time to do much else. Defending our rights becomes part of our baggage, with the result that the sicker we become, the more dogmatic and closed down we often become. Healing and wholeness, the bringing together of our fragmented lives, increasingly gives us the resources, learning and life of trust that further teach us the true value of friendship.

This process of becoming more human as we become more like Christ is helping establish a foundation of authentic community here in CCD, following the example of a social-reconciling-Trinity. Our personal journey toward wholeness allows us to *become* more human, mature and Christ-like while also giving us the capacity to be part of authentic faith community, sharing in *perichoretic* union with Trinity harmony. All that stands in the way of each of us becoming this type of person in faith community is our refusal to change; all we need is an ongoing willingness to change, a willingness continually to become the people faith community needs us to be.

Creation Reconciliation

So to be human is to be *en route*, on a journey, even in death. Our destiny is bound up with the destiny of all those seeking Christ in this world. But the full realization of history, the ultimate reconciliation, is set in motion by creation and personal becoming, finding its culmination in *parousia*, the return of Christ, the fulfilment of all human personhood and destiny. Our life of striving to be reconciled is finally totally fulfilled in Christ.

Our capacity for relationality mirrors our Creator Trinity, for to exist is to coexist. Therefore the human capacity for relationship puts people in touch with themselves, others and the social Trinity – divinity and humanity coexist. For the atonement and return of Christ are both foundations of human reconciliation and immortality. I do not speak only of an endless life but freedom from death (1 Cor. 15:53; 1 Tim. 6:16) and corruption as we know it (Rom. 2:7; 2 Tim. 1:10). So we must always speak of a unified relational individual, one enjoying wholeness, and of a social and cosmic reconciliation and eschatology.

The Bible begins with creation, a relational event focusing on God, nature, the animals and spiritual beings. But, most noticeably, God involved human beings in the creation of the world (Gn. 1:26). Human decisions and actions are honoured and valued by God in our moving into new stages of creaturely development.[2] Israel's God is by nature a social being, functioning within a divine community (Gn. 1:26; 6:1–4; Is. 6:8; Je. 23:18–23; Pr. 8:22–31, etc.). Relationships are fundamental to God.[3] The whole of the Old Testament has a fundamental relational character, focused around God and relationship with Him. But in Christ God has acted in a supremely divine and human relational way (Col. 1:15).[4] Nature also praises God (Ps. 148). For instance, we see in the wilderness narrative that nature has a God-given potential as a vehicle for the healing of the human community (Ex. 16:4–21; 17:1–7, etc.). Accepting that viewpoint, seeing the God-given role of nature, helps us to begin to embrace a less person-centred faith and theology. Human sin may have disrupted the natural order, but it cannot steal nature's capacity to praise God, and human beings, through the praise of worship, are able to help articulate non-human creation praise.[5]

Nature's natural praise is its natural ability to be what God created it to be. By fulfilling its God-given intent, whether as an oak tree or rainbow trout, it praises Creator God. But unlike nature, human beings do not naturally fulfil their Christ-centred potential: this requires an intentional effort to change. As victims of the disease called sin we all have to learn how to become who we were created to be. Each of us must do a journey, with the *Rapha* help of God. By creating space God gives all creatures, along with nature, the opportunity to be what He intended they should be. So together with the whole universe we become who God intended we should be, joining together as the people of God in the praise of Him who created us, an *interdependent mutuality of vocation*.[6] Material reality awaits two things: the return of Christ and our willingness to change to be more in harmony with Christ. Together both reflect our worship of the sociality of divine community.

This intuitive natural capacity to want to form community, by God's help, is a divine wish. In having the capacity to come much closer to others in love, we come much closer to both God and ourselves in new ways. The self-in-personal-relations should develop into the self-in-community. The healing maturing of self only takes place within relationships, within community.[7] Authentic human faith community, where people are able to live healing love and reconciliation, should more and more mirror divine human community until He comes. Let members of Christ Church Deal have the last word.

What community can be

> • Without the relationships, I would not even have begun my journey • Allowing people to love me • Testimonies and stories moving me forward, albeit kicking and screaming –

sorry! ♦ Giving people real space to hurt ♦ Letting others near me ♦ Relationship guidelines: Tell it like it is. You won't be judged for how you feel ♦ Community cannot exist without relationships. The stronger the individual relationships the stronger the community is as a whole ♦ Relationships, they are hard, but you don't see the benefit until after you have made the effort ♦ I have been able to relax and not be suspicious of people, and been able to begin to see damage in myself ♦ I have been able to declare to God what has happened in my past and feel the lifting of the damage ♦ It's very hard! But beneficial ♦ I learned that it was OK to be different ♦ It's just so good to be able to share (and walk) my journey with others ♦ It's the hardest thing in the world to build true relationships; being in community hurts like hell; but it is worth it ♦ Something hit me the other day – I have only just thought of it – I am beginning to 'see' the person behind the face! ♦ I now feel that I am part of the community and am beginning to understand what makes it up and makes it work. I chose to belong and join it ♦ It can take time to lay new foundations ♦ Together it works!

Notes

1 *Oxford English Dictionary.*
2 Fretheim, *God and World*, 277.
3 Fretheim, *God and World*, 17.
4 Fretheim, *God and World*, 301.
5 Fretheim, *God and World*, 265.
6 Fretheim, *God and World*, 275.
7 D. Lane, *Keeping Hope Alive: Stirrings in Christian theology* (New York: Paulist Press, 1996).

Bibliography

Adams, J.E., *Competent to Counsel* (Grand Rapids: Baker Book House, 1970)

Andreassi, J.L., *Psychophysiology: Human behavior and physiological response* (London: Lawrence Erlbaum, 2000)

Angrosino, M.V., 'L'Arche: The phenomenology of Christian counterculturalism', *Qualitative Inquiry* 9 (2003), 6.934–954

Ascough, R.S., *What Are They Saying about the Formation of Pauline Churches?* (New York: Paulist Press, 1998)

Ballard, P., 'The Bible and Christian spirituality today', *Expository Times* 114 (2003), 11.363–366

Banks, R., *Paul's Idea of Community: The early house churches in their historical setting* (Grand Rapids: Eerdmans, 1980/1988)

Barth, K., *Church Dogmatics: Doctrine of the Word of God*, Bromiley, G.W. and T.F. Torrance (tr.) (Edinburgh: T&T Clark, 1956)

Basil of Caesarea, 'Letter 38 4 MPG 32 332a and 333d5–333el, ET' in Wiles, M. and M. Santer (eds.), *Documents in Early Christian Thought* (Cambridge: Cambridge University Press, 1975)

Becvar, D.S., *Soul Healing: The spiritual orientation in counselling and therapy* (New York: Purseus Books, 1997)

Bellah, R.N., *et al*, *Habits of the Heart: Individualism and commitment in American life* (New York: Harper & Row, 1985)

Benner, D.G, *Care of Souls: Revisioning Christian nurture and counsel* (Grand Rapids: Baker Books, 1998)

—, 'Spirituality in personality and psychotherapy' in Aden, L., *et al.* (eds.), *Christian Perspectives on Human Development* (Grand Rapids: Baker Book House, 1992), 171–186

Berkhof, L., *Systematic Theology* (London: Banner of Truth Trust, 1939/1963)

Bietak, M., 'Israelites found in Egypt: four-room house identified in Medinet Habu', *Biblical Archaeology Review* 29 (2003), 5.41–49

Bilezikian, G., *Community 101: Reclaiming the local church as community of oneness* (Grand Rapids: Zondervan, 1997)

Bonhoeffer, D., *Life Together* (London: SCM Press, 1949/1970)

Borgen, P. and S. Giversen (eds.), *The New Testament and Hellenic Judaism* (Peabody, MA: Hendrickson, 1997)

Bosch, D.J., *Transforming Mission: Paradigm shifts in theology of mission* (Maryknowle, NY: Orbis Books, 1991)

Bracken, J.A. and M.H. Suchocki, 'Concluding remarks' in Bracken, J.A. and M.H. Suchocki (eds.), *Trinity in Process: A relational theology of God* (New York: Continuum, 1997), 215–224

Brierley, P., *The Tide is Running Out: What the English church attendance survey reveals* (London: Christian Research, 2000)

—, *UK Church Religious Trends*, Number 4 2003–2004 (London: Christian Research, 2003)

Bright, J., *History of Israel* (London: SCM Press, 1960)

Brown, C.K., 'The integration of healing and spirituality into health care', *Journal of Interprofessional Care* 12 (1998), 4.373–381

Brown, F., et al., *A Hebrew and English Lexicon of the Old Testament with an Appendix Containing the Biblical Aramaic* (Oxford: Clarendon Press, 1907/1962)

Brown, R.E., *The Churches the Apostles Left Behind* (New Jersey: Paulist Press, 1984)

Brown, W.T., *Israel's Divine Healer* (Carlisle: Paternoster Press, 1995)

Buber, M., *I and Thou*, Kaufman, W. (tr.) (New York: Touchstone, 1958/1996)

—, *The Way of Response: Martin Buber, selections from his writings* (New York: Schocken Books, 1966)

Buminovitz, S. and A. Faust, 'Ideology in stone: understanding the four room house', *Biblical Archaeology Review* 28 (2002), 4.32–41

Burrell, D.B., *Knowing the Unknowable God: Ibn-Sina, Maimonides, Aquinas* (Notre Dame: University of Notre Dame Press, 1986)

Butler, J., *The Works of Joseph Butler*, Volume 2, *Fifteen Sermons on Human Nature* (Oxford: Clarendon Press, 1922/1986)

Caird, G.B., *Paul and women's liberty, The Manston Memorial Lecture* (University of Manchester, 1971)

Campbell, R.A., *Elders* (Edinburgh: T&T Clark, 1994)

Carson, D., *Becoming Conversant with the Emerging Church* (Grand Rapids: Zondervan, 2005)

Chan, A.K.Y., *et al.*, *rp*', 'Healing' in van Gemeren, W.A. (ed.) *The New International Dictionary of Old Testament Theology and Exegesis*, Volume 3 of 5 (Carlisle: Paternoster, 1996), 1162–1173

Chancey, M. and E.M. Myers, 'How Jewish was Sepphoris in Jesus' time?' *Biblical Archaeology Review* 26 (2000), 4.18–33

Childs, B.S., *Exodus: A commentary* (London: SCM Press, 1974)

Christians, C.G., 'The sacredness of life', *Media Development* (1998, Online). Available from http://www.wacc.org.uk/publications/md/md1998-2/christians.html (Accessed 26 March 2003)

Chu, J., 'O Father, Where Art Thou?' *Time Magazine* 161 (16 June 2003), 24.22–30

Clark, D., *The Liberation of the Church: The role of basic Christian groups in a new reformation* (Birmingham: National Centre for Christian Communities and Networks, 1984)

Clark, S.B., *Building Christian Communities: Strategy for renewing the church* (Notre Dame: Ave Maria Press, 1972)

Clinebell, H.J., *The People Dynamic: Changing self and society through growth groups* (New York: Harper & Row, 1972)

Coakley, S., 'Rethinking Gregory of Nyssa: Introduction – gender, Trinitarian analogies and the pedagogy of "The Song"', *Modern Theology* 18 (2002), 4.431–444

Cobb, J. and D. Griffin, *Process Theology: An introductory exposition* (Philadelphia: Westminster Press, 1976)

Cobb, J.B., *Reclaiming the Church: Where the mainline church went wrong and what to do about it* (Louisville: Westminster John Knox Press, 1997)

Collins, K.J., *The Scriptural Way of Salvation: The heart of John Wesley's theology* (Nashville: Abingdon Press, 1997)

Collins, P.M., *Trinitarian Theology: West and East, Karl Barth, the Cappadocian Fathers and John Zizioulas* (Oxford: Oxford University Press, 2001)

Cooper, J.W., *Body Soul and Life Everlasting: Biblical anthropology and the monism-dualism debate* (Grand Rapids: Eerdmans, 1989/2000)

Crabb, L., *Connecting: Healing for ourselves and our relationships, a radical new vision* (Nashville: Word Publishing, 1997)

—, *The Safest Place on Earth: Where people connect and are for ever changed* (Nashville: Word Publishing, 1999)

Dever, W.G., *What Did the Biblical Writers Know and When Did They Know It?* (Grand Rapids: Eerdmans, 2001)

Ehrlich, J.D., *Plato's Gift to Christianity: The Gentile preparation for and the making of the Christian faith* (San Diego: Academic Christian Press, 2001)

Eichrodt, W., *Theology of the Old Testament*, Volume 1 (London: SCM Press, 1961/1975)

—, *Theology of the Old Testament*, Volume 2 (London: SCM Press, 1967/1972)

Elliott, M. and C. Dickey, 'Body politics', *Newsweek* (12 September 1994), 24–25

Ellison, H.L., *The Household Church* (Exeter: Paternoster Press, 1963)

Erland, W., 'Shalom and Wholeness', *Brethren Life and Thought* 29 (1984), 145–151

Ernest Wright, G., *The Biblical Doctrine of Man in Society* (London: SCM Press, 1954)

Etzioni, A., *The Spirit of Community: The reinvention of American society* (New York: Touchstone, 1992)

—, *The Spirit of Community: Rights, responsibilities and the communitarian agenda* (London: Fontana Press, 1993/1995)

Faber, R., 'Trinity, analogy and coherence' in Bracken, J.A. and M.H. Suchocki (eds.), *Trinity in Process: A relational theology of God* (New York: Continuum, 1997) 147–171

Ferre, N.F.S., *Swedish Contributions to Modern Theology: With special reference to Lundensian thought* (London: Harper & Bros., 1939)

Feuerbach, L., *The Essence of Christianity* (New York: Harper & Row, 1841/1956)

Fiddes, P.S., *Participating in God: A pastoral doctrine of the Trinity* (Louisville: Westminster John Knox Press, 2000)

Field, A., *From Darkness to Light: How one became a Christian in the Early Church* (Ben Lomond, CA: Conciliar Press, 1978/1997)

Fiensy, D., 'Using the Neur culture of Africa in understanding the Old Testament: An evaluation' in Chalcraft, D.J. (ed.), *Social Scientific Old Testament Criticism* (Sheffield: Sheffield Academic Press, 1997), 43–52

Finkelstein, I., *The Archaeology of the Israelite Settlement* (Jerusalem: Israel Exploration Society, 1988)

Finn, T.M., *Early Christian Baptism and the Catechumenate: West and East Syria* (Minneapolis: Liturgical Press, 1992)

Fitzpatrick, G., *How to Recognize God's Voice* (Fairy Meadows, NSW, Australia: Spiritual Growth Books, 1984/1987)

Ford, L., 'Contingent trinitarianism' in Bracken, J.A. and M.H. Suchocki (eds.), *Trinity in Process: A relational theology of God* (New York: Continuum, 1997), 41–68

Frazee, R., *The connecting church: Beyond small groups to authentic community* (Grand Rapids: Zondervan, 2001)

Fretheim, T.E., 'Yahweh' in van Gemeren, W.A. (ed.), *The New International Dictionary of Old Testament Theology and Exegesis* (Carlisle: Paternoster, 1996), 1295–1300

—, *God and World in the Old Testament: A relational theology of creation* (Nashville, Tenn.: Abingdon Press, 2005)

Gager, J.G., *Kingdom and Community: The social world of early Christianity* (New Jersey: Prentice-Hall, 1975)

Gehring, R.W., *House Church and Mission: The importance of household structures in Early Christianity* (Peabody, MS: Hendrickson, 2004)

Gelpi, D.L., *The Turn to Experience in Contemporary Theology* (New York: Paulist Press, 1994)

Giles, K., *The Trinity and Subordinationism: The doctrine of God and the contemporary gender debate* (Downers Grove, IL: InterVarsity Press, 2002)

Gilligan, C., *In a Different Voice* (Massachusetts: Harvard University Press, 1982/1993)

Gleick, J., *Chaos: Making a new science* (London: Sphere Books, 1987)

Gorman, J.A., *Community that is Christian: A handbook on small groups* (Wheaton, IL: Victor Books, 1993)

Gottwald, N.K., *The Tribes of Yahweh: A sociology of the religion of liberated Israel – 1250–1050 BCE* (London: SCM Press, 1975/1979)

—, 'Sociological method in the study of ancient Israel' in Gottwald, N.K., *et al.* (ed.), *The Bible and Liberation: Political and social hermeneutics* (Maryknoll, NY: Orbis Books, 1993)

Gotz, I.L., 'On spirituality and teaching', *Philosophy of Education*, (1997, Online). Available from

h t t p : / / w w w . e d . u i u c . e d u / E P S / P E S -
Yearbook/97_docs/gotz.html (Accessed 13 January 2003)

Grenz, S.J., *A Primer on Postmodernism* (Grand Rapids: Eerdmans, 1996)

—, *Created for Community: Connecting Christian belief with Christian living* (Grand Rapids: Baker Books, 1996/2000)

—, *Theology for the Community of God* (Grand Rapids: Eerdmans, 2000)

—, *The Social God and the Relational Self: A Trinitarian theology of the imago Dei* (London: Westminster John Knox Press, 2001)

Grof, S. and C. Grof (eds.), *Spiritual Emergency: When personal transformation becomes a crisis* (New York: Penguin Putnam, 1989)

Gunton, C.E., *Enlightenment and Alienation: An essay towards a Trinitarian theology* (Grand Rapids: Eerdmans, 1985)

—, *The Promise of Trinitarian Theology* (Edinburgh: T&T Clark, 1991)

—, *The One, the Three and the Many: God, creation and the culture of modernity* (Cambridge: Cambridge University Press, 1993)

Hanson, P., *The People Called: Growth of community in the Bible* (San Francisco: Harper & Rowe, 1986)

Harnack, von A., *The Essence of Christianity* (Das Wesen des Christentums) (Leipzig,1900)

Harrington, D., *God's People in Christ: New Testament perspectives on the church and Judaism* (Philadelphia: Fortress Press, 1980)

Hartshorne, C., *The Divine Relativity: A social conception of God* (New Haven: Yale University Press, 1948)

Hempel, J., *Theologische Literaturzeitung*, Lambert, W.A. and H.J. Grim (tr.) (Philadelphia: Muhlenberg Press, 1957)

Hengel, M., *The Hellenisation of Judea in the first century after Christ* (London: SCM Press, 1989)

Hennelly, A.T., *Liberation Theologies: The global pursuit of justice* (Mystic, Connecticut: 23rd Publications, 1997)

Holmes, P.R., *Becoming More Human: Exploring the interface of spirituality, discipleship and therapeutic faith community* (Milton Keynes: Paternoster, 2005)

—, 'Spirituality: some disciplinary perspectives' in Flanagan, K. and P.C. Jupp (eds.), *The Sociology of Spirituality* (to be published, 2006)

Holmes, P.R. and S.B. Williams (eds.), *Changed Lives: Extraordinary stories of ordinary people* (Milton Keynes: Authentic, 2005)

Hooker, M.D., 'Authority on her head: 1 Cor 11.10', *New Testament Studies* 10 (1963–64), 410–416

Hull, J., *Hellenistic magic and the Synoptic tradition* (London: SCM Press, 1974)

Hull, J.M., *What Prevents Christian Adults from Learning?* (Philadelphia: Trinity Press International, 1991)

Israel, M., *Healing as Sacrament* (London: Darton, Longman & Todd, 1984)

Jenson, R.W., *The Trinity Identity* (Philadelphia: Fortress Press, 1982)

Johnson, A.R., *The One and the Many in the Israelite Conception of God* (Cardiff: University of Wales Press, 1942)

—, *The Vitality of the Individual in the Thought of Ancient Israel* (Cardiff: University of Wales Press, 1964)

Johnson, D. and J. Van Vonderen, *The Subtle Power of Spiritual Abuse; Recognising and escaping spiritual manipulation and false spiritual authority within the church* (Minneapolis: Bethany House, 1991)

Jungel, E., *The Doctrine of the Trinity: God's being is in His becoming* (Edinburgh: Scottish Academic Press, 1976)

Kasemann, E., *Essays in New Testament themes* (Philadelphia: Fortress Press, 1982)

Kee, H.C., *Who Are the People of God? Early Christian models of community* (Yale: Yale University Press, 1995)

Keefauver, L., *Experiencing the Holy Spirit: Transformed by His Presence – A twelve week interactive workbook* (Nashville: Thomas Nelson, 1997)

Keil, C.F., *Commentary on II Chronicles* (Edinburgh: ET Publishers, 1872)

Kelly, T.M., *Theology at the Void: The retrieval of experience* (Notre Dame: University of Notre Dame Press, 2002)

Kimball, D., *The Emerging Church* (Grand Rapids: Zondervan, 2003)

Kirkpatrick, F.G., *Community: A Trinity of models* (Washington: Georgetown University Press, 1986)

Kitchen, K.A., *On the Reliability of the Old Testament* (Grand Rapids: Eerdmans, 2003)

Kohler, L., *Hebrew Man* (London: SCM Press, 1953/1973)

Kostenberger, A.J., *The Missions of Jesus and the Disciples According to the Fourth Gospel: With implications for the fourth gospel's purpose and the mission of the contemporary church* (Grand Rapids: Eerdmans, 1998)

Kraus, C.N., *The Authentic Witness: Credibility and authority* (Grand Rapids: Eerdmans, 1979)

Lambourne, R.A., *Community, Church and Healing* (London: Darton, Longman & Todd, 1963)

Lampel-de Groot, J., 'The theory of instinctual drives' in Lampel-de Groot, J. (ed.), *Man and Mind: Collected papers of Jeanne Lampel-de Groot* (New York: International Universities Press, 1985), 175–182

Lane, D., *Keeping Hope Alive: Stirrings in Christian theology* (New York: Paulist Press, 1996)

Lee, B.J., 'An "Other" Trinity' in Bracken, J.A. and M.H. Suchocki (eds.), *Trinity in Process: A relational theology of God* (New York: Continuum, 1997), 191–214

Lee, J.Y., *The Theology of Change: A Christian concept of God in an Eastern perspective* (Maryknowle, NY: Orbis Books, 1979)

Lemche, N.P., *Ancient Israel: A new history of Israelite society* (Sheffield: Sheffield Academic Press, 1988)

—, *The Canaanites and Their Land: The tradition of the Canaanites* (Sheffield: Sheffield Academic Press, 1991)

Lewis, C.S., *Reflections on the Psalms* (New York: Harcourt Brace Jovanovich, 1958)

Lindbeck, G.A., 'Confession and community: an Israel-like view of the church', *The Christian Century* (1990), 492–496

Loewe, R., *The social position of women in Judaism* (London: SPCK, 1966)

Lohfink, G., *Jesus and Community*, Galvin, J.P. (tr.) (London: SPCK, 1985)

Lohfink, N., *The Theology of the Pentateuch: Themes of the priestly narrative and Deuteronomy* (Edinburgh: T&T Clark, 1994)

Lovelock, J.E., *Gaia: A new look at life on earth* (Oxford: Oxford University Press, 1979/87)

Lull, T.F., *Martin Luther's Basic Theological Writings* (Minneapolis: Fortress Press, 1989)

Macaulay, R. and J. Barrs, *Being Human: The nature of spiritual experience* (Downers Grove IL: InterVarsity Press, 1978)

Maclaren, D., *Mission Implausible: Restoring credibility to the church* (Milton Keynes: Paternoster, 2004)

MacMullen, R., *Christianizing the Roman Empire* (AD 100–400) (New Haven: Yale University Press, 1984)

Macmurray, J., *The Clue to History* (London: SCM Press, 1938)

—, *The Nature of Religion, St Asaph Conference* (London: SCM Auxiliary, 1938)

—, *Conditions of Freedom* (London: Faber & Faber, 1950)

—, *The Self as Agent* (New Jersey: Humanities Press, 1957/1991)

—, *Persons in Relation* (London: Faber & Faber, 1961)

—, *The Philosophy of Jesus* (London: Friends Home Service Committee, 1973)

Maertens, T., *Assembly for Christ: From Biblical theology to pastoral theology in the twentieth century* (London: Darton, Longman & Todd, 1970)

Malphurs, A., *Leading leaders: empowering church boards for ministry excellence* (Grand Rapids: Baker Books, 2005)

Martin, D.V., *Adventure in Psychiatry: Social change in a mental hospital* (London: Bruno Cassirer Publications, 1962)

Martin, G. and G. McIntosh, *Creating Community: Deeper fellowship through small group ministry* (Nashville: Broadman & Holman, 1997)

Marx, K., *Selected Writings in Sociology and Social Philosophy* (London: Penguin, 1963)

May, G.G., *Care of Mind, Care of Spirit: Psychiatric dimensions of spiritual direction* (San Francisco: Harper & Row, 1982)

McCoy, C.S., *When Gods Change: Hope for theology* (Nashville: Abingdon Press, 1980)

McFadyen, A.I., *The Call to Personhood: A Christian theory of the individual in social relationship* (Cambridge: Cambridge University Press, 1990)

McGrath, A.E., 'Sin and salvation' in Atkinson, D.J. and D.H. Field (eds.), *New Dictionary of Christian Ethics & Pastoral Theology* (Leicester: IVP, 1995), 78–87

McKenna, S., *Introduction to Saint Augustine: The Trinity* (Washington DC: Catholic University of America Press, 1963)

Meeks, W.A., *The First Urban Christians: The social world of the Apostle Paul* (Newhaven: Yale University Press, 1983)

Mendenhall, G., 'The Hebrew conquest of Palestine', *Biblical Archaeologist* 25 (1962), 66–87

Meyers, C., 'The family in Early Israel' in Perdue, L.G. (ed.), *Families in Ancient Israel* (Louisville: Westminster John Knox Press, 1997), 1–47

Middlemiss, D., *Interpreting Charismatic Experience* (London: SCM Press, 1996)

Millard, A., 'Literacy in the times of Jesus', *Biblical Archaeology Review* 29 (2003), 4. 37–45

Miller, H., *Christian Community: Biblical or optional* (Ann Arbor, MI: Servant Books, 1979)

Miller, J.P., *Education and the Soul: Toward a spiritual curriculum* (Albany: State University of New York Press, 2000)

Miller, W.R., 'Spirituality: The silent dimension in addiction research. The 1990 Leonard Ball Oration', *Drug and Alcohol Review* 9 (1990), 259–266

— (ed.), *Integrating Spirituality into Treatment: Resources for practitioners* (Washington DC: American Psychological Association, 1999)

Minar, D.W. and S. Greer, T*he Concept of Community: Readings with interpretations* (Chicago: Aldine, 1969)

Muller, M., *The First Bible of the Church: A plea for the Septuagint* (Sheffield: Sheffield Academic Press, 1996)

Nardin, G., *The Open Family: The vision of the early church* (London: New City, 1996)

Neusner, J., *From politics to piety: The emergence of Pharisaic Judaism* (New York: KTAV, 1979)

Nygren, A., *Agape & Eros* (London: SPCK, 1932/1982)

O'Donnell, J.J., *Trinity and Temporality: The Christian doctrine of God in the light of process theology and the theology of hope* (Oxford: Oxford University Press, 1983)

O'Halloran, J., *Living Cells: Developing small Christian community* (Dublin: Dominican Publications, 1984)

O'Murchu, D., *Quantum Theology* (New York: Crossroads, 1997)

Oden, T.C., *Systematic Theology*, Volume 3 of 4, Life in the Spirit (Peabody, MA: Harper Collins Paperback, 1994/1998)

Oesterley, W.O.E., *The Jews and Judaism during the Greek Period: The background of Christianity* (London: SPCK, 1941)

Ogden, S.M., *The Reality of God and Other Essays* (London: SCM Press, 1967)

Ormerod, N., 'Wrestling with Rahner on the Trinity', *Irish Theological Quarterly* 69 (2003), 213–227

Osiek, C., *What Are They Saying about the Social Settings of the New Testament?* (New York: Paulist Press, 1992)

Osiek, C. and D.L. Balch, *Families in the New Testament World* (Louisville: Westminster John Knox Press, 1997)

Ottoson, M., 'The Iron Age of Northern Jordan' in Lemaire, A. (ed.), *History and Traditions of Early Israel: Studies presented to Eduard Nielsen, May 8th 1993* (Leiden: E.J. Brill, 1993), 90–103

Packer, J.I., *Knowing God* (London: Hodder & Stoughton, 1973)

Pannenberg, W., *Christian Spirituality and Sacramental Community* (London: Darton, Longman & Todd, 1984)

Parry, R., *Worshipping Trinity: Coming back to the heart of worship* (Milton Keynes: Paternoster, 2005)

Perdue, L.G., 'The household, Old Testament theology and contemporary hermeneutics' in Perdue, L.G. (ed.), *Families in Ancient Israel* (Louisville: Westminster John Knox Press, 1997), 223–258

Pingleton, J.P., 'A model of relational maturity' in Aden, L., *et al.* (eds.), *Christian Perspectives on Human Development* (Grand Rapids: Baker Book House, 1992), 101–113

Pinnock, C., *et al.*, *The Openness of God: A biblical challenge to the traditional understanding of God* (Downers Grove, IL: InterVarsity Press, 1994)

Pinnock, C.H., *Reason Enough: The case for the Christian faith* (Exeter: Paternoster Press, 1980)

Plaskow, J., 'Transforming the nature of community: towards a feminist people of Israel' in Bach, A. (ed.), *Women in the Hebrew Bible* (New York: Routledge, 1999), 403–418

Podles, L., *The Church Impotent: The feminisation of Christianity* (Dallas: Spence, 1999)

Pomeroy, S.B., *Goddesses, Whores, Wives, Slaves: Women in classical antiquity* (New York: Schocken Books, 1976)

Prestige, G.L., *God in Patristic Thought* (London: SPCK, 1936/1952)

Preuss, H.D., *Old Testament Theology*, Volume 2 (Edinburgh: T&T Clark, 1996)

Rabey, S., *In Search of Authentic Faith: How emerging generations are transforming the Church* (New York: Random House, 2001)

Rahner, K., *The Trinity* (London: Burns & Oates, 1970)

Rapport, N., 'Community in current use' in Barnard, A. and J. Spencer (eds.), *Encyclopedia of Social and Cultural Anthropology* (London: Routledge, 1996/2000), 136–143

Rasmussen, L.L., *Moral Fragments and Moral Community: A proposal for church in society* (Minneapolis: Fortress Press, 1993)

Reid, M.A., 'Sanctification' in Atkinson, D.J. and D.H. Field (eds.), *New Dictionary of Christian Ethics & Pastoral Theology* (Leicester: IVP, 1995), 756–757

Richard of St Victor, *De Trinitate* (Paris: Les Editions du Cerf, 1959)

Robbins, J. (ed.), *Is it Righteous To Be? Interviews with Emmanuel Levinas* (Stanford, CA: Stanford University Press, 2001)

Robinson, J.A.T., *The Body: A study in Pauline theology* (London: SCM Press, 1952)

Robinson, T.H., *Palestine in General History: The Schweich Lectures of 1926* (Oxford: Oxford University Press, 1929)

Sandbach, F.H., *The Stoics* (London: Chatto & Windus,1975)

Schadel, E. (ed.), *Biblitheca Trinitariorum: The international bibliography of Trinitarian theology* (London: K.G. Saur, 1984)

Schrag, C.O., *The Self After Postmodernity* (Newhaven: Yale University Press, 1997)

Schwobel, C., 'Introduction' in Schwobel, C. and C.E. Gunton (eds.), *Persons, Divine and Human* (Edinburgh: T&T Clark, 1991), 1–29

Schwobel, C. and C.E. Gunton, *Persons, Divine and Human: Kings College essays in theological anthropology* (Edinburgh: T&T Clark, 1991)

Scott, J.J., *Jewish backgrounds of the New Testament* (Grand Rapids: Baker Books, 1995/2000)

Shelton, R.L., *Divine Expectations: Interpreting the atonement for 21st century mission* (Waynesboro, GA: Paternoster, 2006)

Shenker, B., *Intentional Communities: Ideology and alienation in communal societies* (London: Routledge & Kegan Paul, 1986)

Shiloh, Y., 'Four-room house', *Israeli Expeditions Journal* 20 (1970), 180

Skarsaune, O., *In the Shadow of the Temple: Jewish influences on early Christianity* (Downers Grove, IL: InterVarsity Press, 2002)

Stambaugh, J.E. and D.L. Balch, *The New Testament in its social environment* (Philadelphia: Westminster Press, 1986)

—, *The Social World of the First Christians* (London: SPCK, 1986)

Stark, R., *The Rise of Christianity* (New Jersey: Princeton University Press, 1996)

Steele, L.L., *On the Way: A practical theology of Christian formation* (Grand Rapids: Baker Book House, 1990)

Stegemann, E.W. and W. Stegemann, *The Jesus Movement: A social history of the first Christians* (Minneapolis: Fortress Press, 1999)

Strawson, P.F., *Individuals: An essay in descriptive metaphysics* (London: Methuen, 1959)

Strong, A.H., *Systematic Theology: Three volumes in one* (London: Pickering & Inglis, 1907/1962)

Stuhlmacher, P., *Der Brief an Philemon* (Zurich: Benzinger Neukirchen & Vluyn, 1981)

Tertullian, *La pudicite* (De pudicitia) (Paris: Cerf, 1993)

Thompson, J.H., *Spiritual Considerations in the Prevention, Treatment and Cure of Disease* (Stockfield, Northumberland: Oriel Press, 1984)

Tönnies, F., *Community and Association, Loomis*, C.P. (tr.) (London: Routledge & Kegan Paul, 1887/1955)

Torrance, T.F., *Theology in Reconciliation* (London: Geoffrey Chapman, 1975)

—, *The Christian Doctrine of God: One being three persons* (Edinburgh: T&T Clark, 1996)

Tuggy, D., 'The unfinished business of Trinitarian theorising', *Religious Studies* 39 (2003), 2.165–183

Underhill, E., *The Mystics of the Church* (New York: Schocken Books, 1964)

Vanier, J., *Community and Growth* (New York: Paulist Press, 1979)

Vitz, P.E., *Psychology as Religion: The cult of self-worship* (Carlisle: Paternoster, 1977/1994)

Volf, M., *After Our Likeness: The church as the image of the Trinity* (Grand Rapids: Eerdmans, 1998)

Walton, R.C., *The Gathered Community* (London: Carey Press, 1946)

Ward, P., *Liquid Church: A bold vision of how to be God's people in worship and mission – A flexible fluid way of being church* (Milton Keynes: Paternoster, 2002)

Wells, C.R., 'Hebrew wisdom as a quest for wholeness and holiness', *Journal of Psychology and Christianity* 15 (1996), 1.58–69

Wheeler Robinson, H., *The Religious Ideas of the Old Testament* (London: Duckworth, 1913)

—, *Corporate Personality in Ancient Israel* (Edinburgh: T&T Clark, 1981)

Whitehead, A.N., *Process and Reality: An essay on cosmology* (New York: Free Press, 1929/1947)

Whitelam, K.W., *The Invention of Ancient Israel* (London: Routledge, 1996)

Whitson, R.E., *The Shakers: Two centuries of spiritual reflection* (London: SPCK, 1983)

Willard, D., *Divine Conspiracy* (San Francisco: Harper, 1998)

Williams, S.B., *Journeys of Personal Change in a Therapeutic Faith Community: A congregational study of Christ Church Deal, M.Phil. thesis* (Department of Theology: University of Birmingham, UK, 2002)

Williams, S.B. and P.R. Holmes, *Letting God Heal: From emotional illness to wholeness* (Milton Keynes, UK: Authentic Media, 2004)

Winter, G., *Community and Spiritual Transformation: Religion and politics in the communal age* (New York: Crossroads Books, 1989)

Woodbridge, P.D., 'Repentance' in Atkinson, D.J. and D.H. Field (eds.), *New Dictionary of Christian Ethics & Pastoral Theology* (Leicester: IVP, 1995), 730–731

Wright, G. Ernest, *The Biblical Doctrine of Man in Society* (London: SCM Press, 1954)

Wuthnow, R., *Sharing the Journey: Support groups and America's new quest for community* (New York: The Free Press, 1994)

Yaconelli, M. (ed.), *Stories of Emergence: Moving from absolute to authentic* (El Cajon, CA: Emergent YS, 2003)

Young, F.M., *From Nicaea to Chalcedon: A guide to the literature and its background* (London: SCM Press, 1983)

Young-Eisendrath, P. and M.E. Miller, 'Beyond enlightened self-interest: the psychology of mature spirituality in the 21st century' in Young-Eisendrath, P. and M.E. Miller (eds.), *The Psychology of Mature Spirituality: Integrity, wisdom, transcendence* (London: Routledge, 2000), 1–7

Zizioulas, J.D., *Being as Communion: Studies in personhood and the church* (New York: St Vladimir's Seminary Press, 1985/2002)

—, 'On being a person: Toward an ontology of personhood' in Schwobel, C. and C. Gunton (eds.), *Persons, Divine and Human* (Edinburgh: T&T Clark, 1991), 33–45

Author Index

Subject Index

Scripture Index